GARDEN STATE CANOEING

By Edward Gertler
A Paddler's Guide to New Jersey
The Seneca Press
1992

Printed on Recycled Paper

Preface

Perhaps the most unusual thing about this New Jersey guidebook is that its author is a Marylander. But when you think about it, this makes sense. Locals are notorious for overlooking the wonders that are in their backyard. For example, living just outside of Washington, D.C., I am only six miles from the White House. Yet, I have never toured the mansion. So sometimes it takes a pesky tourist to appreciate a place. I've been a tourist in Jersey for a long time.

My oldest recollections of rivers are from New Jersey. My family used to drive up to Wildwood each summer, via a road that went over and by many, many rivers. I was so small then that I had to stand on the car seat to peer out the window to see the wonderful waterways whizzing by. The drawbridges, the lawn-like marshes, the houses that stood on stilts in the water, and the little white boats moored in these houses' watery backyards fascinated me. I decided that I, too, wanted someday to live in a house on stilts and to have a little, white boat of my own on which to poke about in those mysterious channels.

Things don't always turn out exactly as a child dreams. Today I live in a house that sits flush on the ground, 300 feet above sea level, not out in a salt marsh. And my boat is a tiny orange and green canoe, not a white motorboat or sailboat.

But I HAVE managed to poke about on rivers, just as I dreamed and more. More often than not, I have strayed from my original goal — those mysterious channels. I have followed long rivers to the sea, descended into the depths of shadowy canyons, paddled across the Arctic tundra, flushed down roaring rapids, crept through the silent gloom of many a southern bayou, and hitchhiked my shuttles with people who spoke only Serbo-Croatian, French, Polish, or Greek. I have sought out many waterways in many places, but, I have always found a little time to come back and explore yet another little byway in the place that first inspired me.

Just over two years ago, I decided that exploration in bits and pieces was no longer enough. I now wanted to see all of the Garden State. And I wanted then to write a guidebook to these streams, similar to what I had done on Maryland, Delaware, and Pennsylvania. So I set out to methodically explore every possibly canoeable waterway in New Jersey. Countless weekends and thousands of miles later, I am still not quite there. But I have seen enough to write a comprehensive guidebook and give you plenty of ideas for your own adventures.

I take great pride that I have paddled (or portaged) every bit of every stream described in this book, with the exception of a mile on the lower Rockaway and two miles on the lower Batsto. Maybe I can do those next weekend. I have also driven almost every road on the shuttle maps. As a result, I think that you will find this is an exceptionally dependable guide.

Nevertheless, guidebooks are doomed to obsolescence, especially stream guides. By nature, rivers are dynamic and ever-changing: channels shift, trees fall, houses are built, dams wash out, and new fences are strung. So complement this guide with lots of good judgment on the river, scout when there is a question, and carry when there is any doubt.

May this book be the catalyst for many safe and enjoyable trips.

Ed Gertler

Acknowledgments

Even a solo paddler like me has not figured out how to produce a book solo. I called on lots of people for help. In particular, the advice, assistance, and influence of the following people made this guidebook a reality:

- Roger Corbett, whose assistance in my first two guidebooks, prepared me with the know-how for this work;

- Elizabeth Pennisi, a professional journalist, who donated a pair of perfectly good eyes to edit and proof the text;

- Barbara Brown, who specially shot and processed the front cover picture;

- Rick and Barb McKee who generously made their homestead available for use as my northern Jersey base camp;

- Don Rau and Bert Hauser of Word Design, who prepared the camera-ready copy;

- The staffs of the map libraries at the Library of Congress and University of Maryland, who fished out hundreds of topographic maps for my perusal;

- Tom and Paulette Irwin, who accompanied me on most of my Pine Barrens exploration;

- Judy Miller, who advised me on cover design;

- Robert Reiser and Bob Schopp at the U.S. Geological Survey in Trenton, who provided me indispensable hydrological data and gauge information; and

- George Kmetz, New Jersey Department of Transportation, who gave such extraordinary response fulfilling my map orders.

Last, but not least, I want to thank many individuals who will remain anonymous because I have either forgotten their names, never learned their names, or won't mention their names to keep them out of trouble. They fall in three groups. They are the scores of motoring strangers who were kind and brave enough to stop and pick up a funny-looking hitchhiker with a purple paddle in his hand. I could not have shuttled without them. Then there are all the people who live near the put-ins and allowed me to park my boat by their house (sometimes in their house) while I shuttled. Finally, there are all the security guards, policemen, factory workers, and others who bent the rules to let me sneak through, put in at, or camp in places where the "rules" say I should have not. I appreciate their kind hearts and free spirits.

Contents

Chapter 1

Introduction

I have written this guidebook with the expectation that most of its users will be people who live in or near New Jersey. They either are looking for a nearby stream on which to canoe, fish, or explore by other means, or they already have a specific stream in mind, but just want to first know what awaits them. These chapters may also appeal to the armchair explorers, who have no intention of or hope of ever personally floating down all of Jersey's waterways but would like to know just what they would find if they did so. So I have tried, as completely as possible, to inventory the state's canoe routes, thus addressing the diverse (and sometimes perverse) tastes of my readers. As you will see, the menu of New Jersey waterways definitely includes some winners and some losers.

In the following pages, I have attempted to help you not only select a stream, but also plan a successful outing on it. To achieve the latter goal — and recognizing that many beginners will use this book — I was tempted to dedicate much of this chapter to how to canoe. Instead, I have included a few basic tips, but have refrained from trying to cover the topic. The wealth of literature and club, Red Cross, and commercial paddling instruction available in this region can do a much better job than I can. I urge you to use these resources. Those few basic tips that I did include in this introduction will help you better use this guide and understand the information that it provides. I discuss hazards, reading water, judging tides, etc. I have also taken the liberty to preach about conservation, etiquette, and ways that you can help to improve the sport. I beg that you take the time to read and consider the content of those few short pages. The pressures on our water resources grow every year. Only care and energy from you, the user, can assure a rosy future for our pastime. So here is what you need to know.

How To Use This Book

I have organized this book geographically, starting at the northwest corner and working counterclockwise around the state. Where streams have multiple tributaries, I began with the uppermost and worked downstream. I have also divided the state into three major watersheds. Watershed maps precede those descriptions. So if you are searching for a stream to explore in a specific neighborhood, this order will be convenient. If you are looking for a specific stream, use the alphabetical index at the end of the book.

Each river report starts with a (usually) brief **Introduction**. This may locate the stream, identify its outstanding qualities or deficiencies, or inject some historical or contemporary color.

Next the **Section** is identified. I have selected sections most often because of some unifying characteristic, such as quality of scenery, degree of difficulty, or duration of its boatable season. Sometimes the section is just what makes for a good day's run. And on many small streams, it is simply the whole stream. Understand that your trip need not conform to these sections, assuming that there are other points of access. After all, some of my sections will be too long or too short for your tastes. The maps described below will help you tailor your trip.

1

Each section begins with a table of vital statistics — gradient, difficulty, distance, time, scenery, and map number.

Gradient describes how steeply the stream drops. It is expressed as feet per mile and comes from dividing the total drop of the segment by its length. Runnable gradients of streams in this book range from zero on lakes and tidewater to as much as 126 feet per mile in the Rockaway River's difficult Boonton Gorge. Gradients of local whitewater favorites, Pennsylvania's Lehigh Gorge and lower Tohickon Creek, are respectively 20 to 30 feet per mile and 40 feet per mile. Traditionally, even the most daring and skilled paddlers seldom descended streams that exceeded 100 feet per mile. But today, elsewhere in this country, paddlers are negotiating streams as steep as 300 feet per mile without portaging. But that represents the most extreme reach of whitewater sport. If there are significant variations in gradient distribution, I have also included (on the next line) the gradient of the steepest stretch. For example, 1.5 mi. @ 50 means that there is a section that drops 50 feet per mile for a mile and a half.

The gradient is a general indication of likelihood of rapids. The higher the gradient, the higher the probable frequency of rapids and riffles. Sometimes, however, gradient can mislead you. For example, on some rivers, much of the drop is expended in steps, either unrunnable waterfalls or dams. So a stream with a 50-foot-per-mile gradient might actually be a flatwater trip with big portages. You also cannot assume that a stream with a steep gradient is necessarily difficult. For example, there are many small streams with a continuous and evenly distributed drop that gives little more than some bounce and a fast ride. On the other hand, some large rivers with low gradient, but a pool-and-drop configuration, may give you mile-long pools followed by thundering (but runnable) cataracts. So it is necessary to somehow quantify difficulty.

Difficulty is based on the international whitewater rating scale that runs from 1 to 6 and a flatwater scale that goes from A to C. But I have expanded the whitewater numbers to include + and − to improve their precision. I have expressed difficulty as a range (for example, 1 to 3 +) because few rivers stay the same difficulty for very far. If a stream includes a markedly different stretch or one bad rapid, I have set that difficulty off with a comma (for example, 1,4 −). As for the flatwater scale, I have condensed it to just A, feeling that noting variations in current speed would be important to few.

The inventors of the rating scale intended it to be descriptive and objectively applied. Here is what it is supposed to mean.

A. Smooth Water. This may range from a placid pond to the remarkably swift mini-rivers of the Pine Barrens. Keep in mind that this is meant to mean the opposite of rapids and riffles and does not take into account temporary conditions. So the Atlantic Ocean in a nor'easter technically still rates the difficulty A, "flatwater."

1. Easy. Expect short, straightforward riffles usually formed by gravel or sand bars, low ledges, or constrictions of the river. Waves are less than one foot high, and little maneuvering is required. Routes are easy to determine, and all riffles are followed by adequate rescue opportunity.

2. Medium Difficulty. Rapids are more frequent, composed of waves less than two feet high and in regular patterns with easy eddies. There are more rocks and obstructions, but maneuvering is still easy, and rescue spots are still plentiful.

3. Difficult. Rapids are long and require extensive maneuvering. Both ledges and waves are up to three feet high, and waves are often irregular. The course is not always easily recognizable. Rescue opportunities are spaced farther apart.

4. Very Difficult. There are long, pushy, extended sets of rapids with high, irregular waves. Boulders and ledges block the course and, along with powerful crosscurrents, require abrupt and intricate turns. The course is often difficult to recognize, and scouting is often necessary. Rescue is difficult.

5. Exceedingly Difficult. There are long, heavy rapids with high, irregular waves and powerful crosscurrents, or steep, complex, boulder-clogged rapids with poor visibility. Big drops and powerful hydraulics are unavoidable, and ability to catch small, fast eddies is essential for control. Rescue is very difficult, and scouting is often unavoidable.

6. Utmost Difficulty. All the difficulties stated in Class 5 are carried to the extreme. Running such water involves an unusual risk of life.

As you can see, this rating system describes the difficulty of streams or segments of streams. However, paddlers have come to use these numbers to rate rapids also. If you just delete the references to frequency in the above definitions, they work well as a rating scale for rapids.

The problem with this wonderful, objective rating system is that it is used by subjective people such as you, me, and the paddler next door. What often ends up determining a stream's rating are such variables as experience of the rater, size of his or her ego, effect of adverse weather, and the number of wipe-outs, swims, and rolls associated with a particular trip. Also, there has been a trend in recent years, as paddle skills and equipment improve, to downgrade river ratings. As I stated above, people are now running streams with gradients of 300 feet per mile. So what the best paddlers used to call "pushy," "powerful," or "unavoidable" is now run by the masses. So be cautious when considering river ratings given by paddlers whom you do not know well or even given by unfamiliar guidebooks.

To standardize my ratings in this book, I have intended them to describe the given stream at a level of about six inches of runnable water at that stream's gauging point. If you encounter higher or lower water, be prepared for a different difficulty. Since there is no standardization of ratings between various guidebooks, do not count on my application of the rating scale to necessarily match those of other authors. I have tried to take the middle of the road, but the best way for you to get a feel for my ratings is to first try a stream rated well within your ability and then take it from there.

Finally, please note that the 1 through 6 scale is a whitewater rating system only and thus only describes conditions encountered on an ideal, unobstructed stream. In reality, many of this state's small streams are complicated by fallen trees, fences, and other strainers that come and go from year to year. These obstacles greatly increase the difficulty and risk involved in paddling these streams. Then, add to this such factors as water temperature, air temperature, and your physical condition to determine whether you can handle a given class of difficulty on a given day.

Distance is expressed in statute miles and is rounded off to the nearest tenth of a mile. The number describes the distance from one end of a given stream segment to the other, even if there is no convenient access to one of those points. This is all pretty straightforward until one must describe big rivers, such as the Hudson or lower Delaware, or estuaries. For big rivers, the distances are measured from point to point along the centerline of the stream. So the actual distance that you paddle will usually be slightly longer. For wide estuaries or coastal segments with irregular shorelines, the distance represents the route of a paddler traveling about a hundred yards offshore, but who shortcuts across sharp embayments.

Sometimes distance does not tell the whole story. For example, a battle through a mile of the strainer-choked Ridgeway Branch would consume about as much time and effort as eight miles on the Delaware River. And battling a mile into a head wind on Barnegat Bay is far different from floating a mile on the Richardson Gorge, North Branch Raritan. You must vary your time allowances accordingly.

So **Time** is also included, expressed in hours and rounded off to the nearest half hour. This represents paddling and portaging time only. Be sure to allocate extra time for lunch, scouting, and rescue.

Scenery is self-explanatory. I can sometimes be hard to please, especially since I explore many streams in the cold months when there is no foliage to hide the trash, summer homes, industry, and other blemishes.

Maps listed are those applicable to that section. The number corresponds to that on the lower right-hand corner of the map.

Next **Hazards** are listed. The inclusion is usually redundant, but better safe than sorry. You will note that I have often indicated that certain dams or falls are runnable. Unless otherwise stated, if I have declared a drop runnable, it is because I have tried it successfully. As a rule, I discourage beginners and novices from following my lead, because the consequences to the unprepared can be as serious as death in a keeper hydraulic. After all, who knows, maybe I just succeeded by pure luck. On the other hand, experienced paddlers who understand these risks might as well enjoy as much drop as the stream has to offer. But do so at your own risk.

Water Conditions describe the best time of the year and how long after precipitation one can expect to find adequate water in the stream. For example, if I say that a river is most often up from November through May, within two days of hard rain, that means that the river most often rises to, and sustains for the longest time, runnable levels during those months, but those levels are only likely to last for two days after a hard rain. Since I detest driving long miles and endless hours, while wasting gallons of precious gasoline, to find an empty river, the time spans recommended for catching a stream are slightly conservative. The creeks may retain water longer than indicated, but do not count on it.

There is a certain general rhyme and rhythm to favorable water conditions in these streams. Many freshwater streams in this book are small and convey a rapid runoff. You will note that for most of these, the best flow conditions occur between November and May. During those months, large frontal storms — storms that drop large amounts of rain over a wide area — roll through the state. Summer showers, in contrast, can be incredibly heavy, but they often dump only on a few square miles. Also, in summer, vegetation consumes a tremendous amount of moisture that might otherwise run or seep into your river. But during the cold months, most of this vegetation is dormant, so that a given rain has a bigger effect on river levels.

When you look at the streams of the Pine Barrens, they almost always have adequate water. This is because they are fed by a huge, bountiful aquifer (a natural reservoir of water that saturates the soils and rock below). As for the tidal streams, if you can wait a few hours, the tide will return and fill them with enough water.

As mentioned earlier, the rate of flow down a stream can determine its difficulty, not to mention its floatability. Stream flow describes the volume of water that flows by a point in a given time. In the United States, the standard unit of measure is cubic feet per second. Metric countries use cubic meters per second. Since paddlers can seldom measure stream flow, they establish on each stream a point of reference called a **Gauge**. A gauge relates stream height at a given point to flow and canoeability. Sometimes the point of reference is just a joint on a bridge pier, a well-placed rock protruding from the water, or the depth of water in an indicative riffle. A great number of the streams in this book, however, are graced by some sort of numbered staff gauge.

The best of these gauges are United States Geological Survey (USGS) stream flow gauging stations. You can usually identify a full USGS gauging station as an eight- to 20-foot-high, slim, rectangular concrete tower, often located near a bridge. Some others consist of a vertical, corrugated pipe with a green wood or metal box perched on top. These stations contain instruments that measure, record, and sometimes transmit the height of the stream. Many stations also have a readable staff gauge on the outside. The scales on both gauges, inside and out, read the same and are usually set so that they will never measure a negative level. Hence, zero canoeing level on a stream may be, for example, 6.5 feet on a USGS gauge. Generally, paddlers must personally inspect the outside staff on these gauges for a reading. But for about two dozen gauging stations in this book, daily readings are available from the United States Weather Service River Forecast Center in Philadelphia at (215) 627-5575 and in Harrisburg at (717) 234-6812.

Often, the outside staff of the gauging station has washed away. So for the call-in gauges, I have noted whether they are also readable on site. There are many gauging stations that would be very useful, but they neither have outside staffs nor do they transmit their data to the Weather Bureau. But I have sometimes cited these gauges in hope that the USGS will some day replace the outside staffs.

Finally, in addition to these full gauging stations, the USGS also operates water-quality monitoring stations and temporary gauging stations on many more streams. These activities account for why there are so many nice enameled staff gauges on so many of New Jersey's streams and are thus referenced in this book. I have generally taken pains to describe the exact location of these staffs, as they can be easy to miss amongst the mud and weeds. Sometimes the lower ends of these gauges are torn away, rusted, faded, or buried by mud. So add a tape measure and shovel to your paddling gear.

One final word about USGS gauges. The Weather Service performs a tremendous service to the paddling community by making these readings available to us. In Washington, D.C., for example, the Service maintains a 24-hour, multiple-line phone recording, updated twice a day, just for recreational users. The Philadelphia office, lacking a recording, sacrifices valuable personnel time to respond to our needs. In these budget-trimming times, we cannot take these services for granted. So if you use this phone number, please take the time to write the Director of the National Weather Service, 8030 16th Street, Silver Spring, Maryland 20910, and let him or her know how much you appreciate this service. It helps at budget time.

On some popular canoeing streams, or streams with no other gauges, canoeists have established their own, usually by painting marks at one-foot or half-foot increments on bridge piers and abutments. These gauges usually establish their zero marks at the lowest possible level for navigation. However, you should always keep in mind that paddlers possess varying ideas of what constitutes "too low," depending on such variables as the gauge painter's boating prowess, boat materials and durability of construction, and degree of aversion to boat repairs and maintenance. So the boater who runs a river when an unfamiliar canoe gauge reads near zero may be a real gambler. As for my definition of zero, it is the level at which you unavoidably start scraping in more than a few short shallows, unless I have specified otherwise.

For each nontidal stream, I have tried to include a gauge that you can personally inspect and, if possible, a call-in gauge. If there is a call-in gauge only on a nearby stream, I have included that gauge. But that reading must only be regarded as a rough correlation.

Understand that gauges have their limits of usefulness. Unless I have otherwise stated, the recommended gauge level reflects what you need to canoe the stretch of stream near the gauge. High water moves like a big wave, especially on small, flashy streams. So while you may be reading an adequate level at the gauge, 10 miles upstream, the water may have already passed by, and it may already be too low. So it helps to know whether the stream is rising or falling. You may, for example, call Philadelphia on Friday and find that High Bridge is reading 6.7 feet — a fine level. But when you arrive on Saturday, it has already dropped to 6.4 feet — too low for paddling. So it is often wise to start calling gauges two days before you go paddling, to detect a trend. Also, when using the roughly correlated gauges, that is, the gauges on nearby streams or on distant sections of your stream, remember that the correlation holds up best if there is either snow melt or uniform rainfall. So do not count on these gauges in showery summer months.

Maps accompany each river description, primarily to answer shuttle and access questions. Except for the usually exaggerated river widths, the maps are spatially accurate. So that you can tailor the length of your outing to your needs, I have included as many river mileages as possible. These are the little numbers hugging the rivers, and they denote the distances between the little arrowheads. These arrowheads do not necessarily denote access points. Sometimes I have just placed them at landmarks, such as high bridges and mouths of major tributaries, just so you can mark your progress on your trip.

In general though, you can assume that most bridges afford some degree of public access and that those roads that I have included that dead-end at the water will also get you to a public or friendly private access point. I have also occasionally included roads that dead-end at the water, but are not open to the public. I have included these should you need an emergency access point. On tidewater and some of the bigger or more popular rivers, the various levels of government have provided special public access areas for boaters or fisherpersons, often with ramps or parking areas. These are identified, where space permits, as "Access."

As for gauges, I have included most gauges that you must inspect on site and some call-in gauges.

Finally, space constraints prevented me from including all the useful information that I wanted. Parts of this little state are so crowded, that I had to exclude even a few bridges. While these maps should be entirely adequate to conduct a trip, a good street map might also help in the congested suburbs of northeastern Jersey, and I highly recommend a good topographic map for exploring the coastal marshes of southern Jersey.

Geography of New Jersey

New Jersey covers only about 8,200 square miles. But within that modest area, a variety of natural and human influences have molded the interesting selection of rivers in this book.

Starting in the northwest, where the land is highest, you can find mountains — or approximations of such. Over in Sussex and Warren counties, which abut the northwest border, narrow, parallel ridges and wide valleys form an orderly pattern. Geologists call this zone the Ridge and Valley Province. The Jersey portion is the northern end of this landform, which extends south to Alabama. Sandstone, shale, or limestone underlies this topography. This limestone is most striking where it makes up the walls of some of the area's beautiful, old houses. Usually the ridges are wooded, and the valleys, covered with farms. But creeping suburbia is slowly transforming this sleepy, natural character.

In most Appalachian states, the streams that drain the Ridge and Valley section are usually small, shallow, rocky, and swift, with narrow valleys and quick runoff. But in New Jersey, many of the valleys are flat, soggy acres — the remains of glacial lakes. So the rivers of these valleys often move sluggishly and stay up relatively long as water oozes out of the wetlands.

Just to the east is a zone the geologists call the Highlands — an area with topography reminiscent of southwestern New England. Here are even more mountains and valleys, but the uplands are typically broader and made of harder rock such as gneiss. Like the Ridge and Valley Province, part of this area was altered by the glaciers. But here, the lakes and ponds formed by the melting of the ice survive today. Green Pond and Hopatong, Greenwood, and Budd lakes are such remnants. Being closer to New York City, population pressures are proportionately greater on the Highlands. Though plenty of open space remains on the mountaintops of the northeast and on farms of the southwest Highlands, suburbia has established a firm and expanding foothold in this region.

Rivers of the Highlands are small. Sometimes flat and sluggish, sometimes steep and swift, they generally hold their water better than most mountain streams because of the lakes and wetlands they drain. Some of the best whitewater in Jersey, such as that found on the Rockaway, Pequannock, Black, and South Branch Raritan rivers, occurs where these streams drop off the Highlands into the next geologic zone.

This next zone is the Piedmont, also a relatively raised area. Some of it is rolling; some of it is flat. There are even some isolated ridges, such as the two Watchung Mountains. Roughly, U.S. Rte. 1 and the Palisades make up the eastern boundary. Its underpinnings are mostly shale and sandstone, except for the ridges and the Palisades, which are durable basalt, diabase, and other volcanic rock. Its overpinnings are asphalt and concrete, for much of this territory has been buried beneath city and suburb, including the incredible industrial belt that millions of travelers have seen and smelled from the Turnpike. But some rural environment persists in the southern Piedmont of Hunterdon, Mercer, and Middlesex counties.

Gentle landscapes like the Piedmont usually create gentle streams. There are, however, such notable exceptions as the Lockatong and Wickecheoke, which tumble down rapids and falls in order to descend through the highlands that flank the Delaware River. Rivers of the Piedmont usually rise and fall quickly. But where the glaciers visited, leaving huge lakes that ultimately became huge wetlands, flows are far more stable.

The remaining 60 percent of the state lies in the Coastal Plain. As one might expect, this area is typically low and flat. But there are 200- to 400-foot exceptions such as the Atlantic Highlands, Beacon Hill, Arneys Mount, and other subtle, but significant, lumps in the land. The plain is mostly made of loose soils rather than rock. Dull as plains tend to be, the Coastal Plain contains some striking variety.

Most of the soils along the southern and western portion of this area are fertile and retain moisture well. But from Glassboro to Trenton, a dense strip of urbanization locks up this precious farmland resource. Elsewhere, these soils support agriculture, especially the cultivation of fruits and vegetables. The productivity of these farms have earned Jersey its nickname, "The Garden State." About two thirds of the Turnpike passes through this belt, meaning that, for better or for worse, this is what molds part of the world's impression of New Jersey as a flat, boring state. Waterways of this strip are either tiny, overgrown swamp runs or their marshy (at least in their natural state) estuaries.

Much of the eastern half of the Coastal Plain is a 900,000-acre mass of mostly infertile sand called the Pine Barrens. Cranberry and blueberry cultivation thrives here, but little else. Much of the Barrens' area is covered by dry, stunted pine and oak forest that inevitably burns before it gets very big. At times, the same fate befalls housing tracts that developers have foolishly located in this tinderbox.

This area is not dry though, just porous. Falling rain quickly trickles through the coarse sand, doing little for the thirsty vegetation, but collecting below to form a tremendous aquifer. The aquifer, in turn, generously feeds numerous tiny, surprisingly swift, swampy streams. As a result, most rivers of the Coastal Plain have unusually stable flow regimes.

In contrast with the lonely Barrens, the northern end and eastern edge of the plain, including a fragile fringe of sandy barrier islands along the Atlantic, are blanketed by city and suburb. But the southwestern fringe is, by Jersey standards, also lightly populated and also dedicated to agriculture. The waterways of this region are mostly tidal and salty, taking shape as estuaries, marshes, or shallow, open bays.

It takes rain to run rivers, and New Jersey gets its fair share. Southern Jersey averages 45 inches per year; and northern Jersey, 47 inches. The pockets of highest precipitation center around Morris County and Ocean County, with a 48-inch-per-year average. Oddly, the driest spots are at the northern tip of the state and along the southern tier of counties, the low being an average of 40 inches per year. The distribution over the year is fairly constant, ranging from about three to almost five inches per month. The driest months are likely to be February and April while the wettest are July and August. This is an ironic twist, since the stream flows tend to be highest in winter and lowest in late summer.

As for temperature, New Jersey is not Hawaii. Summers are usually hot and humid. Winters are cold, not cool. Nevertheless, the ocean does exert some moderating influence, as shown by the fact that the north gets about three and a half times as much snow as the south. In addition, the vast urban blobs surrounding Philadelphia and New York create a heated microclimate. So dedicated paddlers can, for most of the year, paddle at least somewhere in this damp state.

Coastal Canoeing

As you read through this book, you will see that New Jersey offers a trove of paddling opportunities on its tidal waters. One might think that since this is all flatwater, with no rocks, strainers, falls, and other nasty pitfalls, paddling on bays and estuaries would be a pretty benevolent activity. The truth is, however, capricious tides, contrary wind, and baffling channel morphology can easily make a mess out of a potentially good trip. Just look at what happened to Odysseus.

But do not let this discourage you from exploring these beautiful waters. Just use good sense. Until you develop the knack of paddling tidewater, keep your itineraries short enough that you can reach your destination even if you must fight the tide and wind the whole way. And remember the following tips on how you can adapt to this environment.

First, pay attention to wind. Wind is not just an annoyance; in open water it can be a hazard. It is amazing how much wind resistance you and your boat have, and how small a wave it takes to swamp a canoe. And it is really amazing how wind coupled with cool temperatures and can hurry wet paddlers into hypothermia. So if the day's weather forecast includes small craft warnings or predicts a front passing through, this might be a day to find something else to do. You can also retreat to some narrower, hence more sheltered, streams or plan an itinerary that will keep the wind at your back.

Picking the right craft helps too. A sea kayak can greatly increase your efficiency and margin of safety in rough seas. A keeled or V-shaped bottom is an asset for an open canoe. Also, loading your canoe so that the heaviest end faces the wind reduces the tendency for the wind to turn you.

It is impossible, unfortunately, to accurately predict winds, often even a half hour in advance. But there are resources at your disposal. The Weather Service's regular forecast usually predicts wind velocities and issues small-craft warnings. These are useful, but, like any weather forecast, they should be taken only as a best guess. Take particular note of any forecast of a front passing through, as this also means increased winds are likely, especially in the colder months.

If you have not heard a forecast, make your own. High, wispy clouds; clouds that look like fish scales; and colorful sunrises are often harbingers of impending fronts within 12 to 24 hours. As for the wind at the moment, often just feeling the wind on your face is inadequate to judge wind intensity. While driving to the water, I look for big flags. If they are limp or just stirring, conditions are usually mild. If they are flapping, watch out. Finally, it is now possible to call for up-to-the-minute and on-the-spot reporting of wind conditions via a private service provided by Wind Hot Line. Catering primarily to windsurfers, who delight in windy days, this company reports conditions at Kennedy Park (Somers Point), Sandy Hook, Trixie's Landing (about six miles south of Toms River), Brant Beach (on Little Egg Harbor), and Croton-On-Hudson (Hudson River, 11 miles north of the state line). For more information, write Wind Hot Line, P.O. Box 716, Cambridge, MA or call (617) 864-7940 or (800) 765-4253.

Second, pay attention to tides. Tides mean more than just a rise and fall of water. As the waterways fill and drain during the rise and fall of the tides, they create gradient. And gradient creates current — surprisingly strong currents. So if you start at the wrong place at the wrong time, you will feel as if you are working out on a watery treadmill.

Unlike wind, tides are predictable. The tide changes four times over 24 hours, evenly spaced. The tide coming in from the sea is called the flood tide, the tide going out is called the ebb tide, and the pauses in between are called slack water. You can know in advance when these phases are to occur by consulting a tide table. You can purchase these tables directly from the U.S. Coast and Geodetic Survey in Washington, D.C. or from your local marine supply store.

To understand the use of a tide table, let us take an example. Pretend you want to paddle up the Cohansey River from its mouth on May 1, this year. First you consult this year's table (these are annual publications). It gives the tide schedule at the nearest major point, in this case the entrance to Delaware Bay, on each day of the year. The chart has columns for time of slack water, time of maximum current velocity, and what that maximum current velocity is. The velocity column also indicates the tide's direction, ebb (E) or flood (F). So after checking out May 1, you determine that maximum flood tides will occur at 1110 (tables use military time) and

2331, and that slack waters preceding these tides are at 0812 and 2021 respectively. Now if you want to paddle by daylight, you would choose to time your trip to the first tide and start on the slack at 8:12 A.M., figuring to have a maximum favorable current at 11:10 A.M. and dead slack about six hours after you put in (remember, four tides per day).

But wait! This is the schedule of tides at the Delaware Bay entrance. What about at the mouth of the Cohansey, 45 miles up the bay? It takes longer for the tide change to reach up here. So you now consult an auxiliary table that lists various points up and down the bay and then lists the time difference between that point and the entrance. The lag times vary slightly between ebbs and floods since the Delaware River's inflow always causes a net flow down the bay. So looking up the Cohansey River entrance in the table, you see the time difference at just before flood is + 1 hour, 48 minutes and for maximum flood is + 1 hour, 42 minutes. Therefore, you add these to the schedule at the bay entrance, and now you know that on May 1 you should start heading upstream at 10:00 A.M. (8:12 + 1:48) and will be moving along fastest around 12:52 P.M. and then hitting slack again around 4:00 P.M. This is just the minimum that you can learn from a tide table, but it is enough to canoe by.

If all of the above just seems too complicated for you, you can always take an educated guess by my method. Just go to the bank of the river and see which way the current is flowing. Let's assume that you are near the upper end of the estuary. If the current is toward the sea and little or no mud is showing along the edge, that means that the tide has recently started ebbing and that this is a good time to put in here. If two or three feet of mud are exposed, this means much of the tide has ebbed, and it will soon change direction. So, if possible, go to the other end of the creek to start. This method is not precise, but will generally keep you going with the flow.

Finally, watch where you are going. For while your typical estuary or bay usually gives the impression of substance and depth when viewed from shore, the paddler soon finds that in reality these waterways are often only inches deep with only a narrow, elusive channel barely suitable for even canoe navigation. If you are cognizant, however, of a few basic rules, you can pick your way down these passages with the confidence of a veteran waterman.

First, channels on estuaries, as on nontidal streams, tend to hang to the outside of bends, especially on the lower reaches of the stream where bottom-scouring tidal currents are strongest. Be aware, however, that on tight S-turns, the channel often tends to cut diagonally across to the other side much sooner than on a nontidal river. Even on long, straight stretches, the channels will often wander back and forth. On coastal bays — the water bodies that lie between the barrier islands and the mainland — waters along the backside of a barrier island are almost always shallow. Along the mainland side, little bays and coves are also usually shallow.

Next, look where the waterfowl hunting blinds are. Blinds are usually serviced by motorboats, which need deep water even more than you do. So the conservative navigator in shallow waters might choose to simply zigzag from blind to blind.

Look for man-made markers. The most obvious are channel buoys. These are seldom necessary on any sizable estuary because currents scour out good channels. But on the coastal bays, often the only deep passageways, at least at low tide, are the Intracoastal Waterway and other maintained channels. On upper reaches of estuaries, where channels really start withering, look for strange sticks or clusters of sticks that seem to protrude unnaturally from the murky shallows and seem to follow a line. These are often some waterman's crude buoy system.

Nature sets out markers too. On the extreme upper reaches of estuaries, watch for vegetative patterns. Lily pads, arrowhead plants, etc., usually grow only in shallows. So watch for gaps in the growth, and go for them. On bays, look for birds. If they are wading, not swimming, you know not to head in that direction. You will also learn to recognize a contrast between the textures of wind ripples in shallow and deep water.

Now that you are armed with all this useful information, the first thing you will probably do is go run aground on the mud anyway. At that time, out of the silence, you will probably hear the quack of some mallard ducks. Mallard quacks sound like scornful, irreverent laughing. In this situation, they probably really are laughing at you. But don't worry. If you have had the relative fortune to mess up at low tide, then you just have to wait six hours, and you get lifted off for a second chance.

And one last thing. Probably no discussion on coastal canoeing would be complete without some mention of bugs. New Jersey, like just about every other state, has reason claim the mosquito as the real state bird. Together with various types of biting flies, they can make your tour of the marshes seem like a bad trip to Transylvania. The best cure for biting insects is winter. I do all of my coastal paddling between October and May. A little frostbite is better that a lot of bug bites, and it does not buzz before it strikes you. If you insist on warm-weather paddling, learn to paddle in wind. Wind is an effective mosquito repellent. If you seek a chemical solution, keep in mind that some of the most successful active ingredients are brutal on your eyes, skin, plastic coatings on your clothing, etc. Finally, if you can pick a mild day, just covering up helps a lot.

Good luck.

No Paddler Is An Island

The growing popularity of paddling has resulted in the appearance of paddling communities and clubs in about every sizable town. Is there such a group in your neighborhood? In your best interest and that of the rest of us, I urge you to find the nearest group and join.

Why? A membership in a canoe club will be the best buy for your boating dollar that you will ever find. Besides affording you the chance to meet other people of similar interests, many clubs conduct excellent education programs. Here is an opportunity to quickly acquire techniques that might take you years to learn on your own, and it is free. Clubs serve as a marketplace to buy and sell the sport's highly specialized equipment. This is also the place to keep up with the latest techniques, materials, and other consumer information. If a new hazard appears on a nearby stream, this will be your first chance to learn about it, other than the hard way. If an access problem arises, this is also where to learn about it first. Essentially, a club is your contact with the world of paddling, and no matter whether you boat once a year or every week, or if you are a rugged loner or a group person, you will get the most out of the sport if you keep in touch.

But clubs have another important function — they are the guardian of your special interest. They give you the strength of numbers needed to get your way in this world. It has been clubs that have succeeded in securing special recreational water releases from reservoirs, such as on Pennsylvania's Tohickon Creek and Lehigh River, New York's Esopus Creek, or Massachusetts' West Branch Farmington River. Club input and cooperation has helped guide management decisions on publicly regulated riverways such as the Delaware River and Lehigh rivers. Clubs have helped local rescue squads improve their river rescue capability. Clubs have spearheaded river conservation movements and stopped destructive dam projects. And they have represented us paddlers when boat taxes and user fees threaten.

Essentially, clubs are your river lobby. They are your paddlers' union. Your support of a club, if only in adding your name to its roster, increases its clout to protect your favorite streams and your right to enjoy them with a minimum of interference.

The following are some clubs that serve the area described in this guidebook. Since most club contacts change from year to year, an inquiry at the nearest outdoors specialty shop should produce an address for those clubs that do not possess a permanent address.

Brooklyn, NY: Metropolitan Canoe & Kayak (P.O. Box 021868, Brooklyn, NY 11202-0040)
Chester County, PA: Buck Ridge Ski Club (P.O. Box 179, Bala Cynwyd, PA 19004)
Easton/Allentown/Bethlehem, PA: Lehigh Valley Canoe Club (P.O. Box 2726, Lehigh Valley, PA 18001)
Hunterdon County: Hunterdon County Canoe Club (c/o Hunterdon County Parks, Hwy 31, Lebanon, NJ 08833)
Monmouth County: Monoco Canoe Club
North Jersey: Kayak & Canoe Club of New York (6 Winslow Ave., East Brunswick, NJ 08816)
    Murray Hill Canoe Club
    Garden State Canoe Club
Philadelphia, PA: Philadelphia Canoe Club (4900 Ridge Ave., Philadelphia, PA 19128)
Ridgefield Park: Wanda Canoe Club (P.O. Box 723, Ridgefield Park, NJ 07660)
Trenton: Mohawk Canoe Club
Wilmington, DE: Wilmington Trail Club (P.O. Box 1184, Wilmington, DE 19899)

The Importance Of An Education

Believe it or not, the hapless fellows in the movie "Deliverance" (the suburbanites, not the perverts) are real and common phenomena on our nation's rivers. For it seems that a dumb myth persists in this land. Many individuals believe that the ability to handle a canoe masterfully is instinctive. Unfortunately, too many of these people who have ventured forth to demonstrate their born-to-canoe illusion have become the clients of the local rescue squad, mortician, etc. If you are a raw novice contemplating using this book, you will enjoy it much more if you first accumulate a little education. If you go to the local library or bookstore and obtain a how-to-canoe book, you are on the right track. But you will find it much more effective, efficient, and enjoyable to be taught by a real, live paddler.

It is easy to find instruction in paddling, especially if you live in the big metropolitan areas covered by this book. First of all, you can call your local Red Cross chapter, which usually conducts basic canoeing classes each summer. These courses teach you the details of the canoe and equipment, basic flatwater handling skills, and rescue. Next, contact any of the local clubs listed earlier. Most of these conduct basic flatwater and whitewater paddling classes and offer trips where you can practice your newly acquired skills in the presence of more experienced individuals. Note that even if you do not aspire beyond smoothwater paddling, the knowledge of boat handling and understanding of currents gained from a basic whitewater course will still be of great value to you. Finally, if you have lots of money to spare, there is a fine selection of private paddling schools located as close as Pennsylvania, New York, and Massachusetts, and up and down the Appalachians. In return for your dollar, you receive more intense, advanced, and individual instruction than most clubs afford. These schools also have the advantage of providing your equipment and other logistical needs.

So as you can see, the opportunities to become a master of your craft are there. Please use them.

Save Our Rivers

It is unfortunate, but if something can go wrong with a river, it will. This is especially true in a densely populated region like New Jersey, where lots of people have lots of ideas about how they would like to treat the land. For this reason, it is important that we paddlers take the initiative as watchdogs of our favorite streams. This responsibility is made easier thanks to the existence of a few dedicated organizations, four of which I particularly urge you to support.

1. **American Rivers.** We river lovers are fortunate to actually have an official lobbying organization representing us in the big seat of power, Washington, D.C. It goes by the name American Rivers. This is a small and dedicated band of activists who fight for the preservation of free-flowing streams and fight against needlessly destructive projects such as certain dams, river channelization, etc. They are our David fighting our numerous river-eating Goliaths. Please support them (and help yourself) by joining. Individual memberships are $20 per year, sent to American Rivers, 801 Pennsylvania Ave., S.E. Washington, D.C. 20003. Keep a friend in high places.

2. **American Whitewater Affiliation.** This is a national paddling organization oriented towards whitewater enthusiasts. It has channeled a lot of its energy into preventing hydroelectric projects from destroying prime whitewater streams. While New Jersey whitewater issues have been few, this group has been instrumental in protecting whitewater steams in Pennsylvania, New York, and New England, areas frequented by Jersey whitewater paddlers. Membership is $15 per year, sent to 146 N. Brockway, Palatine, IL 60067.

3. **Natural Lands Trust.** The local governments cannot always plan for or buy up park land as fast as the need arises. Filling some of that void is this Philadelphia-based organization. Its area of interest has been eastern Pennsylvania, Maryland, Delaware, and New Jersey. Its most visible contribution to the latter is protection of The Glades, which surrounds Oranoaken Creek in Cumberland County. Send your contributions or inquiries to Natural Lands Trust, Inc., 1616 Walnut Street, Suite 812, Philadelphia, PA 19103.

4. **The Nature Conservancy.** This group fills a similar function as the Natural Lands Trust, but its emphasis is on preserving ecologically important areas. We paddlers have benefited from this pursuit because the Conservancy has protected a section along the Manumuskin River in Cumberland County. To join or contribute, write The Nature Conservancy, 1815 North Lynn Street, Arlington, VA 22209 (national office) or 17 Fairmount Road, P.O. Box 181, Pottersville, NJ 07979-0181 (New Jersey Chapter).

River Manners

In spite of all the posted lands in New Jersey, most of its streams suffer no access problems. But with the increased popularity of river running, this situation could change, if we do not abide by some basic principles of river etiquette. The following suggestions address most of the sort of actions that have made paddlers unwelcome. Please remember these so that you never spoil the fun for others who follow.

1. When possible, always ask permission to cross, park on, or camp on private land. Most people are glad to share a corner of their land if you just show them this respect.

2. Find a secluded spot for changing your clothes. Public nudity is incredibly offensive to many people, both in backwoods and "enlightened" urban areas, especially when you bare yourself right in front of their house, family, etc.

3. Do not block roads or driveways, even just to slow down for a brief chat. If you cannot find a decent shoulder, keep moving until you do. Otherwise, not only do you obstruct traffic or create a hazard, but also you might get a ticket. Too many times, paddlers have been known to park in and block driveways without permission. Besides being a serious breach of etiquette, you could be responsible for blocking a fire truck or ambulance from its destination. How would you feel then?

4. If you are floating down a creek, and a landowner tells you to "git," then git. Arguing or gesturing obscenely will get you nowhere and will only exacerbate his grudge against paddlers. Besides, you were headed in that direction anyhow. A humble demeanor or apology can often shame a hothead into a more mellow stance.

5. Do not damage those horrible barbed wire, electric, and other fences. They are there to keep a farmer's livestock in during the 99 percent of the year when the creek on which you are floating is only ankle deep. They are not there to hurt you intentionally.

6. Litter leaves hard feelings, so do not litter, even if the stream is already trashy.

7. Be discrete about where you start fires. Ask permission where possible, use other people's fire rings at popular campsites, leave as little evidence of your fire as possible, and, of course, thoroughly douse your fire when you are done.

8. Be nice to fishermen, even if a few of them are not nice to you. Give them a wide berth, do not run over their lines, keep the noise down when passing by, and avoid the popular fishing streams during the first week of trout season. Remember, they enjoy the river as much as you do. And if that does not sway you, remember that there are far more fishermen than canoeists, they are better organized, they have more economic clout, and they have more friends in the state legislatures.

There is another pragmatic motivation for good conduct on and near the river. It has to do with navigation rights. This is a murky subject that varies from state to state. Some states say that if someone owns both sides and the bottom of a stream, he or she owns the water as it flows through. At the other extreme, some states say any stream recreationally navigable, even with obstructions requiring portages, is available for public passage. The definition of public waters even varies depending on whether you are talking about right to navigate, right to fish, or right to pollute.

In my less-than-scholarly investigation of this subject, I was unable to determine the law in New Jersey. We clearly have a right to passage on any tidal waters. And big streams, like the Delaware, are no problem because of precedent set by commercial navigation. But as for small, free-flowing streams, especially these 10-foot-wide cow-pasture brooks, I lack any answer and welcome your input for future editions. In the meantime, tread lightly. A low profile or good behavior may help you to avoid any challenges. Even if we do have a right to paddle on any dribble, if a local sheriff or hotheaded property owner does not know that, you still may be fined, ticketed, or forcibly ejected. And while you might be able get the last laugh in court, why unnecessarily risk ruining what could have been a nice day.

Glossary

In order to communicate with as many people as possible, I have tried to limit the amount of canoe jargon in my descriptions. The newcomer may, nevertheless, still be baffled by a few commonly used river terms. So I have included this brief glossary.

Advanced: Paddler who is competent at maneuvering his or her boat, reading the water, and staying out of trouble in Class 4 or greater whitewater.

Beginner: A person who knows little or nothing concerning basic strokes, canoe handling, and how a river works. Seldom gets out paddling more than once or twice a year.

Braiding: Situation where a stream channel splits, and then the split splits, and then the split splits split, ad nauseam, to form a pattern resembling a braided rope. Such areas can often spell trouble, because narrow and shifting channels are prone to strainers.

Estuary: That portion of a river where it has reached sea level and is thus influenced by the tides.

Hole (A.K.A. hydraulic, keeper, stopper, souse hole, reversal): A foam-filled depression in the water caused by water dropping over a rock, ledge, or weir to displace the water at the bottom of the drop. This results in a recirculating surface current that can slow down or trap boats that enter it. Potentially dangerous.

Intermediate: Paddler who understands the principles of boat handling and the mechanics of river currents, and can roughly move his or her boat to where desired on up to Class 3 water.

Left (or Right): One side as distinguished from the other, when one is facing downstream.

Low-water Bridge: A low concrete slab or culvert bridge designed to function only at low water levels and to accept inundation without damage at high water. A poor man's special, but a paddler's headache.

Novice: Paddler who has learned the basic canoe strokes and simple fast-water maneuvers, such as eddy turns and ferrying, and who understands the nature of currents, eddies, holes, etc., but has not become proficient at using all that knowledge.

Playing: Activity where skilled whitewater paddlers practice precise boat maneuvers by using the current. This includes surfing, hole sitting, and catching eddies for fun. If this still makes little sense, a brief whitewater canoeing lesson or one of those slick whitewater videos now sold in your local boating shop would be worth a thousand words.

Shuttle: Complex car positioning/exchange undertaken by groups of paddlers to make sure that when they reach the take-out, they have a way to get back to the put-in.

Strainer: Any obstacle across the current that allows water to flow through while trapping any floating scum or debris, including boats and boaters. Very dangerous. In this book, I have usually used this term to denote fallen trees, logjams, and brush. I usually separately describe the man-made strainers such as fences and low-water bridges.

Weir: A little dam where water passes over its crest. Do not be deceived by their relatively low height. Often forming powerful holes, they can be every bit as deadly as a big dam or waterfall.

Help Set The Author Straight

Writing a canoeing guidebook is frustrating. I just know that right at this moment, as I write this page, somewhere in New Jersey, a flash flood is moving a rock in a stream bed to somewhere different than where I said it was. Some tree is falling across a stream that I called unobstructed. Some developer is putting up 100 look-alike houses along a stream that I called pristine. The Department of Transportation is probably changing a route number. Some bored delinquents may be shooting holes in the street sign that marks the crucial turn on a complicated shuttle. And shifting gravel probably has caused some gauge to now read two feet off from what I said it should.

It is difficult to nail a moving target. So help me out. Do not be shy. If you find any mistakes or changes, I welcome your comments. Just write Seneca Press, 530 Ashford Road, Silver Spring, MD 20910 and help build a better guidebook. Sure as you will hit another rock, there will be another edition some day.

Further Reading

Good river running does not end at the state line. So here is a list of fine guidebooks that cover some of the nearby areas where Jersey paddlers like to roam.

Keystone Canoeing by Edward Gertler (Seneca Press, 530 Ashford Road, Silver Spring, MD 20910). This describes over 230 streams in Pennsylvania, primarily in the state's eastern two thirds, following the same format as this book.

Maryland and Delaware Canoe Trails by Edward Gertler (Seneca Press). This describes over 110 waterways in Maryland, Delaware, District of Columbia, and a little of Pennsylvania, following the same format as this book.

New England Whitewater by Ray Gabler (Tobey Publishing, Box 428, New Canaan, CT 06840). This attractive and well-written book covers New England's most popular whitewater runs.

Canoeing the Jersey Pine Barrens by Robert Parnes (Globe Pequot Press, Chester, CT 06412). Though covering some of the same streams as this book, Parnes' book provides a more in-depth description of those streams and the natural history of this interesting region.

To further enrich your exploration of New Jersey, here are a few references that make interesting reading. I used these as sources of background information for this book, and I highly recommend them.

New Jersey: A Guide to the State by Barbara Westergaard (Rutgers University Press, New Brunswick, NJ)

New Jersey's Special Places by Arlene Zatz (The Countryman Press, Woodstock, VT 05091

The Pine Barrens by John McPhee (The Noonday Press, 19 Union Square West, New York, NY 10003)

Vegetation of New Jersey by Beryl Robichaud and Murray F. Buell (Rutgers University Press, New Brunswick, NJ)

It Ain't Easy Writing A Guidebook or
Hypothermic Horrors

Those of us who are really hooked on paddling do so almost year-round. We not only tolerate the cold months, but in many ways we find them the best time for paddling. Crowds are down and water is up. When you get away from the city, winter is a beautiful time. You discover that country snow is white, not gray, black, red, or whatever other color is billowing out the stacks of the nearby factories. Golden marshes, brown fields, silvery hardwood forests mottled by ever-greens, and white sycamore bark cast against an azure winter sky can be much more cheery and stimulating than the monotonous green of summertime.

Yet, for all the glories of cold-weather paddling, we should never forget that insidious danger that is always ready to strike — hypothermia. It can kill or maim the unprepared voyageur. Volumes and volumes have been written on the cause, prevention, and treatment of this problem. But I have yet to hear of any intelligent discussion concerning one of hypothermia's most overlooked and underrated consequences: severe, chronic, mind-scarring embarrassment. It is clear we cannot wait any longer for guidance from the medical establishment. I guess I myself will start the ball rolling. So let me tell you about a little known incident on what should have been an average trip on a quiet country brook.

To begin with, this trip was a bad choice. A warm early morning sun and 36-degree temperature served to allay my concerns that this day would be too cold for paddling. It could only get warmer. Right? But by late afternoon, an incoming cold front had sent the mercury plunging to 25 degrees, clouds had covered the sun, and the wind was roaring at probably over 30 miles per hour.

Cold can be sneaky. When you are active, you can be oblivious to it. Just ask any cross-country skier. So the hours of wind chill were never obvious while I vigorously stroked away in the relative warmth of my closed canoe.

But it all became frighteningly telling when I crawled out of my boat at the take-out. I instantly began to shiver. But, worse yet, my hands, which never really felt all that cold while paddling, had lost most of their gripping strength and coordination. The obvious cure would be a warm car.

But I had chosen that morning to leave my car at a more secure location out on the main highway — a three-mile walk from this forlorn spot. Wearing only a wet suit farmer-john bottom (only 1/8th-inch thickness at that), I was neither likely to attract a ride nor stay warm. It seemed that I would be facing a bitter, wind-swept death march. But luckily, I had brought along a pair of warm, baggy wool pants to cover up with.

Life, unfortunately, is never that simple, for these particular pants did not have a zipper, but buttons. Did you ever try to button buttons with numb fingers? Goodness knows I tried, while the whistling wind sucked away more precious calories. I might have had more success performing brain surgery with my toes. So I resigned myself to clutching my pants through a cold, three-mile hike. It turned out though, I wasn't alone.

A short way up the road, I spotted six men sawing firewood (they were not cold). I made the decision in a snap. It was born in desperation. And so, I swallowed my pride and waddled across the road, my pants dropping twice, and said something like, "Hey fellas, I know you're not going to believe this request. But I'm really serious. Will one of you please help me button my pants?" A nervous silence followed as they exchanged funny looks. Five seconds of that type of silence was more than I could bear. So I quickly began to rattle off a detailed trip report, personal biography, and dissertation on the horrors of hypothermia, all the time keeping a careful eye on the nearest fellow holding a chain saw, all in hopes of establishing some level of credibility. My eloquence was astonishing, especially considering that my body temperature had by then sunk to that of a flounder.

I guess I did a good job, as one man finally volunteered. Red-faced, I at least took consolation that my shoes did not need tying too.

So, as I was saying, winter is the greatest time of the year for paddling. You just need to properly prepare for it. I learned my lesson. Hopefully, you will too. Next time I'll take some duct tape along to hold up my pants. How about you?

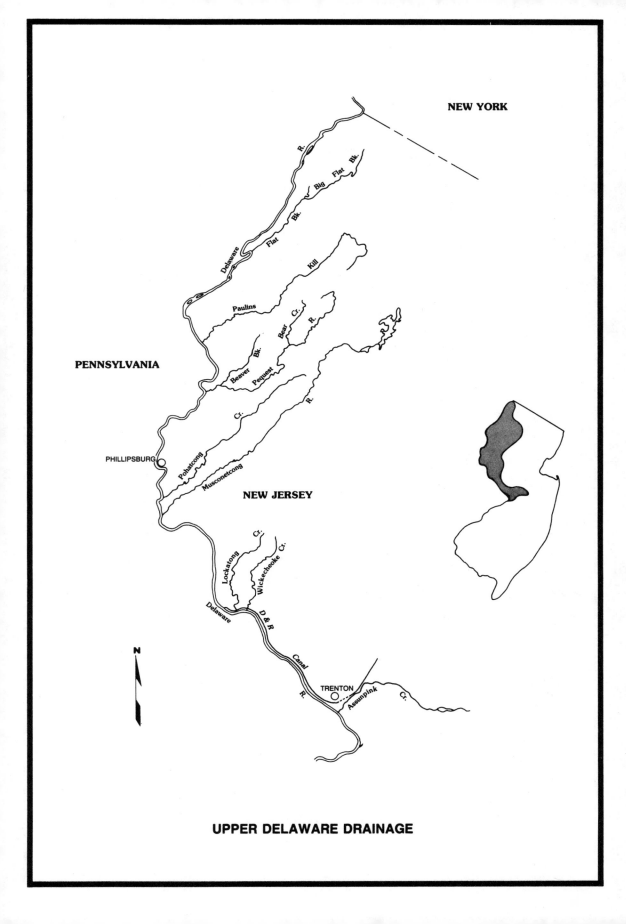

NEW YORK

R.

Big Flat Bk.

Flat Bk.

Delaware

Kill

Paulins

Bear Cr.

R.

PENNSYLVANIA

Beaver Bk.

Pequest

Cr.

R.

PHILLIPSBURG

Pohatcong

Musconetcong

NEW JERSEY

Lockatong Cr.

Wickecheoke Cr.

Delaware

D & R

Canal

TRENTON

R.

Assunpink Cr.

N

UPPER DELAWARE DRAINAGE

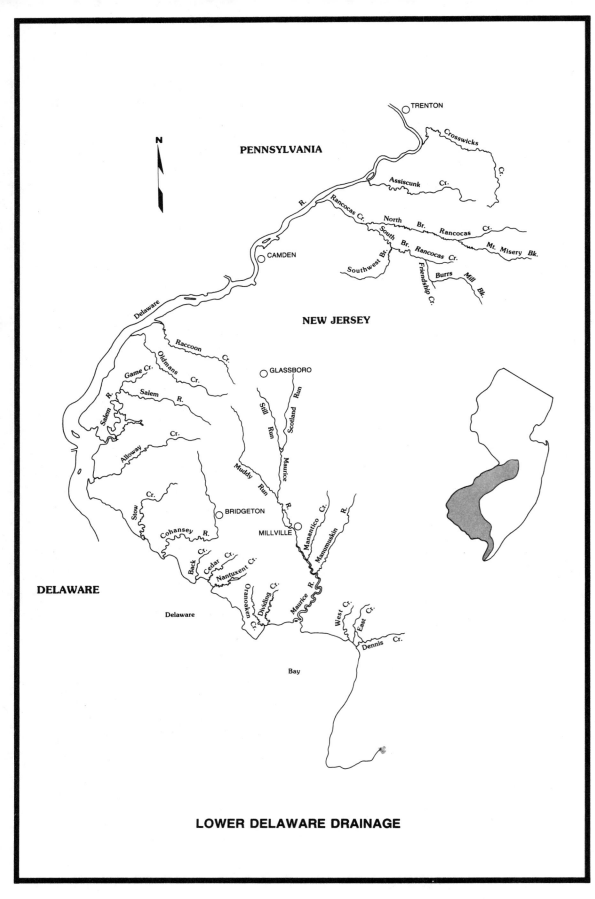

LOWER DELAWARE DRAINAGE

Chapter 2
The Delaware Basin

A little less than half of New Jersey drains west or south either directly into Delaware Bay or indirectly, via the Delaware River. Spanning over 160 straight-line miles from near Port Jervis, New York, to Cape May, New Jersey's portion of the Delaware Basin offers a good cross-section of the state's variety. Its upper reaches consist of a pleasant mix of wooded ridges and rural to semi-rural valleys. Then comes the rolling Piedmont farm country. When it hits the Coastal Plain, the basin becomes part of the great urban corridor, crowded with Trenton, Camden, and every town and suburb in between. Then south of Camden, the basin includes a big chunk of the garden part of the Garden State — a rich agricultural area that is relatively uncrowded.

There is plenty of good paddling here. The centerpiece, of course, is the mighty Delaware River. For thousands, this river has been their first, and maybe even only, taste of canoeing. More serious boaters have long known the joys of the Delaware's swift headwater tributaries. Birders and sportsmen have long headed for the marshy recesses of the lower basin tributaries. And even in urban sprawl, the creeks there provide fine refuges from most of the ugliness and congestion. There should be something here to please you.

The following waterways are described in this chapter:

Delaware River
  Flat Brook
  Paulins Kill
  Pequest River
    Beaver Brook
  Pohatcong Creek
  Musconetcong River
  Delaware & Raritan Canal
  Lockatong Creek
  Wickecheoke Creek
  Assunpink Creek
  Crosswicks Creek
  Assiscunk Creek
  Rancocas Creek
  North Branch Rancocas Creek
    Mt. Misery Brook and Greenwood Branch
  South Branch Rancocas Creek
    Southwest Branch
  Raccoon Creek
  Oldmans Creek
  Salem River
  Alloway Creek

Delaware Bay
  Stow Creek
  Cohansey River
  Back Creek
  Cedar Creek
  Nantuxent Creek
  Oranoaken Creek
  Dividing Creek
  Maurice River
    Still Run
    Scotland Run
    Muddy Run
    Manantico Creek
    Manumuskin River
  West Creek
  East Creek
  Dennis Creek

Delaware River
Flat Brook

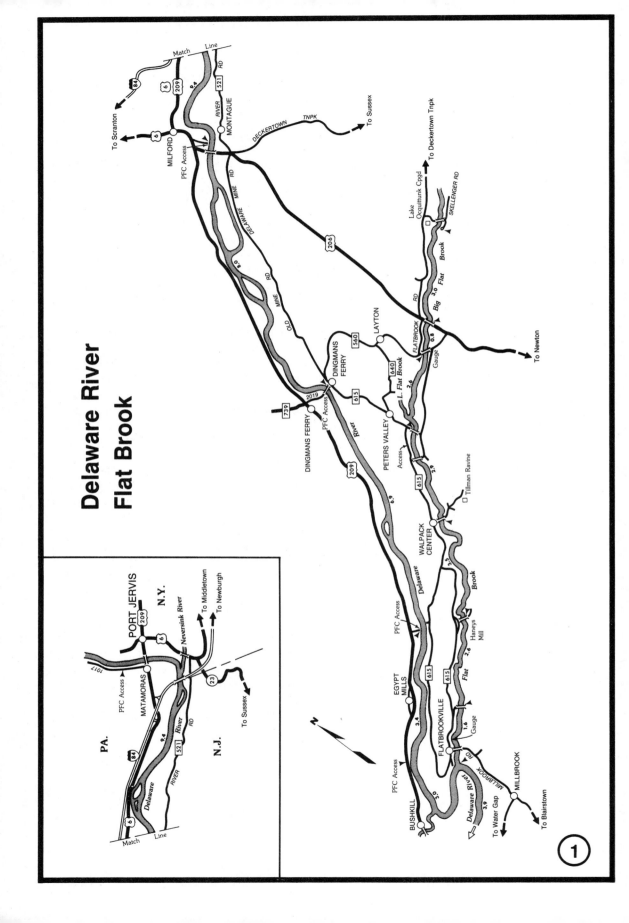

①

Delaware River

INTRODUCTION: The Delaware River and Delaware Bay define New Jersey's western border, molding part of this state's distinctive crooked shape. New Jersey and Pennsylvania share the river, while the section from the Delaware line to the mouth of Alloway Creek belongs entirely to Delaware. Below Alloway, the states split the waters down the middle again.

The waters of the Delaware spring initially from the magnificent 3,000- and 4,000-foot-high peaks of New York's Catskill Mountains, via the river's East and West branches. Further augmented by such Catskill-draining tributaries as the Neversink, Beaverkill, Willowemoc, and Mongaup, and such Pocono-draining tributaries as the Lackawaxen and Shohola, the Delaware enters New Jersey as a big river. The Delaware is officially born at the confluence of the East and West branches, about a mile south of Hancock, New York. From there it flows 197 miles to tidewater, at Trenton, and then sloshes back and forth for another 85 miles to a point south of Salem, where it arbitrarily becomes Delaware Bay.

The Delaware is an anomaly. It is the only major river on the Eastern Seaboard that is not shackled by dams. Major highways seldom follow it very far. Neither do the railroads. Above tidewater, there is only one city on its banks and only a few large towns. There are few big factories along it either, and only four power plants. Not surprisingly, with this absence of development, the water in the free-flowing Delaware is clean and often clear.

Wedged between two of the nation's biggest metropolitan areas, the relatively empty Delaware Valley, with its sparkling, clean river, has long been a prime recreational refuge. The hills surrounding the river's upper reaches are filled with plush resorts, camps, second home developments, private hunting and fishing preserves, and great estates. The immediate river, however, is now partially protected from further unchecked development by the Upper Delaware National Scenic and Recreational River, from Hancock to Port Jervis; the Delaware Water Gap National Recreation Area, from Port Jervis to the Water Gap; Roosevelt State Park, on the Pennsylvania side from Easton to Morrisville; and Delaware & Raritan Canal State Park, on the Jersey side from Raven Rock to Scudders Falls.

These qualities have not gone unnoticed by boaters. Streams just do not come much more popular. Between Hancock and Trenton, there are at least 20 major liveries supplying over 4,000 canoes to eager refugees from the sweltering city. On a hot summer weekend, the boats are often all used. While the worst crowds are on the Hancock to Port Jervis section, over 2,000 boats a day ply the New Jersey section of the Delaware. Add to this population rental inner tubes, rafts, and kayaks, and then a wave of private canoeists, tubers, and kayakers, and an untold number of calloused fishermen on shore, and you have the American version of the River Ganges. So if you want the Delaware to yourself, it is best to visit during the week, after the season, in rotten weather, or after a nuclear war.

Still, the Delaware is Jersey's only big freshwater river. And there are advantages to that. You can always rely on it to have canoeable water levels, even where it rushes over rapids and riffles. And since it is available in summer, it offers one the chance to learn or play on elementary whitewater in the comfort and relative safety of warm weather and warm water. Beginners will be grateful. And finally, it is one of the few nontidal rivers in the state where you will never have to portage or lift over a single fallen tree.

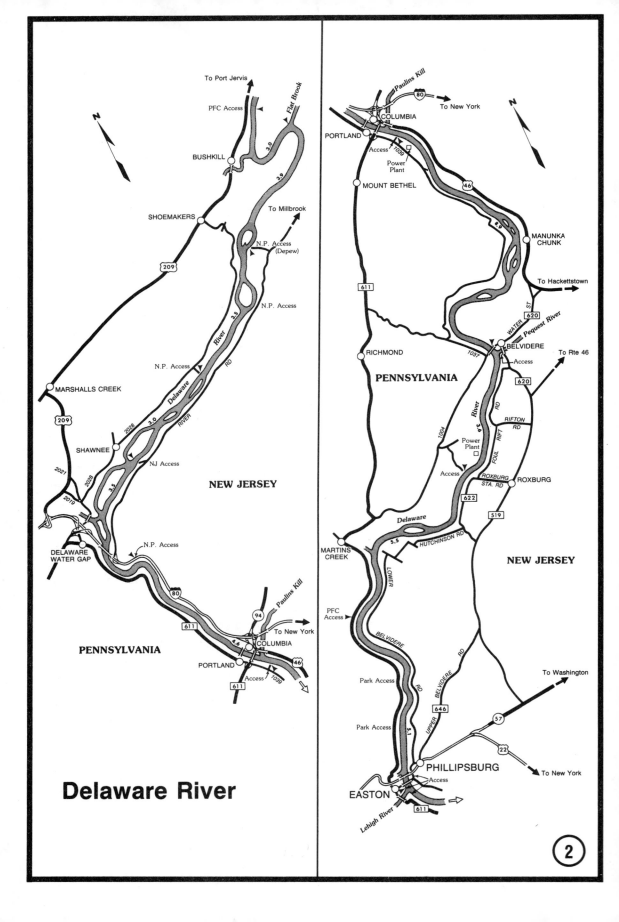

Delaware River

②

Gradient	Difficulty	Distance	Time	Scenery	Map
3	A to 1—	44.6	15.0	Good	1,2

TRIP DESCRIPTION: The Delaware River, the Neversink River, and the New York/New Jersey line converge at the south end of the town of Port Jervis, New York. Just upstream is Matamoras, Pennsylvania. The put-in at this town is at a Pennsylvania Fish Commission access, the only public access point in that tri-state area. Also at Port Jervis, the Delaware makes a 90-degree turn to the southwest. On the right now lies the low and uniform escarpment of the Pocono Plateau. On the left runs the high ridge of Kittatiny Mountain, which peaks at 1,803 feet at High Point, near Port Jervis. The Delaware remains so sandwiched until it escapes through the famous Water Gap.

In many respects, this is the nicest section of New Jersey's Delaware River. It suffers no busy highways along its banks, and the only major highway running up the valley, U.S. Rte. 209, has quieted considerably since through truck traffic was banned between Delaware Water Gap and Milford. This is the only section of river whose banks are unblemished by summer homes. Even the floodplain is free of any buildings. This relative degree of isolation, combined with placid water, makes this stretch ideal for canoe camping. This is especially significant, since few other streams in New Jersey offer much opportunity for legal camping.

Do not take this reach of river for granted. The planners have long dreamed of constructing a huge dam at Tocks Island, a few miles above the Water Gap, to form an comparably huge reservoir that would reach back upstream almost to Port Jervis. The idea was that this reservoir would be thirsty New York City's insurance policy against future droughts. The plan lies dormant now — a victim of questionable benefit-cost ratios, environmental awareness, and recent abundance of water. When the dry years return, however, canoeists can count on this project to again rear its ugly head.

Much of this section is enveloped by the Delaware Water Gap National Recreation Area. The reason for this area is that the Tocks Island Dam came so close to fruition that the Corps of Engineers had already acquired the lands that would be impacted by the project. So keeping this land public not only made sense as a badly needed green space, but it would also simplify reactivation of the dam project, if ever so desired. Regardless of the intended land use, the clumsy acquisition practices of the Corps of Engineers, and then subsequent regulation by the National Park Service, have left a trail of bitterness amongst the valley's inhabitants. This is not the neighborhood in which to walk around bragging that you are a preservationist.

However unfair the acquisition episode was, the river scenery and we the users have benefitted. The subsequent leveling of many riverside houses has restored the banks to a primitive condition that they have not enjoyed for years. Many places where you now may camp would have been posted and developed land in the past. Similar aesthetic qualities on this section's Flat Brook tributary also might not exist were it not for this preservation effort. And as the suburbs continue to inch toward the Delaware, such a huge tract of green space will become priceless.

HAZARDS: None

WATER CONDITIONS: The Delaware is always canoeable, except in winter freeze.

GAUGE: There are USGS gauges at Port Jervis and Montague (call Philadelphia or Harrisburg, or call the National Park Service at 717-588-6637). Levels of 2.3 feet at Port Jervis and 4.9 feet at Montague represent summer low-flow conditions.

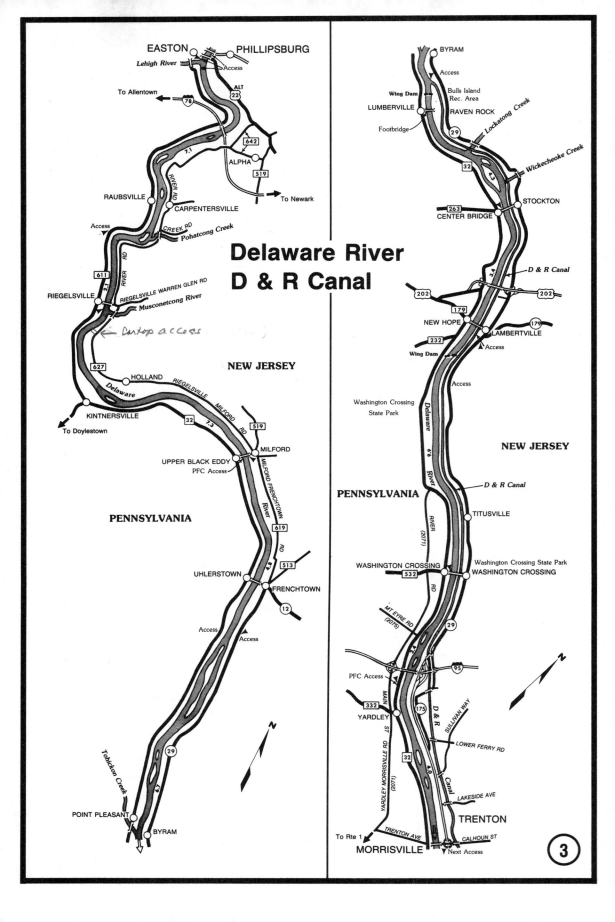

Delaware River
D & R Canal

NEW JERSEY

PENNSYLVANIA

NEW JERSEY

PENNSYLVANIA

EASTON   PHILLIPSBURG
Lehigh River   Access
ALT 22
To Allentown   78   642
7.1   ALPHA
519
RAUBSVILLE   CARPENTERSVILLE
To Newark
Access   CREEK RD
Pohatcong Creek
611
RIEGELSVILLE   RIEGELSVILLE WARREN GLEN RD
Musconetcong River
Cartop access
627
HOLLAND   RIEGELSVILLE MILFORD RD
Delaware   519
KINTNERSVILLE   32   7.3
To Doylestown   MILFORD
UPPER BLACK EDDY   MILFORD FRENCHTOWN RD
PFC Access
619
UHLERSTOWN   513
FRENCHTOWN
12
Access   Access
29
Tohickon Creek   47
POINT PLEASANT   BYRAM

BYRAM
Access
Wing Dam   Bulls Island Rec. Area
LUMBERVILLE   RAVEN ROCK
Footbridge   29   Lockatong Creek
32   4.3   Wickecheoke Creek
263   STOCKTON
CENTER BRIDGE
3.4   D & R Canal
202   202
179
NEW HOPE
232   LAMBERTVILLE
Wing Dam   Access
Access
Washington Crossing State Park
Delaware River
D & R Canal
TITUSVILLE
RIVER (207½)
WASHINGTON CROSSING   Washington Crossing State Park
532   WASHINGTON CROSSING
29
MT EYRE RD (207½)
95
PFC Access   175   D & R
332   SULLIVAN WAY
YARDLEY   LOWER FERRY RD
MAIN ST
YARDLEY MORRISVILLE RD (207½)   32   4.0
Canal
LAKESIDE AVE
TRENTON
To Rte 1   TRENTON AVE   CALHOUN ST
MORRISVILLE   Next Access

(3)

Section 2. Delaware Water Gap (Kittatiny Access) to Easton (Front Street Access)					
Gradient	Difficulty	Distance	Time	Scenery	Map
4	1,2	27.7	9.0	Fair to Good	2

TRIP DESCRIPTION: This section begins in the heart of the Water Gap. To really do this natural landmark justice, you should not just look up at it from a canoe, but also look down on it from the top. A good but aerobic way of doing this is to climb Mount Tammany, which is the end of Kittatiny Mountain on the Jersey side of the gap. The 1,500-foot peak is reached via a blue-blazed trail that branches off of the Appalachian Trail about a half mile north of the river. For more details, either inquire at the National Park Service visitor center in the gap, or pick up an Appalachian Trail map at your local outdoors shop.

Overall, this is the least scenic section of the Delaware this side of Trenton. The Delaware Water Gap, of course, is magnificent, but the interstate highway that passes through it is not. There are three power plants on this reach, and there are long lines of houses on its banks. This section ends in the heart of Easton and Phillipsburg, whose pretty hillside facade is reminiscent of an Old World town.

These are mostly smooth-flowing miles. The occasional rapids and riffles are short and easy, but there is one notable exception — Foul Rift. Located a mile below Belvidere, Foul Rift is a long rapid through a staircase of jagged and diagonal limestone ledges. For a beginner, it can be a nasty place to be, at any water levels.

HAZARDS: None

WATER CONDITIONS: This is always canoeable, except when frozen or flooding.

GAUGE: Check the USGS gauges at Belvidere and Easton (call Philadelphia or Harrisburg). Levels of 3.4 feet at Belvidere and 0.8 feet at Easton represent summer and fall low-flow conditions.

Section 3. Easton (Front Street Access) to Trenton (Old Wharf Access)					
Gradient	Difficulty	Distance	Time	Scenery	Map
3	1,2	50.8	16.5	Fair to Good	3

TRIP DESCRIPTION: Fortified with Lehigh River water from Pennsylvania, the Delaware now cuts through the last of the Appalachian ridges and heads off across the Piedmont to tidewater at Trenton. This is a surprisingly beautiful section, often lined by wooded bluffs and high rock cliffs. There are a few too many houses upon its banks, but many are old and attractive, as are the many small towns along the way. Approaching Trenton, Morrisville, and Yardley, the area becomes increasingly suburban, and then urban. But the neighborhood might have ended up far more crowded had Morrisville been successful, back in 1783, in its bid for being the site of the new nation's capital.

This is also a section of smooth waters and simple, well-spaced riffles. But there are a few splashy surprises. The first, at Raven Rock, is the two-foot wing dam (used to divert water into the Delaware and Raritan Canal) with its wide and wavy chute in the center. Next comes another wing dam, this one below New Hope/Lambertville, with an interesting boulder- and ledge-formed rapid at its foot. Finally, there is Scudders Falls — a low, diagonal reef, above I-95, with a variety of easy chutes. This is a favorite local whitewater play spot. Only a few easy and rocky riffles mark the Fall Line and the Delaware's entry into tidewater, above the U.S. Rte. 1 bridge in Trenton.

Public access points along both sides of this section are relatively plentiful. It is important to

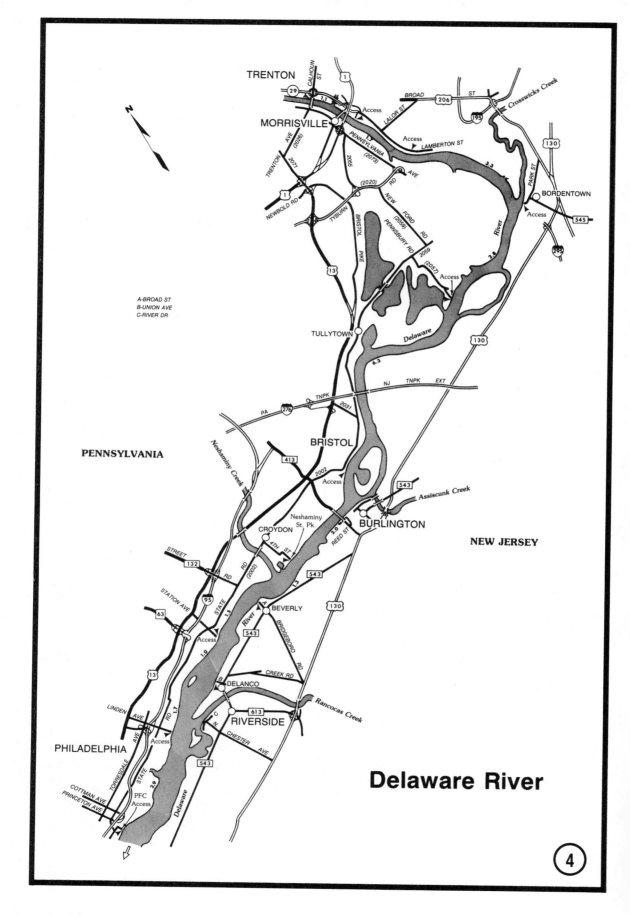

Delaware River

4

note that on this section and Section 2, much of the river bank is privately owned. Particularly during the summer busy season, you should put in and take out only at public launch areas. The normally acceptable access spots, as at bridges and roadsides, just cannot accommodate the throngs that converge on this popular river. Some river towns even have ordinances that prohibit access at bridge rights-of-way.

Finally, it is worth knowing that you can do most of this section without needing a car shuttle. With the Delaware and Raritan Canal running along the Jersey bank from Raven Rock to Trenton and the Pennsylvania Canal running along the Pennsylvania bank from Easton to Morrisville, you can paddle back to your starting point. But heed the following advice. First, make sure that you confirm that the section of canal that you plan to use is watered. Periodic maintenance, leaks, and seasonal drawdowns can leave you with just a damp ditch. Second, keep in mind that both canals have a fairly stiff current. So allow a lot more time for going up the canal than floating down the river. Finally, paddle the canal first. If your itinerary bites off more miles of canal that you can chew, it is better to find this out early, when you already done the hardest leg, rather than later.

HAZARDS: Avoid blundering over the edges of the wing dams at Raven Rock (Bulls Island Recreation Area) and Lambertville. At moderate to high levels, the resulting hydraulics could trap a boat (and boater), so stick to the center. Also, know where they are ahead of time, as low dams are difficult to see until you are almost on their brink.

WATER CONDITIONS: This is always canoeable, except when frozen or flooding.

GAUGE: You can use USGS gauges at Easton, Reigelsville, and Trenton (call Philadelphia or Harrisburg). Levels of 0.8 feet, 2.8 feet, and 8.1 feet, respectively, represent late summer and fall low-flow conditions.

Section 4. Trenton (Old Wharf Access) to National Park					
Gradient	Difficulty	Distance	Time	Scenery	Map
0	A	40.5	20.0	Fair to Different	4,5

TRIP DESCRIPTION: This section will appeal to relatively few. It is tidal, meaning that getting in and out at low tide can be a muddy mess and, for two quarters of the day, the current is going in the wrong direction. And to make matters worse, as the river approaches Philadelphia and Camden, the water becomes filthy, and the air often smelly.

But this section has its virtues too. The reach from Trenton to Burlington is still partially undeveloped and pretty. William Penn's Pennsbury Manor and the waterfronts of Bristol and Burlington are also a pleasure to behold. Getting on into the city, aesthetics are displaced by an interesting array of the technological complexities of the human anthill: the great bridges, a steel mill, loading docks, cranes, shipyards, and ships. Great jet planes zoom in and out of the Philadelphia International Airport. And there is the skyline of the great city, looming behind it all, like the castle of a medieval town. True, it is not as pretty as a rose. But it is an opportunity to view, at a leisurely pace and in a simple and detached way, the high-speed and complex world of which you and I are party. It is fascinating.

If you prepare for this section's peculiarities, you should have a pleasant trip. When you embark on these waters, use the tides, do not fight them. Remember that the shipping channels are for ships, not canoes. Those big freighters move much faster than you do, but they cannot swerve to avoid running over you. Finally, once in Philadelphia and Camden, the shores are often bulkheaded, not to mention privately owned; so you are limited in where you can even get out and stretch. Plan accordingly.

Delaware River

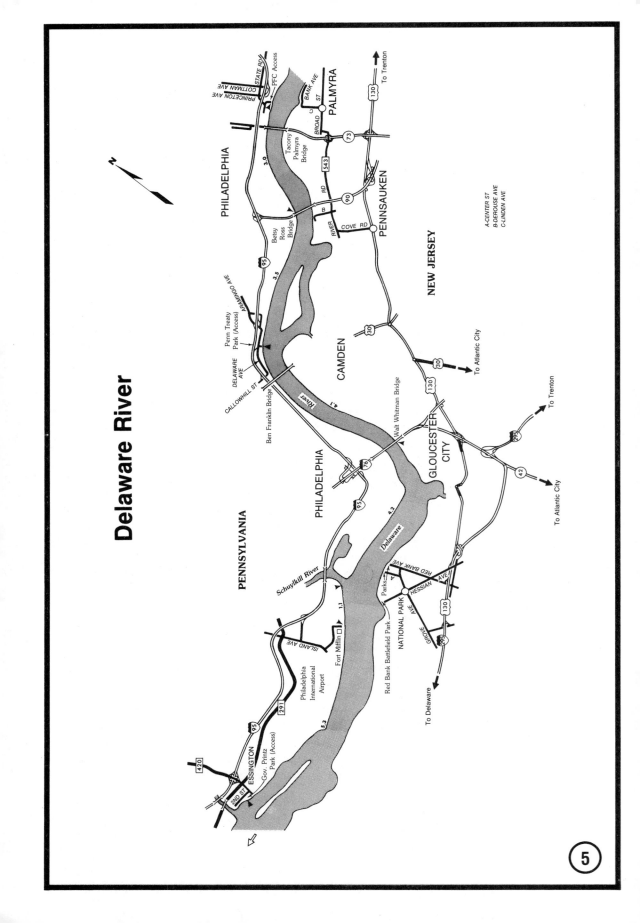

PENNSYLVANIA

PHILADELPHIA

PHILADELPHIA

Schuylkill River

Fort Mifflin

Philadelphia International Airport

ISLAND AVE

291

95

Gov. Printz Park (Access)

ESSINGTON

2ND ST

420

Ben Franklin Bridge

CALLOWHILL ST

DELAWARE AVE

Penn Treaty Park (Access)

ARAMINGO AVE

95

3.3

3.5

Betsy Ross Bridge

COTTMAN AVE

PRINCETON AVE

STATE RD

PFC Access

3.0

River

RD

RIVER

B

COVE RD

543

90

73

BROAD ST

BANK AVE

Tacony Palmyra Bridge

PALMYRA

130

To Trenton

PENNSAUKEN

NEW JERSEY

A-CENTER ST
B-DEROUSE AVE
C-LINDEN AVE

CAMDEN

Walt Whitman Bridge

130

30

30

To Atlantic City

River

1.1

4.1

76

95

4.2

Delaware

GLOUCESTER CITY

295

42

To Trenton

To Atlantic City

130

295

GROVE AVE

HESSIAN AVE

RED BANK AVE

NATIONAL PARK

Parks

Red Bank Battlefield Park

1.1

5.3

To Delaware

⑤

This section has surprisingly good opportunity for boating access, if you are not choosy about which side of the river you will use. The Pennsylvania side seems to have the best selection of public boat ramps or parks. But for the resourceful boater, there are plenty of unofficial launch spots on the Jersey side at little parks, under bridges, by roadsides, etc. For example, the end of this section, at National Park, has three good choices. You can get out at the Red Bank Battlefield Site, a mile upstream at a town park at the end of Center Street in Red Bank, or just a bit farther upstream at the end of Red Bank Avenue in Red Bank. To use this latter spot, you will find that across the street from the League Island Ferry slip (no trespassing) is a playground with a convenient hole in its fence on the river side.

The Red Bank Battlefield is worth including in your tour. This is a county park that commemorates the site of Fort Mercer, where, in 1777, an outnumbered Continental Army defense force repulsed a unit of Hessians. This success delayed the British invasion of Philadelphia and is said to have been a major factor in the French decision to throw their support behind the American Revolution. Part of the riverside Continental defense (and on display) is what was called chevaux-de-frise. This was a heavy timber boom, bristling with sharp spikes, that was strung across the river to float a few feet beneath the surface. Its purpose was to poke holes in any British shipping that attempted to approach Philadelphia. Paddlers who have vied for space on the crowded Youghiogheny or Lehigh rivers during rafting season have no doubt dreamed of the construction of similar contraptions.

HAZARDS: Give commercial shipping a wide berth. Beware of disgusting water quality.

WATER CONDITIONS: Always canoeable

GAUGE: None necessary

Flat Brook

INTRODUCTION: Flat Brook drains the western edge of Sussex County, running parallel to the nearby Delaware River. It gathers its first drops of flow from the south flank of the highest point in New Jersey, a spot which, by the way, is imaginatively named High Point. Flat Brook's valley occupies but a sliver of land between Kittatiny Mountain and a lower, unnamed ridge. This is about as far away from New York City as one can get in northern New Jersey, and there is no fast way to get there either. As a result, Flat Brook is one of the most unspoiled canoe routes in the northern part of the state.

Technically this description covers two streams, as above the inflow of Little Flat Brook, this stream is called Big Flat Brook. The two segments are indeed distinct, so this ephemeral route can match with a wide variety of paddling skills.

Section 1. Big Flat Brook. Skellenger Road to unnamed road due south of Peters Valley					
Gradient	Difficulty	Distance	Time	Scenery	Map
46	1 to 3—	6.4	2.0	Good to Very Good	1

TRIP DESCRIPTION: At its northern end, Kittatiny Mountain spreads out from a narrow ridge to a five-mile-wide plateau that is protected within the bounds of Stokes State Forest and High Point State Park. At the Skellenger Road put-in, near Lake Ocquittunk Campground, Big Flat Brook periodically carries enough drainage from the bogs, swamps, and rolling woodlands of these preserves to float a canoe over its rocky bed. To run from here to U.S. Rte. 206, come prepared with sharp reactions and efficient whitewater paddling skills. The torrent descends over a narrow, mostly cobble bed with almost continuous rapids and with a strong possibility of a surprise strainer in a bad spot. Though some houses perch upon the right bank, partially wooded surroundings and clear water complement the whitewater.

Between Rte. 206 and Rte. 560, the gradient moderates, leaving you time to savor the corridor of hemlock and rhododendron that crowd the banks. Only some scattered fishermen's litter may mar the scene.

Below Rte. 560, the evergreen edge diminishes, revealing a flattening terrain clothed in hardwood forest. As the land flattens, the creek spreads out, that is it braids, thus increasing your encounters with strainers. Some of this area is even swampy. Then just above the finish, Little Flat Brook sneaks in from the right, also via a braided channel, nearly doubling the flow and making the going much easier.

HAZARDS: Expect strainers in fast water.

WATER CONDITIONS: Up only within a day of hard rain, in winter or spring.

GAUGE: There is a staff gauge on the upstream side of the left abutment of Rte. 560 bridge. Consider 2.5 feet as minimum for starting at Skellenger Road. Probably 2.3 feet is OK below Rte. 206.

Section 2. Flat Brook. *Unnamed road due south of Peters Valley to Flatbrookville (Millbrook Road)*					
Gradient	Difficulty	Distance	Time	Scenery	Map
6	A to 1	10.2	3.5	Good to Very Good	1

TRIP DESCRIPTION: Flat Brook now settles down to living up to its name, though there is still a fast current and plenty of riffles. Strainers remain an occasional problem. Some ruins of a milldam at Haneys Mill (about 3.5 miles below Walpack Center) and the weir at the USGS gauging station could possibly create some juicy holes at very high water. But overall, this is a good stretch for novices.

The creek flows in a valley now. Remarkably few people live in this valley, a fact no doubt influenced by its being within the bounds of the Delaware Water Gap National Recreation Area. So you get to enjoy seeing mostly woodlands, weedy cedar-studded fields, and nearby mountain ridges. Clear water reveals a gravel and sand bottom. The little villages of this valley are also pretty, but will be best viewed from the shuttle road.

Millbrook Road falls about a half mile short of the mouth. The final stretch contains more of the lively series of rock garden riffles that starts just above the bridge. If you insist on being a purist, you can take out at the mouth on the right and carry up a gated dirt road to the gate. This is not difficult if your boat is light. Or you can continue down the Delaware almost four miles to the Depew Picnic Area.

If you find yourself with some slack time before or after paddling, this valley offers a few simple distractions to round out your experience. A state natural area preserves the hemlock-filled ravine of Tillman Brook, just east of Walpack Center. Two short walks get you to two pretty, little cascades.

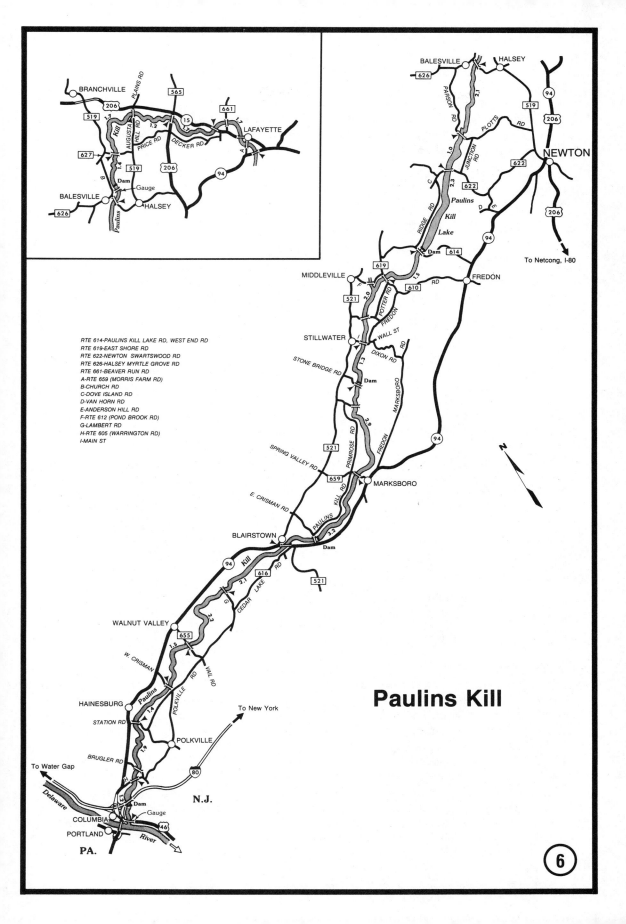

RTE 614-PAULINS KILL LAKE RD, WEST END RD
RTE 619-EAST SHORE RD
RTE 622-NEWTON SWARTSWOOD RD
RTE 626-HALSEY MYRTLE GROVE RD
RTE 661-BEAVER RUN RD
A-RTE 659 (MORRIS FARM RD)
B-CHURCH RD
C-DOVE ISLAND RD
D-VAN HORN RD
E-ANDERSON HILL RD
F-RTE 612 (POND BROOK RD)
G-LAMBERT RD
H-RTE 605 (WARRINGTON RD)
I-MAIN ST

Paulins Kill

N.J.

PA.

6

Peters Valley Craft Village, just north of the Section 2 put-in, offers one a chance to observe craftspersons, buy their wares, or obtain instruction in their discipline. Finally, Millbrook Village, a few miles southeast of Flatbrookville on Millbrook Road, is a recreated late 19th-century village. A self-guided walk introduces you to what life was like back in the dark days before canoes were made of plastic.

HAZARDS: Still watch for occasional strainers, especially at the start. The weir at the USGS gauge demands respect. Avoid both sections during the first week of trout season, and wear lots of orange during fall hunting season.

WATER CONDITIONS: Flat Brook is most likely up in late fall, winter, or spring, within three days of hard rain. It will stay up for a week if that rain falls on already sodden ground.

GAUGE: The staff gauge at Rte. 560 should read at least 2.0 feet. There is a USGS gauging station 0.7 miles upstream of Flatbrookville. You can call Philadelphia or inspect on site (if you can read its sloping, deteriorating wooden staff). A level of about 2.6 feet is minimum.

Paulins Kill

INTRODUCTION: The old New Jersey survives somewhat in the valleys and rolling hills of Warren and southwestern Sussex counties. This is still relatively open country where you will still find working farms, owned and run by the same families that have done so for generations. The towns remain small and compact with beauty and charm equal to the better-known villages of New England. And suburban housing tracts, shopping malls, etc., are still mostly over the horizon. Change has been taking place in these parts, including in the valley of the Paulins Kill. But rather than the countryside being swallowed in chunks by your typical large-scale housing developments, numerous single new houses are popping up here, there, and everywhere. So far, most of the development has kept to the high ground and is mostly invisible from low spots, like creeks. So one nice way to enjoy the best of this setting is by paddling the Paulins Kill.

Section 1. Lafayette (N.J. Rte. 94) to Stillwater (Main Street)					
Gradient	Difficulty	Distance	Time	Scenery	Map
7	A to 2	16.6	5.0	Good	6

TRIP DESCRIPTION: Much of this segment could be called a micro-stream. The down side of smallness is that such streams are subject to such liabilities as excessive strainers and ephemeral runnable levels. The up side is that such streams often enjoy such assets as intimacy with their surroundings and variety and changeability of that scenery. This is especially true if you start at Rte. 94, where in return for the pleasure of two zesty flushes of whitewater (Class 2) located behind and then a mile below Lafayette, you must also put up with a quiet stretch that festers with fallen trees and logjams. Certainly, most novices would be happiest if they start no higher than the Rte. 15 crossing a mile northwest of Lafayette.

Launching at Rte. 15 puts you on a gentle and meandering course through grassy meadows. Low banks allow good views of farms and wooded hills. After passing Rte. 206, the stream turns southwest and leaves busy Rte. 94. It follows a quiet path through hilly terrain, typically a setting of pastoral hillsides and wooded bottomlands. Both fields and woods are dotted with red cedar, and an occasional rock outcrop puts a hard edge on this otherwise soft landscape. The water is usually placid, but riffles do pop up, and watch out for a four-foot milldam about a mile below Rte. 519 (carry).

Three-mile-long Paulins Kill Lake begins abruptly just above Parson Road. Hemmed in by steep hillsides, these are initially attractive waters. But house-lined shores below Swartswood Road (Rte. 622) are a disappointment. This is partly compensated for by strikingly dense stands of hemlock on the hillsides to the left. The 12-foot dam that forms this pool has an easy carry on the left. From here the stream returns to the isolated fields, woods, and hills. This remaining passage is also easy except for a braided section above Stillwater, where strainers in the now more powerful current can be dangerous.

HAZARDS: Watch for a four-foot weir at the site of Bales Mill, which is about a mile below Rte. 519. Carry or — though not advised for the inexperienced — run the millrace on the right. The dam at the end of Paulins Kill Lake is easily carried on the left. Fallen trees may occur throughout this section, but they are particularly concentrated just below Lafayette and starting about a mile above Stillwater. Barbed wire fences are a possibility in pastoral areas.

WATER CONDITIONS: Paulins Kill is most often up in late fall, winter, and spring. The first few miles will only stay up for about 24 hours after a hard rain. The rest will stay up for two days and maybe even longer if the ground is saturated.

GAUGE: There is a staff gauge on the left abutment of the unnamed road bridge that crosses at Bales Mill. It should read over 3.0 feet to start at Rte. 94, and probably 2.6 feet is enough for passage below Rte. 519 (if you do not mind scraping in the rapid at Bales Mill). Also, enough water to float through the rapid just above Beaver Run Road (Rte. 661) will get you through the entire section.

Section 2. Stillwater (Main Street) to mouth					
Gradient	Difficulty	Distance	Time	Scenery	Map
8	A to 2	17.7	6.0	Good	6

TRIP DESCRIPTION: It is a bit easier to find this section with adequate water. To Blairstown, the stream continues to wander through a sparsely populated landscape. This is mostly open farm country bordered by low, distant ridges. But now and then there are interludes through wooded ravines. The waters flow pretty quietly, but be prepared for some riffles and even some tricky little rapids. Formed by old milldam debris and natural ledges, these pop up between Rte. 659 and Blairstown. There is also a runnable two-foot weir at Stone Bridge Road and an unrunnable 10-foot weir on the upstream end of Blairstown. The passage through Blairstown, an attractive community, is mostly trashy and unappealing from the water.

The remainder of the Paulins Kill offers scenery similar to that above Blairstown, but the surroundings are more populated. Bridge enthusiasts will be treated to the sight of the high railroad viaduct below Hainesburg. The water remains smooth, again with scattered rapids and riffles. Near the end, the creek slows in a big pool. It is formed by a 20-foot dam just below I-80. The carry on the right, around the dam and a hydroelectric station, is easy. Take out at U.S. Rte. 46, just above the mouth.

HAZARDS: You can run the two-foot weir at Stone Bridge Road over the center or via the old millrace on the right or easily carry around. Portage both the big weir in Blairstown and the dam at Columbia on the right. Barbed wire fences and trees are still a possibility throughout.

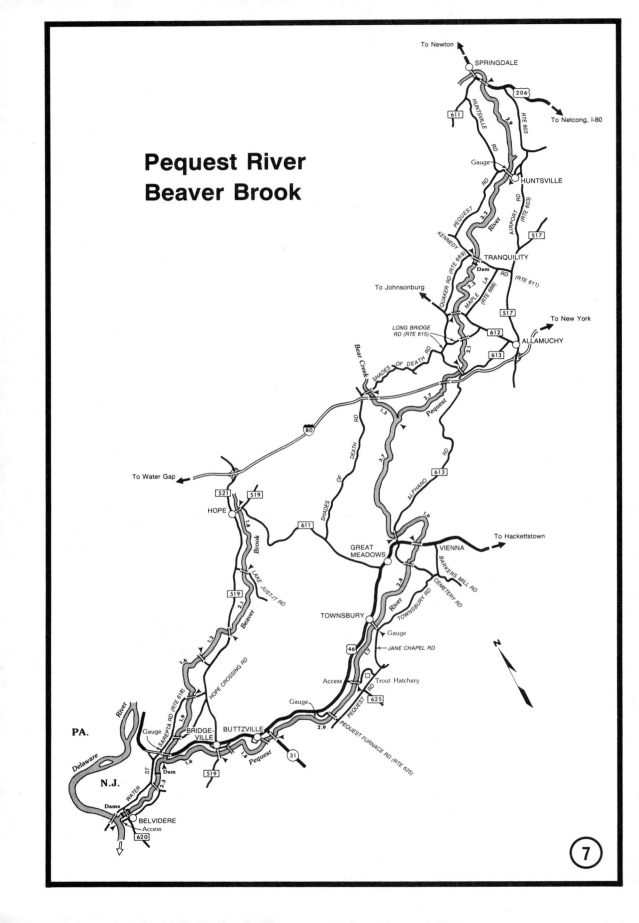

Pequest River
Beaver Brook

WATER CONDITIONS: This section is most often canoeable in late fall, winter, and spring. If weather has been dry, it may stay up for two or three days after a hard rain. But if weather has been wet, it will stay up for seven to 10 days.

GAUGE: The staff gauge on the left abutment of the U.S. Rte. 46 bridge in Columbia should read at least 1.3 feet and the USGS gauge in Blairstown (about a quarter mile above N.J. Rte. 94 on right bank), if they ever replace the staff gauge, should read at least 2.2 feet. Roughly, the USGS gauge at Flatbrookville on Flat Brook (call Philadelphia) should read at least 2.5 feet.

Pequest River

INTRODUCTION: The author was first attracted to the Pequest Valley because of the names. The lure of driving at the base of Jenny Jump Mountain on Shades of Death Road to get to Allamuchy or Tranquility was just too much to resist. It was worth the trip, for he found a truly beautiful valley drained by a wonderful stream.

The name Pequest is Native American for "open land," which still proves to be descriptive. The Pequest starts in a swamp just south of Newton in Sussex County. After a false start to the north, it zigzags southwestward almost 32 miles down a flat and often soggy valley to feed the Delaware River at Belvidere. Its valley is still predominately farm country whose black soil from drained wetlands produces bountiful yields of celery, onions, lettuce, and sod. It is easy to reach via I-80 and relatively easy to catch up, thanks to the many still swampy acres of its watershed. Graced with some exceptionally unspoiled scenery and some good novice whitewater, this should be the springtime destination for many paddlers.

Section 1. Springdale (U.S. Rte. 206) to Great Meadows (U.S. Rte. 46)					
Gradient	Difficulty	Distance	Time	Scenery	Map
4	A to 1+	18.5	6.5	Good to Very Good	7

TRIP DESCRIPTION: The upper Pequest offers many miles of easy paddling in a beautiful and tranquil setting. In fact, it even flows by a town named Tranquility. In wet weather, you can start as far up as U.S. Rte. 206, which amazingly is only about five miles from the head of the creek. The clear but tannin-stained water proceeds to wind through maple swamps and marsh meadows. The higher ground beyond is usually in pasture, and few buildings are visible. It is an unspoiled landscape. The cruising is not quite as unspoiled. While with one exception this is a smoothwater run, the strong current will carry you into some fallen trees, low-water bridges, and fences. Be prepared. The one whitewater exception comes as you near Huntsville, where a blind rapid rushes through a braided, tree-strewn course. This spot could be dangerous, as could the strong roller at the gauging station weir just downstream.

The soggy landscape continues on past Huntsville, but more farms appear along the edges. The village of Tranquility greets you with a beautiful old grist mill and a portage (left) around its weir. Though tributaries continue to swell the Pequest's channel, you can still expect some more low-water bridges, fences, and trees, at least as far as I-80. An easy rapid interrupts the quiet water near I-80, and I-80 just plain interrupts the quiet. But below that road, the Pequest meanders off into Bear Swamp.

Bear Swamp is just a shadow of its old self, since much has been drained for agriculture. In fact, much of the stream between Bear Creek confluence and Rte. 46 appears as if it was once, long ago, channelized. While a pleasant enough stretch, this section is often bracketed by high, wooded, mud banks that limit your view, and the cleared timber of a private road has disrupted a few miles of the scenery to your right. So it is not as pretty as the upper creek, but at least it is far from the busy roads. However, as you approach Great Meadows, even that quality may be compromised by obnoxious noise from a nearby dragway.

An alternate entry to the Bear Swamp segment can be had by putting in on Bear Creek at Shades of Death Road. This is a twisting brook that flows between high, mud banks. The setting is largely woodsy. The water is smooth with a few brief riffles, and several deadfalls will require carries.

HAZARDS: This section has a fair number of strainers. The worst spots are just below Rte. 206 and when approaching Huntsville. The gauging station weir just above the bridge in Huntsville, while not high, is sharp and may have a strong reversal. The sharp five-foot weir at Tranquility Mill is definitely a carry (left). Finally, beware of an old, low railroad bridge just above the lower Long Bridge Road crossing.

WATER CONDITIONS: This is easiest to catch in late fall, winter, and spring. Above I-80, it usually stays up only for about two days after a hard rain. Below I-80, it is passable almost any time during those seasons.

GAUGE: There is a USGS gauge at Huntsville, on the right bank a few feet above the bridge. Roughly, 3.0 feet would be minimum to start at Rte. 206. Also, very roughly, the USGS gauge on Section 2 should be at least 2.5 feet to start at Rte. 206 and at least 1.8 feet to float below I-80.

Section 2. Great Meadows (U.S. Rte. 46) to mouth					
Gradient	Difficulty	Distance	Time	Scenery	Map
21	A to 2	13.1	4.0	Fair to Good	7

TRIP DESCRIPTION: A different stream now takes shape. The swampy terrain gives way to hills, some farm-covered, some forested. Busy Rte. 46 or other roads are often, if not in sight, within hearing, and there are more villages and houses.

But the Pequest compensates by drawing your attention to its whitewater. After a placid warm-up as far as Rte. 46 below Great Meadows, the creek begins gently tumbling downhill. Riffles and easy rapids run continuously at times. At moderate levels this is a delightful slalom through rock gardens, patches of small boulders, and islets. Below Bridgeville, a crumbling three-foot weir has a runnable chute in the center. Approaching and passing through Belvidere, the Pequest stairsteps over one marginal and two unrunnable weirs. Those who put up with these portages will be treated to a ledgy, relatively voluminous drop just above the mouth. If you go this far, the best take-out is about a hundred yards down the Delaware where a path leads up to a tiny (public) fishermen's access area at the foot of Front Street. Allow some time to wander about this picturesque river town and county seat.

HAZARDS: Anticipate possible strainers on island channels. Just above N.J. Rte. 31 at Island Park, a low private bridge to an island could be a problem at high water. Just downstream, but also above Rte. 31, is the high concrete arch of an old railroad bridge. Directly underneath it and hovering above a better-than-average rapid is a low steel plate girder bridge that, at higher water levels, will lack adequate clearance. Approach cautiously. Weirs in Belvidere are as follows: The first is a sharp, three-foot drop about a half mile below Beaver Brook. At low levels one can clunk over it, but at high levels a powerful reversal would discourage such attempts. A five-footer and a six-footer in Belvidere are definitely carries. Finally, with its proximity to the road, this is a good stream to avoid on the first week of trout season.

WATER CONDITIONS: This is most often up in late fall, winter, and spring for three to four days after a hard rain. But if the weather lately has been consistently wet, it will stay up for about a week.

GAUGE: There is a USGS gauge about three miles above Buttzville on Pequest Furnace Road (Rte. 625), just after it forks off of Rte. 46. The staff is attached to the old bridge abutment just upstream. Approximately 2.1 feet would be minimum level. Or you could use the staff gauge on the upstream end of the left abutment of the bridge at Townsbury. This should be at least 2.0 feet (at minimum levels the staff is out of water). Two useful gauges for sizing up conditions from afar are the USGS gauges on the South Branch Raritan at High Bridge and on Flat Brook at Flatbrookville (call Philadelphia for both). Roughly, levels over 6.5 feet at High Bridge suggest enough water to float this section, and look for over 7.1 feet to get you down all of Section 1. Levels of over 2.6 feet at Flatbrookville should indicate enough water for Section 2.

Beaver Brook

INTRODUCTION: You may have guessed by its name that this is not one of the major waterways of the world. Even with all its turns and oxbows, there are relatively few miles separating Beaver Brook's source near Blairstown from its confluence with the Pequest River near Belvidere. But size is not everything. For here is a stream that drains possibly the prettiest remaining rural landscape in north Jersey. So even if you cannot catch that necessary wet spell to create canoeable waters, go there anyway with a bicycle or good walking shoes and enjoy it while it lasts.

Section 1. Hope (Rte. 519) to mouth					
Gradient	Difficulty	Distance	Time	Scenery	Map
14	A to 2—	8.5	3.5	Very Good	7

TRIP DESCRIPTION: Hope is a nice place to start a trip. Founded by Moravians in 1769, this old crossroads retains a sizable and beautiful collection of sturdy stone structures, including a restored mill and splendid arch bridge. That bridge (Rte. 519), which spans Beaver Brook, has stood there since 1807. Put in about a hundred yards downstream of the stone bridge where the creek bumps briefly against Rte. 611.

The following miles wind through woods, swamps, marshy meadows, and pastures. Insignificant banks allow good views of Jenny Jump Mountain and other low hills. The countryside is lightly populated with most houses, often old and pretty ones, scattered up along Rte. 519. The stark remains of another old mill grace the left bank at Sarepta Road (Rte. 618).

But paddling Beaver Brook has its price. It bristles with obstacles — fences, trees, and low-water bridges, and some of the barbed wire fences are especially nasty. Most of this run is characterized by smooth, swift water. But there is a good set of rocky rapids starting at Lake Just-It Road, and the last mile down to the Pequest has almost continuous easy rapids.

HAZARDS: Lots of strainers and lots of resultant short portages. In particular, watch for a surprise strand of barbed wire near the end of the rapid below Lake Just-It Road and a pair of especially taut strands at Hope Crossing Road and shortly below.

WATER CONDITIONS: This run is most often canoeable in late fall, winter, and spring within a day of hard rain. But during a good wet spell, it can hold its water for as long as four or five days following the rain.

GAUGE: There is a USGS gauge on the right bank a quarter mile above U.S. Rte. 46 along Sarepta Road. It should read at least 2.7 feet.

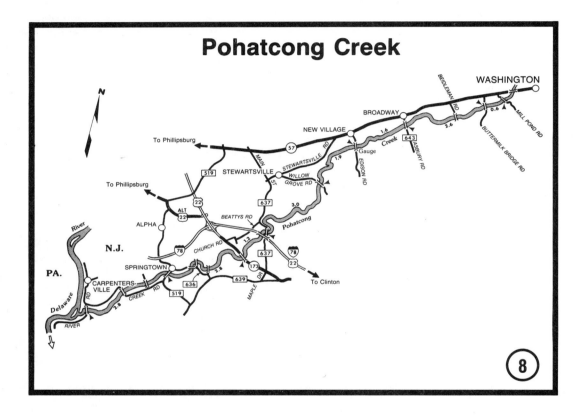

Pohatcong Creek

INTRODUCTION: Pohatcong Creek is an ephemeral country brook that flows down a narrow limestone valley that parallels the valley of the Musconetcong. It starts just west of Hackettstown and finishes near Carpentersville, a few miles down the Delaware from Phillipsburg. Pohatcong offers a pleasant novice run with all the expected problems and rewards of canoeing such a tiny stream. It is a fine destination if you are certain that buckets of rain have fallen on Warren County.

Section 1. *Mill Pond Road to River Road*					
Gradient	Difficulty	Distance	Time	Scenery	Map
14	A to 1, 2	16.5	5.0	Fair to Very Good	8

TRIP DESCRIPTION: This is a fine way to enjoy the peace of a beautiful and fairly uncluttered rural valley. The scenery evolves with the miles. Initially the surroundings are relatively flat, first covered by cornfields, then pasture. Then below I-78, the stream is entrenched in a narrow inner valley with largely wooded cover. Moderately low banks afford good views of the countryside, though at times great thorny thickets of multiflora hem you in. You will float by many beautiful, old farm houses, barns, and mills, often built of the native limestone. Other interesting cultural features are three long, dark, stone tunnels that carry your creek under the high railroad grades that cross the valley. At this time, the most significant blemishes on the creek are limited to a trailer park and the far too usual smattering of streamside trash heaps and old farm junk.

Pohatcong has frequent riffles formed by its rocky bottom and a few boulder patches. The only real rapid is the product of rubble from the washed-away dam at Kennedy Mills, below Rte. 173. Surprisingly, for this part of the world, there are no intact dams or weirs on this run. Not surprisingly, logs, logjams, and barbed wire fences may occur throughout the course, though they usually are infrequent. You can avoid a particularly nasty bunch of strainers by starting no higher than Buttermilk Bridge Road. Another spot at which to exercise caution are the ruins of a concrete weir somewhere between Edison Road and Willow Grove Road. It bristles with rebars. And expect a portage around what seems to be a permanent logjam against an old railroad trestle five or six miles into the trip.

River Road, where there is an easy take-out and parking on the left, is not the exact end of the Pohatcong. The creek meanders another quarter mile through floodplain forest to the mouth, where there is no access. Often when the Pohatcong is canoeable, the Delaware will be high also and its slackwater will be backed up all the way to River Road.

HAZARDS: The most likely problem will be periodic strainers, including the perennial logjam at the above-mentioned trestle. Watch for rebars in an old weir.

WATER CONDITIONS: The runoff in this valley is swift. So get there within a day of hard rain even during winter or spring.

GAUGE: There is a USGS gauge at Edison Road. This is a stubby concrete building on the left bank upstream of the bridge. A staff gauge is attached to a concrete buttress. It should read at least 1.5 feet. You can also use the concrete footing on the left side of the pier of the Asbury Road bridge. The top should be less than five inches out of the water.

Musconetcong River

INTRODUCTION: When you look at the Musconetcong on the map, it is deceptive. Spanning a straight-line distance of about 35 miles from its source in Lake Hopatcong to its mouth at Riegelsville on the Delaware, it looks like a major waterway. But it is not. Drawing runoff from only a slender valley, it never develops into anything more than a creek. The name Musconet-

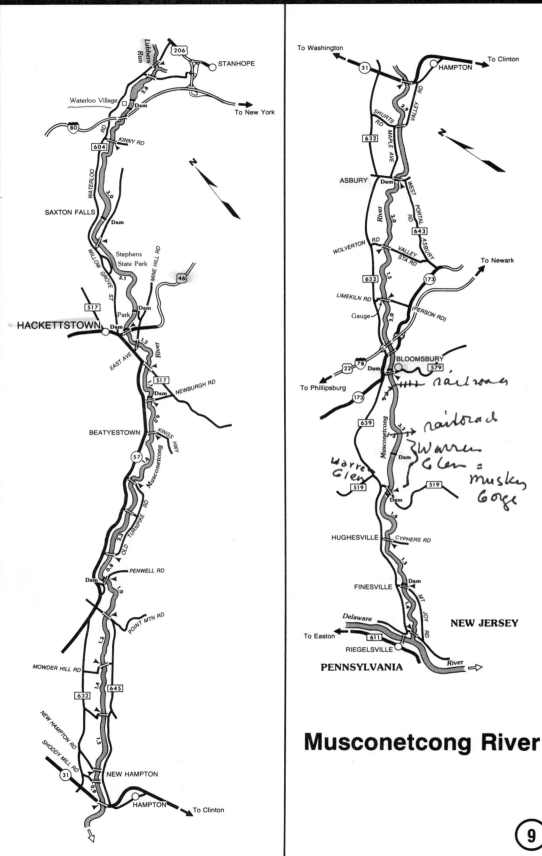

Musconetcong River

cong is Native American for "rapidly running river." In spite of numerous dams and weirs, that is still true. So when you add enough water to its rocky bed, this stream will give you a nice ride. But remember, with plentiful access, this stream is also a favorite with anglers. So check the stocking schedules and time your trip accordingly.

Section 1. Confluence Lubbers Run to Hackettstown (U.S. Rte. 46)					
Gradient	Difficulty	Distance	Time	Scenery	Map
15	A to 1	8.9	3.5	Fair to Good	9

TRIP DESCRIPTION: The put-in is about a mile and a half above historic Waterloo, on Waterloo Road where it crosses Lubbers Run. Starting as a rushing, alder-lined brook, that phase lasts only about a mile before slowing in the marshy backwaters of the first of Waterloo's two weirs (a two-footer and then a six-footer, both carried on the right). And while you are carrying, you might take an interest in exploring the restored 19th-century iron-mining village that lies just up the bank. Unfortunately, to do so you will have to return by road and pay the admission charge like all the other tourists. Proceeding onward, a little taste of free-flowing water leads you into the long backwater of Saxton Falls Dam. Carry the 12-foot barrier on the right, passing by a restored lock of the old Morris Canal. After that, you can enjoy a long stretch with current and long, rocky riffles through Stephens State Park. Floating on into Hackettstown, a two-foot weir offers runnable chutes in the middle at moderate levels and on the right at high levels. Finally there is another pool, and it is formed by a five-foot weir just above Rte. 46. Carry on the left. Or if you do not plan to continue past Rte. 46, the best take-out is on river right, back about 200 yards above the dam, at a town park. This is reached via Rte. 604, Willow Street (road to Waterloo Village). Look for a sign saying "Alumni Field."

  The aesthetics through here are mixed. While the quaint historical structures at Waterloo and wooded passage through the state park are certainly pretty, too much streamside development and ambient road noise characterizes much of this stretch. So combined with all the necessary portages, many paddlers would gladly forego this reach.

HAZARDS: You will need to portage two weirs at Waterloo, one at Saxton Falls, and one in Hackettstown.

WATER CONDITIONS: This river's response to rain is quite variable. Coming off of dry weather, it may stay up for three days after a hard rain. But if the ground is saturated, it will stay up for a week to 10 days. Its season is generally late fall, winter, and spring.

GAUGE: There are none on this section. Judge the riffles along the road in Stephens State Park or the rapid below Saxtons Falls Dam (if you can float through the latter, you will do just fine). For a good estimate, there are USGS gauges upstream of Bloomsbury on the Musconetcong at Limekiln Road on Section 2 (you must visit this) and at High Bridge on the South Branch Raritan (you can call Philadelphia for this). Levels of 2.2 feet at Limekiln and 6.5 feet at High Bridge should indicate adequate water.

Section 2. Hackettstown (U.S. Rte. 46) to Bloomsbury (N.J. Rte. 173)					
Gradient	Difficulty	Distance	Time	Scenery	Map
11	A to 1 +	22.1	7.5	Fair to Good	9

TRIP DESCRIPTION: The most noteworthy characteristic of this section is that it has fewer portages per mile than any other section. The put-in is also somewhat special as Hackettstown is the home of Mars Candy Company. Probably Mars' most famous product is M & M Candy, the main constituent of gorp. The author is convinced that some of his paddling associates actually subsist on a diet of only gorp, granola, and beer. If you fit into this description, then you might consider a trip to Hackettstown and the Musconetcong on the level of a holy pilgrimage.

Once you shake free of Hackettstown, this is an attractive passage. The often low and wooded banks allow you to enjoy views of farmland and distant ridges, though nearby roads support a sizable but spread-out population. Perhaps the prettiest part of this segment is an isolated ravine below Penwell where the creek flows past wooded slopes that are just littered with boulders. The most unexpected but ugly sight on this reach is that of an old, rusting tank farm.

This stretch is graced with plenty of riffles and easy rapids. The liveliest spot is the chute, on the right, through the breach in a weir just above N.J. Rte. 31. You will have to duck under, or maybe even carry, the East Avenue bridge in Hackettstown. A four-foot weir above Newburgh Road has a runnable chute on the right at moderate levels. Also, keep right to negotiate the ruins of an old weir just below the final Old Turnpike bridge. But plan on carrying the six-foot weir at Penwell and a five-foot weir beneath the curving concrete bridge at Asbury (carry on right, behind graphite mill).

HAZARDS: There are weirs above Newburgh Road and Penwell Road and beneath Asbury Road. The low bridge in Hackettstown can be troublesome.

WATER CONDITIONS: Above Rte. 31 (Hampton), conditions are about the same as for Section 1. Below Rte. 31, adequate levels persist for another several days in wet weather.

GAUGE: The USGS gauge at Limekiln Road should read at least 2.1 feet to start at Hackettstown and 1.8 feet to start at Rte. 31. Or you can just judge by the riffles that you can see from the nearby roads. Also, a good estimate can be had from the USGS gauge at High Bridge on the South Branch Raritan (call Philadelphia). A level of 6.5 feet is good for the top and 6.2 feet is good for doing below Rte. 31.

Section 3. Bloomsbury (N.J. Rte. 173) to mouth					
Gradient	Difficulty	Distance	Time	Scenery	Map
14	A to 2 +	8.3	4.0	Fair to Good	9

TRIP DESCRIPTION: This last section has the most personality. You can enjoy an exciting start with a plunge over the sloping six-foot weir at the bridge in Bloomsbury or a dull start by just putting in downstream on the left. After passing a few farms, the river wanders through remote forest and slinks through two long, creepy, stone tunnels beneath high railroad grades. The second tunnel marks the beginning of Warren Glen — an attractive rock-strewn ravine where the stream is plugged at midpoint by a 25-foot dam. The dam diverts water down a canal to a paper mill. If you come here at low flow, all of the river will be going into the canal, giving you the choice of a long portage or paddling down the canal and portaging along the railroad tracks around the mill. Either option is undesirable and involves some degree of trespassing. Assuming enough water is flowing over the dam, the easiest of your portage options is, if you do not suffer from fear of heights, ascending the big stone steps on the left side of the spillway. Needless to say, do not fall.   *descending?*

From the dam to the mill, the river descends over a rocky and bouldery bed to form continuous rapids that are Class 2 + at low levels and would only become more exciting at higher levels. The whitewater ends all too soon, in a pool, because about a hundred yards below Rte. 519 the stream is backed up by a sloping eight-foot weir. Once again, the weir diverts water into a canal on the left that leads to another paper mill. And once again, at low flows your choice is to either carry a half mile downstream (via the highway), drag down the dribbling stream, or paddle the canal and portage through the paper mill (which would no doubt be frowned upon by the paper company). At good flows, your inconvenience is limited to a short, easy portage around the right side of the weir. More riffles follow, and then you face a last portage, this one around a dangerous weir at the bridge in Finesville. The remaining two miles are fast and riffly, with some easy chutes through the ruins of old weirs. Watch for spikes. These final miles pass through a well-populated area. But if you are interested in old mill factories, you might enjoy it. At times of high water, the backwater of the Delaware extends a few hundred yards up the Musconetcong.

HAZARDS: Watch for four weirs or dams, three of which are definite carries. Beware of spikes in rubble of old weirs on lower few miles.

WATER CONDITIONS: The season is usually late fall, winter, and spring. To do the diversion-depleted passages through Warren Glen and below Rte. 519, catch within two days of hard rain following dry weather or within six days of hard rain during a wet spell. Otherwise, this section is passable almost any time from November through May, unless weather has been particularly dry.

GAUGE: The USGS gauge at Limekiln Road should read at least 2.4 feet to avoid hardship at the diversion dams. Otherwise, about 1.7 feet is enough to float this section. Roughly, corresponding levels at the USGS gauge at High Bridge on the South Branch Raritan (call Philadelphia) are 6.6 feet and 6.1 feet.

Delaware and Raritan Canal

INTRODUCTION: Most of the waterways described in this book were put where they are by Mother Nature. Admittedly, some have been straightened, deepened, drained, or altered in other imaginative ways by man. But they still generally represent the natural path of drainage. Here now is a totally artificial waterway.

The Delaware and Raritan Canal connects those two rivers. It starts at Raven Rock, about three miles up the Delaware River from Lambertville. The canal follows the Delaware River to Trenton, disappears beneath the city, and emerges on the north side of town. It cuts over to and follows the Millstone River to the Raritan River and then follows the Raritan to tidewater at New Brunswick. Its total remaining length is 56.5 miles, of which about 51 miles are reasonably canoeable.

This was once a bustling commercial artery, connecting New York and Philadelphia back when other means of transportation moved at a snail's pace. Work started on the main canal in 1830 and was completed in four years. The main canal ran from tidewater on the Raritan River at New Brunswick to tidewater on the Delaware River at Bordentown. The section from Raven Rock to Trenton was originally designed as a feeder canal to supply water for the main canal. But it was soon improved for navigation, allowing a brisk trade in Pennsylvania coal. From the beginning, the canal faced competition from the ever more superior railroads, but it managed to remain profitable as a bulk carrier for many years and, even when profitability ceased, it continued operating, lasting until 1932. It might have just become another weed-filled memory, but in 1944 the State of New Jersey recognized that here lies a potential water supply aqueduct for thirsty North Jersey. So the state commenced repairs and has kept the canal in condition ever since. Better yet, the state came to recognize the recreational potential of this waterway and in 1974 created the Delaware and Raritan Canal State Park. So we now have a story with a happy ending.

This is a great waterway for beginner canoeists. There are no rocks, rapids, falls, weirs, or strainers. If you need help, civilization is always nearby. Lots of access points allow you to keep your trip short. And you do not necessarily need a shuttle. While nothing is idiot proof, this is about as secure a place for a first-time outing as you will find (outside, maybe, of a two-foot-deep duck pond, and even there, the ducks might bite you).

Section 1. Raven Rock to Trenton (Lower Ferry Road)					
Gradient	Difficulty	Distance	Time	Scenery	Map
2	A	18.8	7.0 down	Fair to	3
			20.0 up	Good	

TRIP DESCRIPTION: The trip can begin at the head of Bulls Island, where the canal entrance quietly branches left from the Delaware. With over 70 million gallons per day (about 105 cfs) committed to water supply utilities, this is a significant arm of the river. Bulls Island is not just a geographical name, but also a state recreational area with a large, conveniently located campground. Because a lock blocks the way only about three quarters of a mile into the trip, many would choose to start at the canoe access area at the vehicle entrance to Bulls Island.

It is really worth emphasizing that this segment of the canal is best as a one-way paddle. With a starting elevation of 70 feet above sea level and the hefty volume of flow, there is a strong current surging down the narrow channel. The current velocity is comparable to that of the parallel Delaware River at moderate levels. While it is certainly possible to paddle up the canal, progress will be slow. If you are planning a circuit trip, it is a good idea to start at the lower end and thus paddle against the current first, so that you do not commit yourself to more than you can manage on the return leg.

While canoeists who go with the flow will find this a relaxing trip, there are a few flaws. Besides the lock at Bulls Island, there are locks at Stockton and New Hope. You cannot, unfortunately, lock through as they did back in the good ole days, so you will face some short carries. Also, you will need to get out for three or four low bridges.

The aesthetics along this stretch is only fair. Busy N.J. Rte. 29 parallels and usually hugs this route. The upper miles of this section are the prettiest, because there is actually a little buffer between the road and the canal. Also, the countryside is less developed. As you approach Trenton, noise and congestion become increasingly difficult to ignore.

There are some pretty towns along the canal, particularly Stockton and Lambertville. Back in the operating days of the canal, Lambertville functioned as a point of entry to the canal where coal-laden barges from the Pennsylvania Canal, which follows the other side of the river, could transfer to the Delaware & Raritan and continue on to New York. Lambertville was a gritty industrial town. Now long since gentrified, dirty, stinky ironworks, cotton mills, grist mills, lumber mills, and even a rubber plant have all disappeared or have become restaurants, condos, art galleries, etc. Both of these towns, however, show their best face to the streets, not the canal. So you might want to stop and ramble.

Lower Ferry Road is by no means the end of this portion of the canal. It is just the last official access point with good, convenient parking. If you are curious, skilled, and adventuresome enough, you can push on another four miles to Willow Street in the heart of Trenton. After Willow Street, the canal disappears beneath the city. The positively last place where you can enter or leave the canal is at Sullivan Way, a mile downstream of Lower Ferry Road. Below there the canal is entirely confined by high chain-link fences. In such a setting, a paddler quickly begins to feel like an animal in a zoo (in fact, someone actually tossed the author a peanut). As you progress downstream, the neighborhood becomes increasingly congested and run-down. Graffiti decorates walls of buildings. Trash litters the banks, and styrofoam, balls, plastic, and other flotsam carpet the surface. Bridges get lower and lower, but all have just enough clearance for a low boat with a skinny paddler to squeeze beneath. These are often old concrete bridges whose undersides drip with hundreds of soda-straw stalactites that would do justice to Carlsbad Caverns. As you try to squeeze under these bridges, these calciferous wonders will inevitably crumble into your hair and eyes and down your collar, along with all the spiders and bugs that have established a habitat in this shadowy little ecosystem. But in surmounting these challenges, you will have discovered the true meaning of life, reality, Trenton's deepest and darkest secrets, and, most importantly, why the author recommended that you end your trip at Lower Ferry Road. Next time, listen to him.

HAZARDS: With the strong current, some low bridges could easily flip a beginner.

WATER CONDITIONS: Except in rare periods of maintenance or if a major leak appeared, there is always plenty of water.

GAUGE: None

Section 2. Trenton (Whitehead Road) to New Brunswick (Landing Lane)					
Gradient	Difficulty	Distance	Time	Scenery	Map
1	A	32.4	13 down	Fair to	37,40,41
			17 up	Good	

TRIP DESCRIPTION: The canal emerges into daylight at Mulberry Street, a mile upstream of Whitehead Road. This is an ugly mile, with the U.S. Rte. 1 Freeway literally forming the east bank and a string of commercial and industrial structures rising above the trash-strewn west bank. Add to this a unique form of canoe slalom: ducking under the 80 low-slung steel I-beams that span the channel to shore up the freeway's retaining wall, and you have one masochistic mile that few paddlers would regret missing.

While Section 1 is the old feeder canal, Section 2 is what remains of the canal proper. This reach provides a slightly more pleasant canoeing route, being easier to negotiate and generally prettier. One reason that it is easier is because it is wider and deeper, hence slower. You can paddle it in either direction with ease. Another improvement is that it is less obstructed. Though locks are spaced at about the same frequency, there are fewer low bridges. Access is plentiful, and a nice towpath always accompanies the route. This section is prettier because it has more roadless reaches. Also those roads that are there are often less busy, and fewer miles bear much nearby development. So more of the peaceful, old-time flavor remains.

From Whitehead Road, the canal heads up the Assunpink Valley and then cuts across the subtle divide for about three miles to pull alongside Stony Brook at Port Mercer. Aesthetically speaking, it gets off to a slow start, leaving behind the ugly development, but being plagued by the roar of nearby Rte. 1. But after about a mile and a half, things quiet down as the canal passes through woods and countryside which, unfortunately, are slowly transforming into suburbia. Coming up beside Princeton, the canal spans the Millstone River by aqueduct and then closely follows the right shore of Lake Carnegie, offering the paddler good views of the lake.

Between Lake Carnegie and the Raritan, the path is fairly quiet. About the only ugly spot is by the quarry near Kingston. Generally there are woods on the left and a mix of woods, country-side, and scattered houses on the right. Where roads cross the canal and valley, there are often attractive little villages dating from the canal era and, hence, of traditional architecture. Because the canal runs along the edge of the valley, one always has the illusion of being up high.

After the canal pulls beside the Raritan, the parallel roads become busier, and there is more nearby development. The roads bring more noise and trash. There are some ugly clusters of commercial structures concentrated near Bound Brook, but, on the other hand, there are also some pretty old houses spread out along the way. Overall, this last section is pleasant to the end. It is a particularly good destination during autumn, when colorful foliage, canal structures, and old houses make for some calendar-quality scenes.

The end of the line comes about a quarter mile past Landing Lane bridge, where again the canal disappears underground. Because there is no real place to park here or at Landing Lane, you have two choices. The best is to go to the very end of the canal, where there is a spillway to the Raritan. You can carry down to and paddle across the river and then take out at Johnson Park. The other choice is to double back 3.5 miles to Five Mile Lock. The first choice is easier than it sounds.

HAZARDS: None. But if the wind is right, fragrances from a steakhouse between New Brunswick and Bound Brook may cause irrational and even dangerous behavior in someone who has paddled all day and had nothing better to eat than gorp.

WATER CONDITIONS: Barring drawdowns for repairs, this section is always runnable (except when frozen).

GAUGE: None

Lockatong Creek

INTRODUCTION: Every November, hundreds of whitewater-crazed boaters turn out for a water release on Tohickon Creek in Bucks County, Pennsylvania, crowding themselves out in a paddling frenzy in the rapids of a four-mile stretch of that stream. Few of these enthusiasts realize that Tohickon is not unique, that after a hard rain several other streams that cut down through the Delaware River's high palisades can also offer a garden of whitewater delights. Two outstanding examples flow almost directly across the river from Tohickon, in Hunterdon County. The uppermost of these is Lockatong Creek, which enters the Delaware just below Raven Rock.

Section 1. N.J. Rte. 12 to Rte. 519					
Gradient	Difficulty	Distance	Time	Scenery	Map
7	A to 1	4.4	1.5	Good	10

TRIP DESCRIPTION: While most paddlers only seek these waters for excitement, those desiring more placid paddling will find that a nice novice run exists before Lockatong plunges to the Delaware. Most of the route is smooth, though riffles do take shape towards the end of the run. One must be prepared, however, to stop for strainers on this rivulet.

This is certainly a pretty outing. The surrounding country is a relatively flat plateau, and much of it is visible over the creek's low banks. Though this is farm country, only a few farms are visible from the creek. Otherwise, it comes across as a woodsy passage.

HAZARDS: Expect a few strainers.

WATER CONDITIONS: Catch within 24 hours of a hard rain in late fall, winter, or spring.

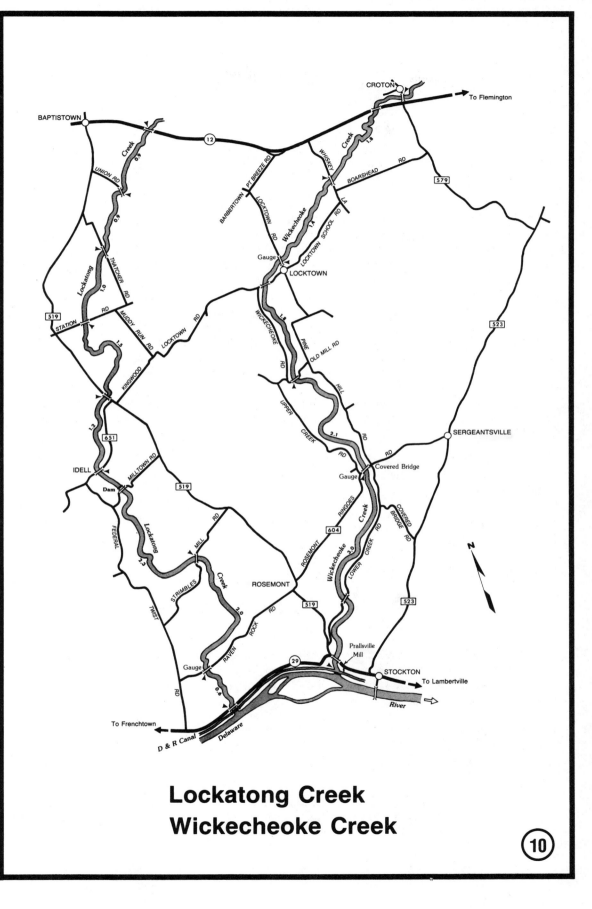

Lockatong Creek
Wickecheoke Creek

10

GAUGE: Judge by the riffle at Rte. 12 or check the staff gauge on the downstream side of the left abutment of Raven Rock Road. It must read at least 6.0 feet.

Section 2. Rte. 519 to N.J. Rte. 29					
Gradient	Difficulty	Distance	Time	Scenery	Map
63	1 to 3 +	6.1	3.0	Excellent	10

TRIP DESCRIPTION: This is the most beautiful whitewater run that New Jersey has to offer. The first mile is a warm-up. Just be ready to quickly exit when the creek makes a hard left-hand turn under Rte. 651. Immediately below is a falls. Carry on the right. Continuous rapids then quickly lead you to a dam and two more falls. And it soon becomes apparent that this is a ledgy stream. These are often jagged reefs where your decision to run or carry may be determined by how tough the materials are that your boat is constructed of. There are diagonal drops, sloping drops, and just plain complicated drops. The above difficulty rating is emphatically for relatively low levels. High water could transform this reach into a hole-ridden horror story.

As for scenery, there is indeed ample opportunity to appreciate it from the short pools, eddies, and portages. The stream cuts a shady gorge where hemlocks thrive at the base of dark, jagged cliffs. Though there are some houses on the nearby slopes, as the miles pass, this run begins to feel very remote. Bridge enthusiasts will admire the rickety iron truss of Raven Rock Road. It has stood there since 1878.

In the final mile, the slopes diverge, and the channel begins to braid about a more gravelly bed. So you should be particularly alert now for strainers. Finish at a roadside rest on the left and upstream side of Rte. 29.

HAZARDS: Some difficult drops could have pinning potential. This being a small stream, watch for strainers, especially near the end.

WATER CONDITIONS: Same as Section 1

GAUGE: Use the staff gauge on Raven Rock Road. As on Section 1, the level should be at least 6.0 feet.

— Wickecheoke

Wickecheoke Creek

INTRODUCTION: Wickecheoke Creek enters the Delaware River less than two miles downstream of the mouth of the Lockatong. Slightly larger than the Lockatong, it also cuts a beautiful and whitewater-filled gorge as it descends to the Delaware. Do both of these in a day and it will be a day you will fondly remember.

Section 1. Croton (Rte. 579) to Delaware & Raritan Canal					
Gradient	Difficulty	Distance	Time	Scenery	Map
43	A to 3	10.1	4.0	Good to	10
1.75mi @ 85				Excellent	

TRIP DESCRIPTION: This trip starts off with a few miles of mostly just fast flatwater and riffles. But it is spiced with a strong chute through a crumbling weir, a possible logjam-formed drop, and, approaching Locktown, an ominously steepening gradient. So tacking on these few extra miles serves as a recommended warm-up. You will be additionally rewarded with a mostly remote passage through deep woods. There are some fine tree specimens back here, but networks of old crumbling stone walls remind you that this is anything but old growth forest.

Locktown, an attractive cluster of fine old houses, marks the beginning of the real whitewater. From here until the end, the rapids are almost continuous. A stream bed of ledges and big rocks form dozens of jagged drops. Shortly below Locktown, there is a falls and three more big drops that might also be called falls. As on the Lockatong, what you do or do not run depends on how much you are willing to abuse your boat. And also as on the Lockatong, to attempt this course at high water would only add frightening holes and pushiness to the challenge. All this excitement takes place in a gently-sloped gorge. There are quite a few houses down there and, unfortunately, many no trespassing signs. But one beautiful and unspoiled section between Scott School Road and Green Sergeant Covered Bridge is free of houses and signs. This covered bridge is the last remaining in New Jersey. Below the covered bridge, the rapids are easier, though they are still continuous. Take out at the Delaware & Raritan Canal lock access area behind old, restored Prallsville Mills along N.J. Rte. 29. Wickecheoke here actually feeds into the Delaware and Raritan Canal, rather than pass underneath. As a result, the left side of the canal is a sloping spillway to the Delaware. You clearly will want to avoid this dangerous drop.

Save some time to explore the mill complex at the mouth. Though originally established in 1711, the structures that you see now were built later and consist of a grist mill, linseed oil mill, and sawmill. The main mill is now an art gallery.

HAZARDS: Beware of jagged rocks, possible strainers, and the canal dam at the end.

WATER CONDITIONS: Catch within 24 hours of a hard rain in late fall, winter, or spring.

GAUGE: There are staff gauges on the Locktown Road bridge (downstream face of left abutment) and on Sergeant Bridge (downstream end of right abutment). Consider 0.5 feet and 2.5 feet respectively as minimum. Respective levels of one foot and three feet are exciting but reasonable levels at which to attempt this challenging run.

Assunpink Creek

INTRODUCTION: Assunpink Creek is an unusual stream, as it is the only one that the author has ever found that flows out of the east to cross (well, at least clip) the Fall Line. It is born in rural Monmouth County and flows from there into and down the heart of Trenton. Few would expect a nice canoe stream to flow through Trenton, and that turns out to be an accurate assumption. But for those who seek to avoid the beaten path, and maybe even like to live dangerously, this stream may be for you.

Section 1. U.S. Rte. 130 to Whitehead Road					
Gradient	Difficulty	Distance	Time	Scenery	Map
5	A to 1	9.8	4.0	Good to Fair	11

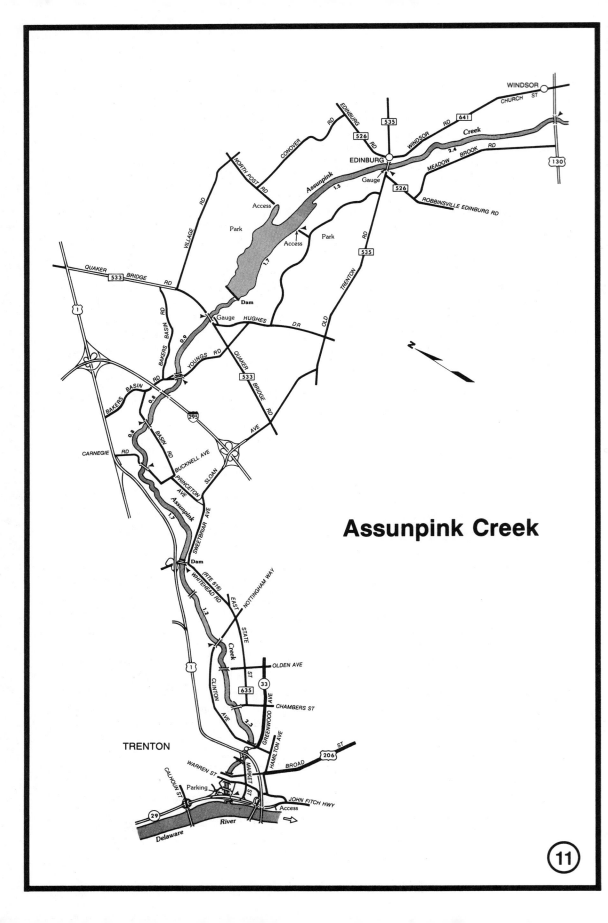

Assunpink Creek

11

TRIP DESCRIPTION: Surprisingly, from U.S. Rte. 130 to Whitehead Road, Assunpink makes a mostly attractive canoe route. The first few miles flow unnaturally straight, probably having been channelized in the distant past. But the banks are still low, so you can enjoy pleasant views of farms and woodland. The water is fast and mostly smooth, with few woody obstructions. That fact is unusual for a tiny coastal plain stream, further evidence of human tampering.

After passing under Rte. 535, Assunpink slows in the head of a long pond. The surrounding land is all within a large county park. Sometimes swampy and sometimes solid shores, with patches of forest or grassy knolls just beyond, create a pleasant setting. Only the presence of those ubiquitous high-voltage power lines mar the view. The park has a boathouse and launching ramp for those just interested in this pond. As for those passing through, the dam, a fairly big earthen structure, is easily portaged to the left of the spillway. This returns you to a short but particularly wild swamp passage that lasts until Quaker Bridge Road.

Below Quaker Bridge Road, civilization begins to close in. Busy highways, more power lines, neighborhoods, and even Amtrak's high-speed trains become part of the experience. But all along, a pleasant buffer of swampy woods pad the impact. The creek continues to be easy, obstructed only by few deadfalls. But watch out for a powerful, sloping chute beneath the old bridge just upstream of Youngs Road. The final portion of this section slows in a pond formed by a dam just above Whitehead Road. You can take out on the left brink of this drop (convenient but small parking area there), or back upstream, on the left, along Sweetbriar Road.

HAZARDS: The sloping chute beneath the bridge above Youngs Road could cause an ugly broach on the bridge piers. Carry if you have any doubts about your ability to negotiate this. The seven-foot weir just above Whitehead Road would best be portaged. The dam at Mercer County Park is not normally a hazard, just an obstacle. But stay off of the spillway. Expect to encounter some fallen trees. Finally, be aware that this is actually a stocked and well-fished trout stream. So avoid this place during the first week of trout season.

WATER CONDITIONS: The best period to catch any sustained high water is from November through April. The stream will stay up anywhere from two to six days after a hard rain, depending on how wet the ground already is.

GAUGE: A staff gauge at Rte. 535/526 (downstream end of pier) should read at least 1.9 feet. Better yet, there is a USGS gauging station just above Quaker Bridge Road (Rte. 533). To reach it, turn off Quaker Bridge Road just south of its bridge over Assunpink onto Hughes Drive. Go only a few feet and then turn left onto a small, paved road (sign says, "Hunter Education Center"), and go straight back to the creek and a sheet metal gauging station shed. Its staff gauge, attached to a vertical beam in the stream bed, should read at least 4.3 feet, though you may scrape in the riffle at the gauge.

Section 2. Whitehead Road to mouth					
Gradient	Difficulty	Distance	Time	Scenery	Map
8	A to 2	3.6	1.0	Bizarre	11

TRIP DESCRIPTION: This segment is for the curious and adventurous, but keep in mind that it could be dangerous. The big city now completely envelops the creek and shows no mercy. Factories, commercial buildings, and decaying neighborhoods line the banks. Worse yet, extraordinary quantities of trash smother the banks, trees, and stream bed. Even the city park has been popular as an illegal dump. Then comes The Tunnel.

For about a thousand feet, two curving parallel box tubes carry Assunpink beneath the ugliness. The entrances, unfortunately, tend to collect debris. When the author last cruised these waters, logs jammed against the left tube had formed a dangerous vertical drop of about four feet into a churning hydraulic. A more gradual and passable descent was available on the right tube. But on a more recent visit, the left entrance was wide open and the right was completely clogged. So bring a saw as you may need to hack your way into the tunnel. Once inside the tube, it is dark and scary, but usually uncomplicated. Rumors of 15-foot alligators, albino water moccasins, and stalactites of stinging carnivorous slime hanging from the ceiling have never been substantiated (yet).

When you emerge into the blinding daylight, you find yourself in Mill Hill, a renovated, gentrified neighborhood (talk about other side of the tracks!). But high, unscalable retaining walls separate you from the outside world. And now the creek begins to break over riffles, and outcrops of Fall Line rock appear. The creek tumbles over a big, gnarled ledge with a strong chute on the right with a sticky hole and then hurtles you into the mouth of another tunnel. This one is shorter but, with the noisy whitewater echoing off the walls, it is equally intimidating.

Back into the light again, it is an easy float down more riffles to the Delaware River. Take out on the right, above N.J. Rte. 29 and the mouth, by ascending a 20-foot embankment to a municipal parking lot (access from Willow Street).

HAZARDS: Lack of portage opportunity really commits one to the uncertainties of the tunnels. So avoid in high water and bring along adequate equipment (i.e. ropes, saws, carabiners, lamps, etc.).

WATER CONDITIONS: Same rules of thumb apply here as on Section 1.

GAUGE: The gauges and levels for Section 1 still apply. There is also a USGS gauge at Chambers Street. It is difficult to reach, but you can call Philadelphia Weather for a reading. It should read at least 3.7 feet.

Crosswicks Creek

INTRODUCTION: If you are looking for a pretty creek to canoe near Trenton, this stream may be for you. Crosswicks starts on the fringe of the Pine Barrens, just north of Fort Dix. It follows a great arc through rich farm country and manages to avoid suburbia almost to its tidal finish at beautiful, old Bordentown. Canoeable much of the year, Crosswicks presents an opportunity to conveniently enjoy some woods, wildlife, and quiet. And maybe you will even have a creek to yourself.

Section 1. New Egypt (Rte. 528) to Groveville (Groveville Road)					
Gradient	Difficulty	Distance	Time	Scenery	Map
3	A to 1	16.3	9.0	Good	12

TRIP DESCRIPTION: For the most part, this section offers one a green, woodsy corridor through attractive farm country. But you see little of those farms as there is usually at least a facade of trees hugging the banks. Typically Crosswicks meanders and even braids about a flat and soggy forested bottomland. You will spot some fine old trees down there. The bottomlands are bracketed by steep hillsides, here and there forming bluffs that tower as much as 50 feet above the stream. You typically see few houses from the water and the most ubiquitous signs of civiliza-

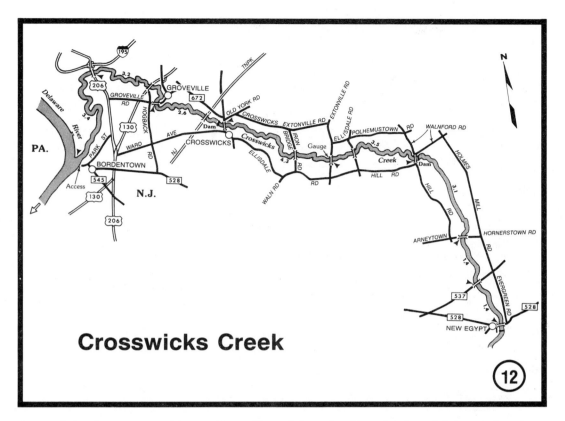

Crosswicks Creek

12

tion are irrigation pumps and hoses. Generally trash is noticeable only where it is jammed against deadfalls.

If you start at New Egypt, a pretty little country town, the best put-in is at the park on Lakeview Drive, river left about a hundred yards above Rte. 528. Navigation of Crosswicks is relatively easy. Fallen trees and logjams are a recurring annoyance, but less a problem than on most streams this size. It would not take too much sawing to vastly improve the canoeing on this creek (hint, hint). There are occasional pea gravel-formed riffles and, below Walnford Road, a tortuous 50-yard-long man-made rapid formed by the debris of someone's illegal tire dump. Only in Jersey can you run a rubber rapid. There are some little drops too. Just upstream of Walnford Road there is a beautiful, restored grist mill, and it has a runnable 18-inch weir. The tiny weir at the USGS gauging station at Extonville Road forms an easy chute. Finally, about a hundred yards below the bridge in the village of Crosswicks, by the old crumbling mill factory, is a four-foot wooden weir with a runnable sluice on the right, that is, depending on whether any debris is jammed there. So approach with caution. Tidewater starts somewhere between the Turnpike and Groveville Road.

HAZARDS: The weirs at Walnford Road and in Crosswicks have potential for trouble, especially if the water is high. Strainers could also present a danger at higher levels.

WATER CONDITIONS: Except in the driest of years, Crosswicks Creek usually carries canoeable flows continuously from November through the end of May. In any normal year, the rains keep it up through most of June and July also. With some wet weather, it will stay up for several days at a time even in August through October.

GAUGE: There is a USGS gauging station on the right bank just upstream of the Extonville Road bridge. It has two staffs, one attached to the downstream face of the concrete abutment on the right and one on the upstream face. They differ by about 0.2 feet at moderate or low levels, and if this gauge ever becomes available by phone, the upper staff reading is what you would hear. You want to see roughly at least 2.6 feet on the upper staff to start at New Egypt, but on the lower reaches of the creek probably 2.4 feet is passable.

Section 2. Groveville Road to mouth					
Gradient	Difficulty	Distance	Time	Scenery	Map
0	A	6.6	2.0	Fair to Good	12

INTRODUCTION: The remaining miles of Crosswicks Creek are all tidal. Houses crowd the stream as it flows through Groveville, but the scenery improves below as marshlands spread out on both sides. The high ground beyond supports a sewage treatment plant, houses, and roads, but distance softens the impact. These wetlands are worth poking around in. The trip can end at a town park and ramp at the foot of Park Street in Bordentown. This is a pretty and historic settlement, dating back to 1682, with many restored houses and tree-shaded streets. Allow some time to linger.

HAZARDS: None

WATER CONDITIONS: This is tidal, so it is always canoeable (except when frozen).

GAUGE: None needed

Assiscunk Creek

INTRODUCTION: Assiscunk Creek (Native American for "clay-at") is a tiny tributary of the tidal Delaware, entering at Burlington. It flows through a surprisingly thinly populated patch of land that is dedicated largely to horse farms and agriculture. The creek reflects little of this, wrapped up in its own riverine environment. So we can enjoy a surprisingly pleasant canoe path less than 25 miles from downtown Philadelphia.

Section 1. Jacksonville Hedding Road to mouth					
Gradient	Difficulty	Distance	Time	Scenery	Map
5*	A	8.8	6.0	Good	13
*above tidewater					

TRIP DESCRIPTION: The first half of this run is a freshwater, free-flowing brook. In spite of its small size, it is congested by relatively few deadfalls or other strainers, though inexperienced or lazy paddlers might still find the going rough. The paddler sees mostly woods and a few farm fields, except where a new landfill crowds the creek just below the start. The noise from I-295 and the New Jersey Turnpike are the biggest detractions of this run.

A pleasant surprise of Assiscunk Creek is that its tidal section is also largely natural. Tidewater starts somewhere approaching Old York Road. Marshes soon replace solid banks and widen. Except

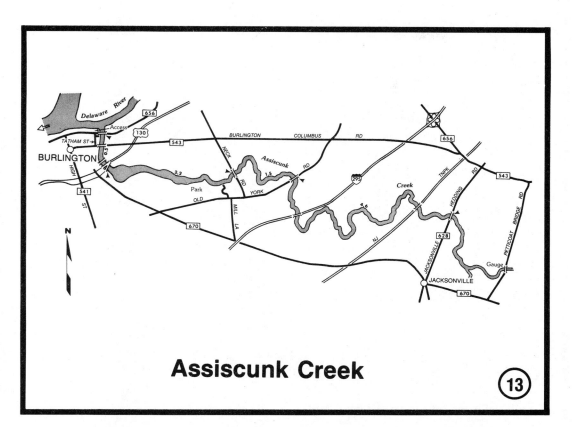

Assiscunk Creek

(13)

for a housing development at Neck Road, the wetlands are backed up by wooded high ground, with much of the south side protected by a county park. In the final mile, the scenery turns urban and once again road noise fills the air. You can take out at the foot of East Union Street (off Tatham Street) in Burlington or at the municipal boat ramp (fee may be charged in season), just a few yards down the Delaware River from Assiscunk's mouth.

HAZARDS: Strainers

WATER CONDITIONS: This is usually runnable from November through June.

GAUGE: There is a staff gauge attached to the downstream face of the left abutment of Petticoat Bridge. This is the next bridge upstream of the suggested put-in. Be careful here as the approach is steep, slippery, and thorny. Zero canoeing level is probably about 2.2 feet.

Rancocas Creek

INTRODUCTION: A broad, fan-shaped configuration of micro-streams oozes out of central Burlington County's Pine Barrens and focuses its flow on a point halfway between Mount Holly and Willingboro. It is there that Rancocas Creek is born. Rancocas (named after a local Native American tribe) is only about eight miles long. It is all tidal, so one cannot appreciate the substantial

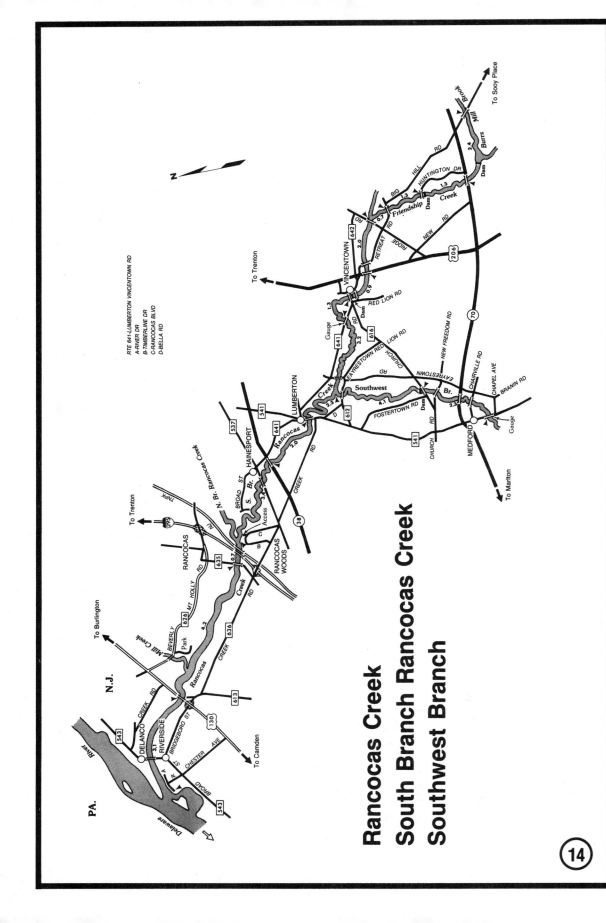

Rancocas Creek
South Branch Rancocas Creek
Southwest Branch

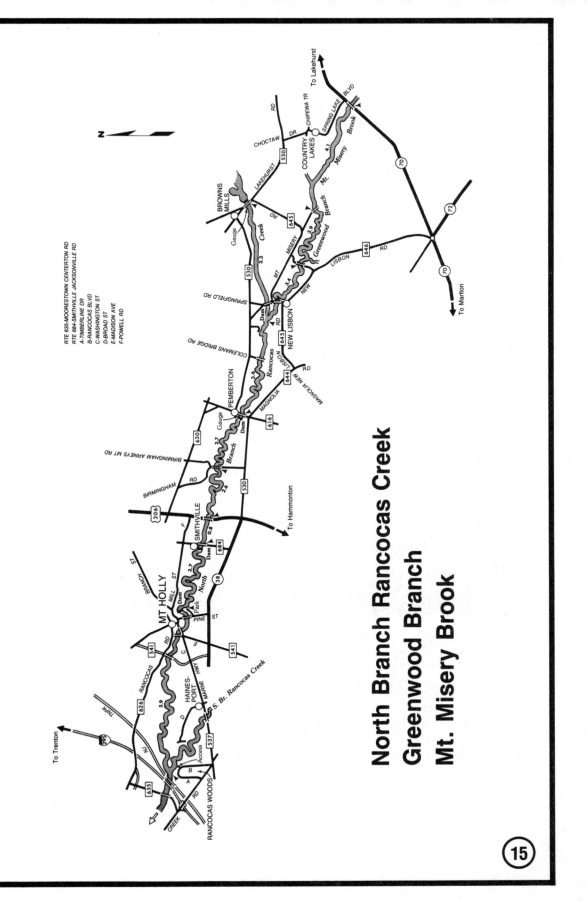

North Branch Rancocas Creek
Greenwood Branch
Mt. Misery Brook

RTE 635-MOORESTOWN CENTERTON RD
RTE 684-SMITHVILLE JACKSONVILLE RD
A-TIMBERLINE DR
B-RANCOCAS BLVD
C-WASHINGTON ST
D-BROAD ST
E-MADISON AVE
F-POWELL RD

15

flow that it draws from that great Pine Barrens aquifer. It being so close to Philadelphia and more the domain of motorboats than canoes, you will be surprised to find the Rancocas to be a reasonably nice place to paddle.

Section 1. Confluence North and South branches to mouth					
Gradient	Difficulty	Distance	Time	Scenery	Map
0	A	8.0	3.0	Good	14

TRIP DESCRIPTION: The best place to start this trip is on the South Branch about a quarter mile above its confluence with the North Branch. There is an obscure boat ramp here, behind Rancocas Woods' sewage treatment plant, at the intersection of Timberline Drive and Magnolia Road. Finding this spot may be your day's biggest challenge.

As far as U.S. Rte. 130, Bridgeboro, the setting is pleasant. The south side of the river is almost all marsh, with just a wooded skyline beyond. You can find in these marshes some of Jersey's largest remaining stands of wild rice, mostly along the first mile of this section. The north bank, in contrast, supports a lot of development. Still about half of the north bank remains wooded and appears wild. The final two miles to the mouth are fairly developed on the high ground of both sides. If you choose to follow Rancocas to its mouth, take out along the south side in Riverside, along River Drive, somewhere down river of Chester Avenue. At low tide, this can be a messy and mucky take-out. But mess and muck aside, at least one visit to Riverside is worth anybody's time just to see the classic clock tower on an old factory at Bridgeboro and Broad streets. The worst aspect of visiting Rancocas is that it is difficult to escape the drone of traffic noise from the Turnpike, I-295, and Rte. 130.

This should be a beginner's trip. You can keep it simple by using the tide and wind. The width of the Rancocas and its northwest course make it particularly susceptible to wind. So let these factors determine at which end you start. Finally, this seems to be a popular motorboat river. Best advice is keep to the edges.

HAZARDS: Motorboats

WATER CONDITIONS: This is all tidal and always deep enough for a canoe.

GAUGE: None

North Branch Rancocas Creek

INTRODUCTION: Traditionally, the North Branch seems to have been the most canoed branch of the Rancocas. Depending on the section you travel, it can be as pretty or as ugly as any stream in South Jersey. You have many miles from which to choose.

The creek starts in the Pine Barrens of Lebanon State Forest and Fort Dix Military Reservation, near Browns Mills. It gathers a canoeable flow quickly, and it even has a canoeable-size tributary, Greenwood Branch. But the North Branch always remains a small stream. For its first 17 boatable miles, its swift water follows a twisting path, across pine woods, farm country, and then suburbia. Tidewater begins at the upper end of Mount Holly. Then, in its final five and a half miles, a sluggish estuary fattens to the broad Rancocas Creek that one sees from the Turnpike.

Gradient	Difficulty	Distance	Time	Scenery	Map
3	A	17.2	7.0	Very Good to Poor	15

TRIP DESCRIPTION: The put-in at Browns Mills is at the base of the dam that lurks beneath the Rte. 530 bridge. You can find parking on the left bank (beware of sharp drop-off from road to lot, if you have a low-riding vehicle) and launch from either side. The tiny ribbon of clean, tea-colored water that speeds off into the woods promises much. So the numerous jams and deposits of trash from streamside party spots and the backyards of some of the streamside inhabitants is especially sickening. But quickly enough, you will shake free of the unsightly nearby houses and trash as the North Branch burrows into seemingly remote forest. The banks here are usually high and dry, as they are along most of this creek. The best of this reach blossoms as a long, narrow, cedar-bound pond near New Lisbon. If it were not for the heavy and low-flying air traffic from McGuire Air Force Base, it could pass for a piece of Canada. To paddle these first few miles below Browns Mills, be prepared to work with a strong current, a very narrow channel, and sharp bends. Deadfalls, or at least overhangs, are always possible, though usually this stream is well sawed out.

From New Lisbon to Pemberton, the North Branch continues its scenic route through the woods with little development visible. The weir that forms the pretty pond upstream of New Lisbon lies immediately below Rte. 646 (New Lisbon Road). The chute on the left is runnable, though most would be advised to carry (right side is the lesser of the evils). Shortly downstream, Greenwood Branch comes in from the left, adding noticeable elbow room. Entering the village of Pemberton, whose main street is graced by a pretty display of old buildings, the creek again slows in a millpond. A diagonal weir, split by an island, forms this pond. Carry around the left end. You want to avoid the right channel because it is blocked by the ruins of an old steel bridge. Those just starting at Pemberton can follow a road on the left bank and put in at a park by the old weir.

The remaining miles from Pemberton to Mount Holly are seldom as scenic or as isolated as the river above. They start with another mile or so of woodland setting. But at Birmingham, a large chemical plant occupies both banks. Far uglier than the plant though is the clot of houses that begins to line and crowd the banks around Evansville (Rte. 206). With bulkheaded banks, trash, and a bountiful display of plastic lanterns, signs, every tacky lawn ornament imaginable, etc., you now know what Venice, Italy, would have looked like if its founders had been from New Jersey. This sort of development plagues much of the North Branch on down to Mount Holly.

One pleasant interlude from the above blight is Smithville. Smithville is what remains of a once-thriving 19th-century industrial town. As a river traveler, you will see on the left a crumbling old factory; straight ahead, a mill weir (carry right); and on the right, a short chain of company houses and a mansion. You should allow time for a tour of the latter.

Smithville's roots go back to the 1770's with the establishment of the first of many mills. Initially there were grist mills and sawmills, and the place was called Parkers Mills. Then came the textile mills, and it was called Shreveville. Finally, an industrialist from New England, Hezekiah Bradley Smith, bought the town in 1865, developed it into a national center for the production of woodworking machinery, and gave the place its present name. He later diversified to produce a popular line of bicycles, bringing further fame to this remote South Jersey settlement. And all through this period, water power from Rancocas ran much of the mills' machinery.

Mr. Smith distinguished himself not only as a talented businessman, but also as a socially progressive manager. In an era of American industrial history when sweatshops were the norm and when the average laborer was considered cheap and expendable, Mr. Smith offered his work force top wages, shorter hours, improved housing, and other perks. Mr. Smith's successor added to this list a unique improvement for his commuting staff. During the 1890's, the company built and operated a bicycle railroad between Mount Holly and Smithville. Too bad it was not a successful venture. Think what fun this would have made shuttling the Rancocas.

Upon entering Mount Holly, the creek slows in another pool. A town park appears on the left, at the head of which a road comes right to the river's edge. Take out here, unless you plan to continue to tidewater. Just around the bend, about a quarter mile above Pine Street, is the last weir, with an easy carry on the left. The tide starts just below.

HAZARDS: Weirs at New Lisbon, Pemberton, Smithville, and Mount Holly all require carries. Strainers are a possibility in the first few miles.

WATER CONDITIONS: This stream is probably always passable, though it is common to have low enough flows in August and September to create shallow spots and to expose annoying and normally submerged snags.

GAUGE: There is a staff gauge on the downstream edge, right side of the Rte. 530 bridge at Browns Mills. Zero is unknown, but levels in excess of 5.6 feet are certainly fine. There is a USGS gauging station at Pemberton (call Philadelphia or inspect on site) with a staff gauge on the right face, downstream abutment of the Rte. 530 bridge. Zero is unknown, but probably lurks around 1.4 feet. Anything over 1.6 feet is just fine.

Section 2. Mount Holly (Pine Street) to mouth					
Gradient	Difficulty	Distance	Time	Scenery	Map
0	A	5.4	2.0	Fair to Good	15

TRIP DESCRIPTION: Though Mount Holly is a pretty town, there is little indication of such from the creek. Where it passes through downtown, the channel is confined within concrete walls. Near the end of this man-made stretch, below Washington Street, there is a little sluice-gate weir. Treat with caution.

Below town the surroundings are largely natural. This is partly so because a large portion of both banks is within the preserve of Rancocas State Park. The lower North Branch is usually bordered by extensive wetlands, mainly marsh. Most high ground outside the park is occupied by houses. Noise from the nearby New Jersey Turnpike significantly reduces the appeal of this section.

There is no access to the mouth. The best option is to ascend the South Branch a quarter mile to the public access in Rancocas Woods at Timberline Drive and Magnolia Road.

HAZARDS: The little sluice-gate weir at the end of the concrete channel in Mount Holly is exposed at low tide. It could be a site for a nasty broach.

WATER CONDITIONS: This is tidal, so it is always up enough to float a canoe.

GAUGE: None

Mount Misery Brook and Greenwood Branch

INTRODUCTION: Tired of repeating the same old Pine Barrens trips? Want to escape the obnoxious crowds of the Wharton Forest area? Then this combination may be for you.

Mount Misery Brook gushes out of the piney desolation of Lebanon State Forest. It bears that discouraging name only for about three miles before merging with Bridge Branch to form Greenwood Branch. Greenwood Branch ultimately feeds the North Branch Rancocas Creek just below New Lisbon. These branches and brooks together form a diminutive, isolated, and challenging canoe trail. But this just may provide the escape that you were looking for.

Section 1. N.J. Rte. 70 to New Lisbon (Rte. 646)					
Gradient	Difficulty	Distance	Time	Scenery	Map
3	A	10.7	8.0	Fair to Very Good	15

TRIP DESCRIPTION: There is a reason that this stream is so lightly traveled. It is difficult. Mind you, it is not a cellulose hell like Ridgeway Branch or the North Branch Metedeconk. Just difficult. Though this may sound like an oxymoron, Mount Misery Brook would best be described as advanced flatwater paddling. Typically this is a swift, extremely tortuous, and narrow stream that bristles with overhanging vegetation. The route, surprisingly, is seldom blocked. You just have to constantly hustle, draw, pry, push, and duck to keep from getting tangled, poked, twanged, and pinned. It is a continuous slalom.

Mt. Misery winds about in a narrow, semi-swampy bottomland that is surrounded by sandy pine barrens. The vegetation along the stream is impenetrable, thorny, and generally deciduous with a smattering of cedar trees. Towards the end, the forest recedes at the head of some old cranberry bogs, and the stream meanders about tussocky meadows. This is a welcome respite from the tunnel-like confinement of the upper creek.

With the subtle inflow of Bridge Branch, the route changes. The channel is roomier now, usually passing through a flooded swamp dominated by red maples. Initially the channel is unnaturally straight as it flows through the site of more old cranberry bogs. It then resumes its traditionally twisting course to the extreme. As the stream grows larger, so do the trees of the swamp, and some of these trees inevitably fall across the creek. So paddlers can expect at least several liftovers, maybe more. One low road bridge may also require a carry.

All of Mt. Misery Brook and the Greenwood Branch down to Lower Mill (the second road bridge) is nearly wilderness. There are no houses or other structures. There is, however, a disappointing quantity of junk back here, including old cars and many old tires, usually dumped where sand roads penetrate to the edge of the stream. It is a painful contrast.

A significant tributary, Bisphams Mill Creek, further swells Greenwood Branch just above Lower Mill. There is a state access at this bridge. From there on, the going is really easy and usually unobstructed. This remaining section, unfortunately, is also mostly lined with houses. So it is not particularly attractive or wild. There is an easy take-out on the left at New Lisbon.

If you choose to continue the remaining 0.65 miles to the North Branch, there is a three-foot, sloping weir with a respectable hydraulic beneath the Rte. 646 bridge. It is runnable at moderate levels, but watch for spikes. The first take-out below the confluence is behind Burlington County Community College. To reach this spot, follow Rte. 646 out to Rte. 530 (blue water tower) and turn left. Go 0.1 miles and turn left into the first college entrance (College Drive). Follow until the road bends to the right, and then turn left onto a dirt road to an abandoned brick building. An easy take-out is right behind the building.

HAZARDS: You must deal with strainers, a low bridge, and the weir beneath Rte. 646.

WATER CONDITIONS: This route is most likely up in late fall, winter, and spring, except after prolonged dry spell.

GAUGE: None on creek. If there is enough water on the upstream side of the Rte. 70 bridge to float you, then you have an adequate level. Roughly, a level of over 1.8 feet at the USGS gauge on the North Branch at Pemberton (call Philadelphia or inspect on site), means plenty of water. What corresponds to a zero level is unknown.

South Branch Rancocas Creek

INTRODUCTION: Flowing entirely within Burlington County, the South Branch gathers its flow from the heart of the Pine Barrens and from the Coastal Plain to the west. Its extreme headwaters are on its tributary, Burrs Mill Brook, near Chatsworth. This is the same area from which issue the popular Wading and Batsto rivers. But the South Branch never turned out as good as those Wharton Tract streams. Instead of flowing through the wilderness, it heads for the big city, and as a result, it suffers a lot of wear and tear. And even on segments where it has remained beautiful and wild, it has found few friends to saw it out and keep it easily canoeable. So the South Branch has never experienced the popularity of the North Branch.

The creek has three distinct sections. There is the upper part, which you would only want to paddle sections of. There is the middle, which would be acceptable to most people. And there is the lower, tidewater, which offers only marginal compensation for one's efforts. Additionally, the South Branch has a canoeable tributary, the Southwest Branch, that makes a nice alternative trip for the middle section. Surely you can find a good time somewhere in this system.

Section 1. Sooy Place Road to Ridge Road					
Gradient	Difficulty	Distance	Time	Scenery	Map
6	A	5.7	6.0	Poor to Excellent	14

TRIP DESCRIPTION: The canoeing on this stream always starts on the tributaries. The upper South Branch is too small to paddle. But a few miles east of Vincentown, it is swollen to canoeable proportions by a canoeable-sized tributary, Friendship Creek. The upper Friendship Creek is also too small to paddle. But a few miles south of N.J. Rte. 70, it is swollen to canoeable proportions by a canoeable-sized tributary, Burrs Mill Brook. This series of brooks, canoeable in size, if not always in reality, make up most of this section.

The highest potential put-in is the road from Rte. 70 to Sooy Place, over Burrs Mill Brook. If you are a veteran of South Jersey canoeing, the tiny, tea-colored brook that you behold should look no more ridiculous a canoeing objective than the put-ins for the Mullica, Batsto, or Wading.

But why then do you see so many canoeists lined up at those other put-ins, while you stand here at Burrs Mill Brook all cold and alone? Perhaps because just downstream this creek burrows into a terrible, tangled swamp. The brook maintains a deep enough channel or channels, but its waters are repeatedly strained through thorns, brush, and fallen trees. And unlike the wonder streams of Wharton, no navy of good Samaritans have put a saw to this potential canoe trail. The swamp is beautiful though, as is the pine and cedar covered high ground beyond. It is all so nice, but you will only be cursing. Then, after filtering through this mess for about a mile, the path opens up in the backwaters of a marshy pond. It is a pretty pool that could pass for the Canadian wilderness were it not for just two houses. The paddle across the pond ends with a carry around a four-foot weir. A short and easy passage through the woods merges into another pond, this one even prettier than the last — visually a wilderness. But the noise and sight of busy Rte. 70 end the optimistic illusion.

A forgettable interlude with classic South Jersey suburban sprawl follows. The pool continues past the Rte. 70 bridge, but is now set in the heart of a large housing development called Leisuretowne. Isolated evergreen shores are now replaced by the sight of house after house. This long pond turns out to be formed by only a two-foot rubble weir, but it is unlikely that you will have enough water to run it. There follows a short, free-flowing stretch and another pond, enveloped by densely packed houses. A sloping four-foot weir forms this pond. There is seldom enough water to slide down its concrete face, which may be for the best, since a hazardously placed bridge pier below could make for a nasty broach.

The South Branch finally shakes free of ticky-tacky civilization and meanders through a strip of glades, probably the bed of a former pond or cranberry bog. Fringed by woods, this short reach is as pretty as any on the Mullica or Wading. Approaching Retreat Road/Big Hill Road, the creek returns to the woods. The woods develop into a beautiful hardwood swamp. There are some big trees down here, and complementing the understory are thick groves of holly. A lot of wood, unfortunately, has fallen across the channel, forcing many carries, some quite difficult. When the South Branch finally sneaks in above Ridge Road, the additional flow greatly reduces the blockages.

HAZARDS: A weir above Rte. 70 and another at Huntington Drive (in Leisuretowne) require carries. There are numerous strainers at the start and in the last mile. Also, a low footbridge below Huntington Drive and a pipe crossing at Retreat Road are too low for clearance. Finally, beware of killer poison ivy in that last swamp, growing on the liftover trees, of course.

WATER CONDITIONS: This usually has enough water any time between November and early May.

GAUGE: There is a staff gauge below Vincentown (Section 2) at Rte. 641, right abutment, downstream end. A good level is about 2.7 feet. Zero is unknown.

Section 2. Ridge Road to Lumberton (Rte. 541)					
Gradient	Difficulty	Distance	Time	Scenery	Map
3	A	9.7	5.0	Good to Fair	14

TRIP DESCRIPTION: This is the best overall portion of the South Branch for canoeing. Strainers are far fewer than above and their number decreases with each mile. After the confluence with the Southwest Branch, they are seldom found. The scenery on this reach is different from that upstream. The surrounding land begins to rise and the bottomlands or swamps narrow. Between late fall and spring, when the foliage is bare, you can see that the countryside beyond is farmland. You leave the country and wilderness briefly at Vincentown. This is a pretty, New

England-like village approached via an old millpond. The pond ends with a five-foot weir (at Race Street) and a carry. Much of the passage below Vincentown is wooded and undeveloped. With the surrounding ground higher, 30-foot, beech-covered bluffs grace many bends. Below the Southwest Branch, though, the riverside becomes more populated. On these last miles, the South Branch quietly slips into its tidal form.

The best take-out in Lumberton is about 200 yards upstream of Main Street (Rte. 541) bridge on the right at a side stream and old bridge. You reach this by car by turning east off Main Street onto Landing Road and going about 50 yards.

HAZARDS: Watch for a weir at Race Street in Vincentown and be prepared for strainers throughout.

WATER CONDITIONS: This reach is canoeable all year, except in extreme drought.

GAUGE: There is a staff gauge on the Vincentown Lumberton Road (Rte. 641) bridge, downstream side, right abutment. Zero is unknown, but 2.5 feet is a perfectly adequate level.

Section 3. Lumberton (Rte. 541) to mouth					
Gradient	Difficulty	Distance	Time	Scenery	Map
0	A	5.3	2.0	Fair to Poor	14

TRIP DESCRIPTION: This section is all tidal, so plan the direction of your trip accordingly. With even more development and road noise than the tidal section of the North Branch, this reach is disappointing. Still, there is some nice marsh scenery and, where protected by Rancocas State Park, some undisturbed wooded shores. If you are ascending this section, it is easy to make a wrong turn at a subtle fork about a mile above the mouth. Bear left there.

Regarding access, there is none at the mouth, but about a quarter mile upstream there is a public ramp on the south bank. It is approached by land from Timberline Drive at Magnolia Road in Rancocas Woods. The best access point in Lumberton is described in Section 2.

HAZARDS: Motorboaters

WATER CONDITIONS: This is all tidal so, except when frozen, it is always runnable.

GAUGE: None

Section 4. Southwest Branch. Medford (Rte. 541) to mouth					
Gradient	Difficulty	Distance	Time	Scenery	Map
3	A	6.4	4.5	Good to Fair	14

TRIP DESCRIPTION: This is a nice, alternate way to start a South Branch trip, though it would be even nicer if some party would come saw it out. Except for the house-lined banks of the pool above Kirbys Mill (Church Road), the setting is mostly natural. Usually the high-banked creek flows well back in the woods, with only an occasional house. Often one side shapes up as a beech-covered bluff. At one spot it emerges from the wild as it passes a golf course.

Navigating this typical Coastal Plain creek has all the typical pros and cons. On the pro side, the Southwest Branch is, at normal levels, a gentle stream. The water is smooth, though at low levels there are some tiny pea gravel-formed riffles to negotiate and snags to dodge. On the con side, there are those strainers. Fallen trees are a too-frequent annoyance, particularly between Kirby Mills and Eayrestown Road. Count on several carries. Upstream of Kirby Mills, where the backwater of a weir smooths things out and slows things down, the path is generally unobstructed. That weir at Kirby Mills warrants a carry, which gives you an opportunity to inspect the restored mill on the left. There is no access at the mouth of this stream, so continue on down the South Branch Rancocas a bit over two miles to Lumberton.

HAZARDS: Carry on the left the six-foot weir at Church Road. There are lots of strainers.

WATER CONDITIONS: This is usually passable any time except in late summer of a dry year.

GAUGE: There is a staff gauge on a pipe stand, upstream right of Rte. 541 in Medford. You want at least 3.8 feet.

Raccoon Creek

INTRODUCTION: Raccoon Creek is a Gloucester County waterway that flows from just outside of Glassboro to the Delaware River, joining about a mile and a half below the Commodore Barry Bridge. It passes through a variable landscape that is the center of a major fruit-growing area, the edge of a major petrochemical belt, and everywhere, home to new industry and creeping suburbs. Add to all that the presence of the New Jersey Turnpike and I-295, and it is amazing that a nice canoe stream could still exist here. But it does. And with exits off those busy highways only a mile away, you could not ask for a more convenient stream to reach.

Section 1. Mullica Hill (U.S. Rte. 322) to Russell Mill Road					
Gradient	Difficulty	Distance	Time	Scenery	Map
7	A to 1	3.4	2.0	Good	16

TRIP DESCRIPTION: At only three and a half miles, this is not a run that will satisfy hyperactive paddlers. Its defining characteristic is that it is nontidal. It has little in common with Section 2.

This section starts in Mullica Hill, a picturesque town of about a thousand people, where it seems as if every building is either a craft or antique shop. The put-in at Rte. 322 is actually beneath the span of N.J. Rte. 45 (following permission from property owner, of course). With initially what seems like a steep gradient, i.e., by South Jersey standards, the 15- to 20-foot-wide ribbon rushes down dozens of riffles. The riffles are usually formed by bars of pea gravel. With the fast spots often complicated by overhanging vegetation, you had better know how to handle your canoe in fast water before venturing here. But what is really amazing about this section is the relative lack of obstacles. You can count on several liftovers. But if you compare this with just about any other stream, this small, the upper Raccoon seems like the Panama Canal.

This is a very pretty section. The creek flows almost entirely through forest, where there are plenty of big hardwoods, some perpetually green hollies, and those wonderful silvery stands of beech that dominate so many hillsides. And yes, there are hillsides here. Though officially called the Coastal Plain, the surrounding land is very rolling and, especially in the first mile or two, 30- to 50-foot bluffs crowd the stream. The banks are also usually high, of mud or sand, and are overgrown to a jungle-like degree. There are a few houses down here. Otherwise, you get to enjoy solitude. At high tide, the Russell Mill Road take-out marks the start of tidewater.

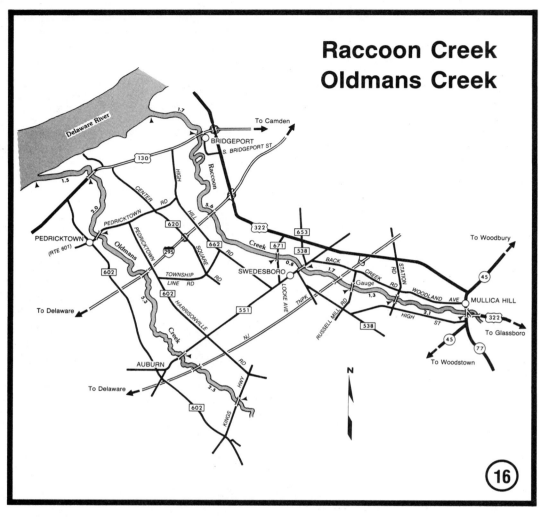

**Raccoon Creek
Oldmans Creek**

HAZARDS: Strainers

WATER CONDITIONS: Above Tomlin Station Road, Raccoon Creek is usually only passable within two days of hard rain between November and early May. Below Tomlin Station Road, adequate water may last for an additional two days.

GAUGE: There is a staff gauge on the downstream side of the left abutment of N.J. Rte. 45 in Mullica Hill. There is a USGS gauging station on the right bank just below Tomlin Station Road. Respective levels of 1.4 feet and 7.6 feet should float you over all the riffles (except the rocky riffle at Rte. 45). The section between Tomlin Station Road and Russell Mill Road is probably negotiable as low as 1.2 feet and 7.2 feet.

Section 2. Russell Mill Road to Bridgeport (U.S. Rte. 130)					
Gradient	Difficulty	Distance	Time	Scenery	Map
0	A	8.1	3.0	Fair to Good	16

TRIP DESCRIPTION: The evidence of your arrival on tidewater comes suddenly and strikingly. The channel immediately widens, high banks disappear, and marshes spread out on both sides. By far, the prettiest reach is above Swedesboro. Here the lush and dense marsh is framed by wooded slopes, while Swedesboro looms in the distance, dominated by a church steeple rising above a cluster of white houses. On closer inspection, however, Swedesboro (which was started as a Swedish colony) shows only its drab side to the river. But you pass through quickly. The channel narrows here for about a mile and is hemmed in by relatively high, solid, and overgrown banks. Then the creek balloons to a wide expanse of marsh, side channels, weed-choked shallows, and, at low tide, mud flats.

Sometimes this change is obscured by high, overgrown banks or berms. These were formed by dredge spoil deposited when they straightened the channel long ago. But generally you get a wide open view which allows you to see both the good and the bad. The good includes distant fields and woods, the graceful arc of the Commodore Barry Bridge, and even Pennsylvania. The bad includes an industrial park, housing tracts, and a chemical plant. With all these acres of wetlands, a trip down Raccoon Creek can be rewarding for birders. In fact, the author has even observed a pair of bald eagles here (by the chemical plant of all places).

Navigation is generally easy. You should do the section between Russell Mill Road and Rte. 551 only at high tide or when the upper river is high. At low tide, the creek does not reach sea level almost until Rte. 551, running in a shallow and almost channelless manner over a sandy bottom with sand riffles. Without good flow from above, you will be doing a lot of walking.

Starting at Swedesboro, the stream is always navigable, even at low tide. At low tide the channel is usually easy to follow. Possible points of confusion are just below I-295 (bear left) and the hairpin loop at the chemical plant (you can follow the loop or short-cut its base). At high tide many of the side channels and lagoons are then passable, increasing your opportunity for side trips, both deliberate and accidental. Take out along South Bridgeport Street just upstream of the railroad bridge or at Rte. 130 by the bridgekeeper's house. There are still 1.7 miles of more of the same below Rte. 130, but there is no access at the mouth.

HAZARDS: None

WATER CONDITIONS: This is passable any time on a high tide. At low tide, the stretch above Swedesboro requires the water conditions necessary to paddle the upper part of Section 1.

GAUGE: At low tide, use the staff gauges from Section 1 for the stretch above Swedesboro. You probably want at least 1.3 feet and 7.4 feet respectively to float over the worst shallows.

Oldmans Creek

INTRODUCTION: Oldmans Creek defines part of the western border between Gloucester and Salem counties. It starts just southwest of Glassboro, only about a mile from the head of Raccoon Creek. It finishes in the lower Delaware about four miles upstream from Penns Grove. Mostly a tidal canoe trail, this is a lackluster waterway.

Section 1. Kings Highway to U.S. Rte. 130					
Gradient	Difficulty	Distance	Time	Scenery	Map
0	A	9.8	4.5	Fair to Good	16

TRIP DESCRIPTION: The suggested put-in at Kings Highway is above tidewater. Do not try starting any higher, as most of the route is a swampy, cellulose obstacle course. Even the first three quarters of a mile below Kings Highway can be trying. There are some more strainers and tangled spots, but it does not take a paddling Houdini to negotiate them. The reward for starting your trip on this final free-flowing section is enjoying the pleasure of a small stream, some attractive woodsy surroundings, wetlands, hilly terrain, and only a few houses back in those woods.

Tidewater is immediately noticeable as the stream abruptly widens. The surrounding ground stays initially high, but after Rte. 551, marshes bracket the route. The high ground beyond is occupied by woods, fields, and houses. As the marshes widen, so does your field of vision. This, unfortunately, treats you to the sight (and sound) of a lot of distant industry. Particularly obnoxious is the drone of the large refinery across the Delaware River.

The take-out at Rte. 130 is poor, especially if you have been running with the tide, because there will be high, exposed, black mud banks to surmount. Probably the best bet is on the right about 50 yards below the bridge. There is an old, abandoned ramp here that is not too slippery to ascend.

The remaining mile and a half to the Delaware is of little redeeming value. The marshes have been filled with dredge spoil that is covered with phragmites. There is no access at the mouth. So you can either double back to Rte. 130, paddle four miles down the Delaware to Penns Grove, or paddle up the Delaware a mile to where a good dirt road comes almost to the river's edge. This road, probably private, branches off of Rte. 130 about a third of a mile east of the bridge over Oldmans Creek.

HAZARDS: You must deal with strainers in the first mile.

WATER CONDITIONS: Most of this is runnable year round. But the upper mile could get too low in late summer and early fall.

GAUGE: There is a staff gauge on the right upstream piling of Kings Highway bridge. Minimum is unknown, but anything over 4.0 feet is just fine to negotiate that short nontidal section.

Salem River

INTRODUCTION: If somebody told you that there was a beautiful canoe stream only six miles from the center of Wilmington, Delaware, only two miles from the huge DuPont chemical plant at Deepwater Point, New Jersey, and only a mile from the point where busy U.S. Rte. 40, I-295, and the New Jersey Turnpike all merge, would you believe it? Go wet your paddle in the Salem River, and find out the truth.

The Salem River starts in eastern Salem County near the crossroads of Pole Tavern. Its natural path is an inefficient one, traditionally joining the Delaware only after paralleling that river for several miles along the west side of the county near the town of Salem. But its real path has been engineered into efficiency by the DuPont Corporation, via the Salem Canal. Several decades ago, DuPont, needing a good water supply for its huge Chambers Works Plant at Deepwater Point, constructed a diversion dike across the channel and marsh just downstream of what is now Rte. 540. To deliver this water, DuPont dug a canal to the Delaware River, where the Memorial Bridge now crosses. Just above the mouth of the canal, DuPont built a low dam to block the tide.

This has allowed the upper Salem to flow in only one direction (into the plant's water intake) and thus become essentially a long and narrow freshwater reservoir. With little flushing action

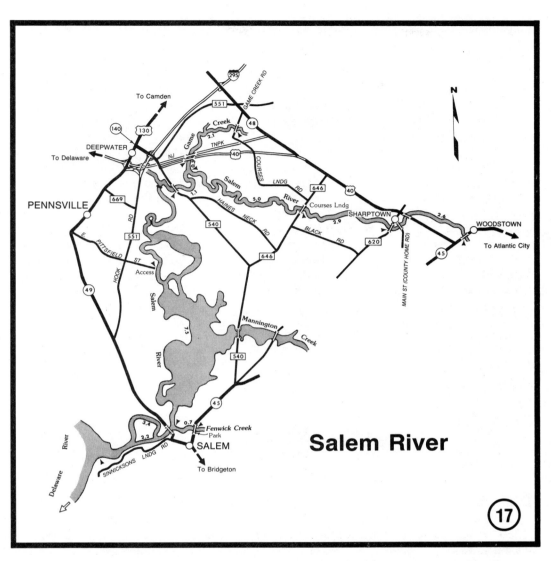

Salem River

below the diversion dike, the lower Salem resumes only as an inches-deep, sluggish puddle or as mud flats. But it reconstitutes itself after about a mile and provides many more miles of good canoeing. So this is really a tale of two rivers.

Section 1. Sharptown (Rte. 620) to Rte. 540					
Gradient	Difficulty	Distance	Time	Scenery	Map
0	A	9.0	4.0	Good	17

TRIP DESCRIPTION: First of all, it is possible to start as far up as where U.S. Rte. 40 crosses on the west end of Woodstown, if you are into hardship. The river up here is just a brook, certainly narrow enough to be easily blocked by any trees that fall into it. And there are many. The water is fairly swift with many little gravel-formed riffles. The mostly forested setting is pleasant, with a high bank on one side and low floodplain on the other. It might be possible to forget civilization down here were it not for an annoying volume of trash in and along the creek.

Deadfalls are still a problem for about the first mile below the first recommended put-in, Rte. 620. But the woodsy/swampy setting is fairly nice, though on weekends the peace will probably be disturbed by continuous chatter from the loudspeaker of a nearby auction. When the river abruptly widens, that signifies that you have reached the level of the man-made pool. To Courses Landing (Rte. 646), there is usually a high, steep, wooded bank on the left and marsh or swamp on the right. Those wishing to avoid that first relatively congested mile can instead start at Rte. 646 and first paddle upstream. Since there is usually little current, this will be an attractive option for many. Below Courses Landing, the surroundings are mostly wetlands, ranging from maple swamp to marsh, with combinations of the two in between. Occasional houses appear on the high ground, including one particularly trashy farm. A nearby power line and increasingly loud highway noise are this reach's other flaws.

Branching off of Salem River, about a mile above Rte. 540, is Game Creek. This tiny tributary offers an attractive side trip of about two and a half miles each way, through mostly a maple-studded marsh. Between Rte. 40 and the farm at Game Creek Road, the setting appears delightfully wild and remote. But your ears, unfortunately, tell you otherwise as the stereo noise from I-295 on one side and the Turnpike and Rte. 40 on the other penetrates the peace.

HAZARDS: Anticipate trees on the upper reaches.

WATER CONDITIONS: The Salem is always runnable below Rte. 620, except during winter freeze. Above Rte. 620, try during late fall, winter, or spring after a wet spell or within a few days of hard rain.

GAUGE: None

Section 2. East Pittsfield Street to mouth					
Gradient	Difficulty	Distance	Time	Scenery	Map
0	A	9.6 or 10.8	5.0	Good	17

TRIP DESCRIPTION: The end of East Pittsfield Street is a public landing. It is by no means the head of navigation. Even at low tide you can make it at least two miles upstream.

Between the put-in and N.J. Rte. 49, the Salem meanders about a huge expanse of marsh and enters a series of lake-like stretches of open, shallow water called Pine Island Meadow, Kates Creek Meadow, and Mannington Meadow. Generally, the channel follows the western edge of these waters. The open water is surrounded by broad marshes of mostly phragmites. The marshes are bordered by high ground bearing both hardwood forest and cultivated land. Well-spaced, old farm houses and barns grace the landscape. As on the upper river, only the drone of distant highway noise breaks the serenity.

Salem is a good place to end your trip, though good take-outs are difficult to find. Probably the best option is to ascend Fenwick Creek for a half mile to N.J. Rte. 45 bridge, where there is a town park on the south bank. Though Salem is a pretty town, its waterfront is ugly. And the marshy surroundings below town are only mediocre. Depending on whether you follow the big loop below town or take the shortcut (hence the variable distance given above), it is 2.1 or 3.3 miles from Rte. 49 to the mouth. There is no access at the mouth, but you can find a spot to exit along Sinnicksons Landing Road along the south bank.

HAZARDS: None

WATER CONDITIONS: This is always canoeable.

GAUGE: None

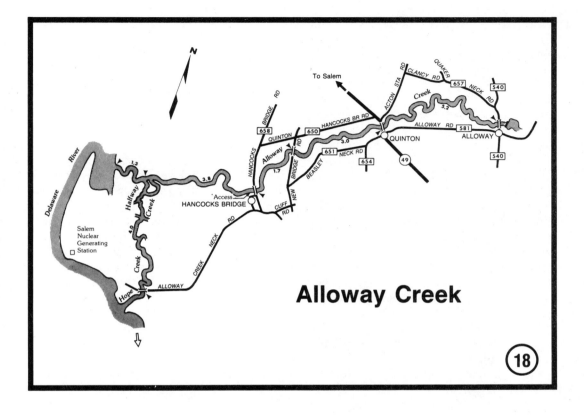

Alloway Creek

INTRODUCTION: Alloway Creek is a mostly tidal Delaware River tributary located a few miles south and east of Salem. It is typical of many estuaries in this area — a fine place to sample the great outdoors without getting too far from civilization or its reminders.

Section 1. Alloway (Rte. 540) to Hancocks Bridge					
Gradient	Difficulty	Distance	Time	Scenery	Map
0	A	9.9	3.0	Good	18

TRIP DESCRIPTION: The trip gets off to a nice start with an easy put-in. At the northeast end of the Rte. 540 bridge, a dirt road will get you right to the water's edge. This point is not quite the head of navigation. So you might enjoy starting with a side trip up the remaining quarter mile of this estuary. It is a tight, woodsy passage that ends at the foot of a dam. Heading downstream from Rte. 540, the creek winds through an attractive hardwood swamp decorated with a touch of cedar. Unfortunately, surrounding high ground is often occupied by houses. The swamp inevitably yields to marsh, usually vast stands of phragmites bordered by clumps of cedar trees. It is a big marsh, though usually you will not be able to see beyond the waterside wall of reeds.

Hancocks Bridge is a historic village whose claim to fame is a Revolutionary War massacre of 30 militiamen in their sleep. A much safer place to sleep now, this is the last point of access to Alloway Creek. The town has a nice boat ramp, but there is a fee for its use. To paddle to the mouth it is still another 5.2 or 6.2 miles, depending on whether you bypass one oxbow bend.

The creek below Hancocks Bridge offers a scenery of strange contrast. On one hand, you have the usual green (or tawny in winter) marsh, the waterfowl, the solitude, and the big sky. On the other hand, you have the huge hyperbolic cooling tower and the domed containment structures at the Salem Nuclear Generating Station and the attendant high-voltage power lines radiating outward. It is as if the Martians had invaded the marsh.

While there is no access to the Alloway below Hancocks Bridge, there is access to nearby Hope Creek. So by deft navigation through a maze of tidal guts, you can branch off Alloway Creek and take out where Alloway Neck Road (the road to the power plant) crosses Hope Creek. To accomplish this, you might want to bring along a good map, like the Taylors Bridge 7½-minute quadrangle sheet (from USGS), or even the New Jersey Department of Transportation's Salem County highway map is adequate. The traverse starts about four miles below Hancocks Bridge where there is an oxbow loop on the left. The main channel cuts straight across the loop. Continue down the main channel about 300 yards to where the loop returns, a point which is about a half mile above a power line crossing, and turn left into that channel. Ascend that channel about a half mile until you see a channel on the right (Halfway Creek). Ascend this, bearing left at the first fork. A winding half mile farther and you come to a four-way confluence of channels with an old, crumbling shack on the left. You go straight, which puts you on Hope Creek, and just follow the current out from there. Be resigned to the fact that you cannot do this trip entirely with the current. Ideally you should ride an outgoing tide out of Hancocks Bridge. You will then have to fight the current in the oxbow loop and that first side channel. But at the four-way confluence you again go with the tide. It is about an eight-mile trip from Hancocks Bridge to Alloway Neck Road.

Finally, if you are really ambitious, have an outgoing tide, and have calm weather, you could make a lovely trip starting at Hancocks Bridge, cutting through to the Delaware via Hope Creek, and then traveling along the beautiful, marshy shores of Mad Horse Creek Fish and Wildlife Management Area to finish at Bayside. This would be a 16-mile trip. Strong paddlers could do this on a single tide.

HAZARDS: Like most Delaware tributaries, the tidal currents can be most powerful. At Quinton, a narrow bridge constricts the flow to almost a rapid. So beware of the bridge piers and, if riding an outgoing tide, steer clear of some low pilings in the water just upstream.

WATER CONDITIONS: Being tidal, Alloway always enough water for navigation.

GAUGE: None

Delaware Bay

Delaware Bay is the lower estuary of the Delaware River, separating Delaware from New Jersey. It starts about eight miles south of Salem, at a line running from the mouth of New Jersey's Hope Creek to Delaware's Liston Point. Its junction with the Atlantic is defined by Cape May on the northeast and Cape Henlopen on the southwest. The bay covers roughly 700 square miles. In contrast to its famous neighbor to the southwest, the Chesapeake Bay, the funnel-shaped Delaware Bay has a most regular shoreline. On both sides of the bay, these shores barely exist, being just inches above sea level. If predictions of global warming and resultant sea rise hold true, the Year 2100 edition of this guidebook will need to include a much expanded description of this expanding waterway.

This is a scenic edge of New Jersey. Most of the bay is bordered by a one- to two-mile-wide swath of marsh, broken only by a well-spaced string of little resort villages and one power plant. The state has set aside many acres of these wetlands as public fish and wildlife management areas. Behind the marsh is mostly farm country. So next to the Pine Barrens, this area offers the least congested conditions in this congested state. The potential value to an outdoorsperson is obvious.

The unsheltered shores of the bay make a fine destination for sea kayakers, though on those all too infrequent calm days, it is just as good for canoeists. The scenery is consistent throughout — open water and distant ships on one side and the edge of the marsh on the other. The ubiquitous resort villages do little to enhance the view, but they are almost all small and quickly pass from view.

In planning a trip, you will need to consider wind, tide, and access. That day's prevailing wind should determine the direction of your trip. In these open waters, you must not only deal with the power of the wind, but also the resulting waves. Also, flooding of the marshes by wind-generated extra-high tides can completely eliminate any possibility of getting out of your boat anywhere between villages.

Tidal currents on the narrow upper bay are significant, so you also should try to paddle in the same direction. On the lower bay, they are still evident, but weak. Tidal range is relatively small, only a few feet, so approaching the shore at low tide is rarely a problem. Remember that if your itinerary includes both the shore of the bay and a segment on one of its tributaries, the tidal currents on the tributaries are invariably strong. As you have now probably realized, if you are going to successfully juggle winds, tide, and hours of daylight into an energy-efficient trip, you are going to have to be flexible about your itinerary.

There are few points of public access to the bay. Most are found a few miles back up the tributaries, and even they are relatively few. So your best options are those resort villages. In the season, usually a courteous request will get you permission to launch from private property. In the off season, there is often nobody around to ask, but discrete trespass usually works. You can find your way around just fine with a county road map, though keep in mind that some of these villages are linked to high ground by some poorly maintained roads. There are usually signs to warn you of such conditions. Also be aware that wind-driven high tides can sometimes flood these roads. Plan accordingly. The following are mileages between major access points or mouths of tributaries for one who follows the curves of the shore.

Segment	Miles
Salem R. to Alloway Cr.	5.4
Alloway Cr. to Hope Cr.	6.0
Hope Cr. to Bayside	8.5
Bayside to Cohansey R.	4.8
Cohansey R. to Sea Breeze	3.2
Sea Breeze to Back Cr.	3.8
Back Cr. to Cedar Cr.	1.7
Cedar Cr. to Nantuxent Cr.	1.3
Nantuxent Cr. to Gandys Bch.	1.3
Gandys Bch. to Dyers Cr.	1.3
Dyers Cr. to Fortesque	2.7
Fortesque to Dividing Cr.	8.5
Dividing Cr. to Maurice R.	3.6
Maurice R. to East Pt.	2.2
East Pt. to Thompsons Bch.	1.9
Thompsons Bch. to Moores Bch.	2.4
Moores Bch. to West Cr.	2.2
West Cr. to East Cr.	0.8
East Cr. to Dennis Cr.	0.8
Dennis Cr. to Bidwell Cr.	2.5
Bidwell Cr. to Reeds Bch.	0.8
Reeds Bch. to Pierces Pt.	2.4
Pierces Pt. to Rte. 642	2.7
Rte. 642 to U.S. Rte. 9	5.6
U.S. Rte. 9 to Cape May Pt.	3.4

Stow Creek

INTRODUCTION: Forming part of the border between Salem and Cumberland counties, Stow Creek is your average small Delaware Bay tidal tributary. It is neither wilderness nor heavily developed. It is off the beaten track; yet you will probably still be sharing it with somebody else — perhaps a hunter, trapper, or fisherman. It can be a beginner's delight or, with adverse wind or tide, anyone's nightmare. All things considered, Stow Creek is a fine paddling destination that, hard to believe, is less than 20 miles off the Turnpike.

Section 1. Rte. 623 to Bayside (Goslin Road)					
Gradient	Difficulty	Distance	Time	Scenery	Map
0	A	11.3	4.0	Good	19

TRIP DESCRIPTION: First of all, if the tide is high or on the rise, by all means head upstream (north) from Rte. 623. This is by far the prettiest section of Stow Creek. There are about two canoeable miles above the highway, but there is no access at the head of navigation. So you must negotiate this as a round trip. After passing a few houses and a trailer park, all within sight of

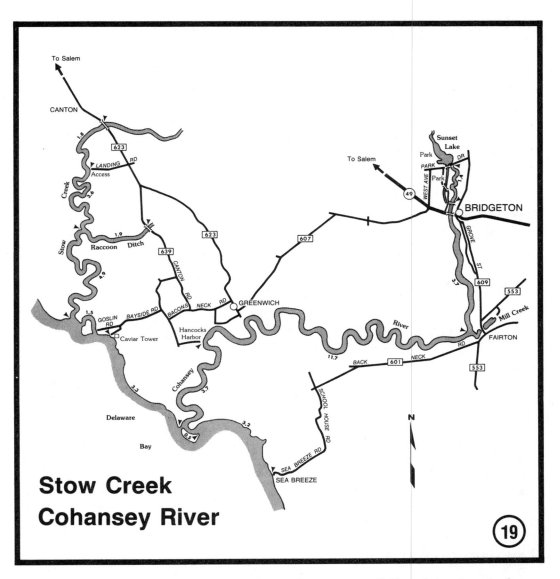

Stow Creek
Cohansey River

(19)

the highway, the ever-narrowing creek meanders up first past some fields and then into the forest. On both sides of the water there is marsh, also ever narrowing, and beyond the marsh is dry ground that rises about 20 feet above the water. Come here during the cold months, and the surrounding woods are particularly beautiful thanks to a thriving green understory of American holly. Absent from the scene are buildings, power lines, and even the typically ubiquitous duck blinds. As you approach the head of the tidal creek, the turbid estuarine water yields to the clear flow of the swampy headwaters. Around this point there is a sudden transition from marsh to swamp, and soon afterwards the tangled branches that border the channel knit together and force you to turn back.

The downstream journey from Rte. 623 to the Delaware Bay is all out in the open. Great loops guide you through a wide marsh of cordgrass and phragmites. The high ground beyond bears scattered farm houses, fields, and a distant line of hardwood forest with a spotty cedar fringe. The route is generally easy to follow, though at high tide or on a flood tide, it is possible to take a wrong turn into a side channel. If you really want to avoid such problems, bring along a USGS topographic map (Canton, 7½-minute quadrangle).

When you reach the bay, turn left, and then after a quarter mile, turn left again up what seems to be another river. This is actually just what remains of a final loop of Stow Creek before reaching its original mouth. If the bay is rough, you will probably want to finish at the foot of Goslin Road in Bayside. But if you can make it another half mile eastward, down the coast, there is a more public take-out option at an observation tower. Called "Caviar Tower," this spot marks the site of a big caviar processing plant that stood back in the days when huge sturgeon slinked about the depths of the bay and when Bayside was a real town.

HAZARDS: None

WATER CONDITIONS: The combination of low tide and low water in the upper creek might reduce how far you can ascend above Rte. 623. Otherwise, it is always runnable.

GAUGE: None

Cohansey River

INTRODUCTION: The Cohansey is a larger than average tributary of the Delaware Bay, draining the northwest end of Cumberland County. For the greater portion of its length it is tidal. And that is mostly where it is canoeable.

You will find the Cohansey to be an attractive paddling destination that combines nicely with some conventional terrestrial sightseeing. For the head of navigation is near Bridgeton, a more than 300-year-old town whose claim to fame is possessing New Jersey's largest historic district. This district includes more than 2,000 buildings that preserve the varied architecture of the 18th, 19th, and early 20th centuries. And to round out your historical sojourn, beyond the bounds of this district, there is a reproduction of a Native American village in this town's huge city park.

In fact, if historic preservation interests you, then the fun does not stop at the Bridgeton city line. The whole of Cumberland County is a delight. Because these nice estuaries that you want to paddle were once the only good means of access and transportation, this well-watered end of the state was also the end first settled. As a result, even in the smallest or most forgotten towns or crossroads, you will find old churches, graveyards, and houses, often proudly displaying plaques that proclaim their dates of origin.

So snoop around.

Section 1. Bridgeton (Park Drive) to mouth					
Gradient	Difficulty	Distance	Time	Scenery	Map
0	A	21.0	9.0	Good	19

TRIP DESCRIPTION: The Park Drive put-in presents you with some choices. Park Drive runs along the crest of a long milldam that marks the head of tidewater and backs up an attractive, almost mile-long pool called Sunset Lake. With a park protecting its west shore and an attractive residential neighborhood on the east, you may enjoy launching at the amphitheater parking lot and just paddling around the lake.

If you plan only to go downstream from Park Drive, you have two choices. You can park at the left downstream end of the dam and put in on the river below the main spillway. In floating from here to downtown Bridgeton, this route gives you a taste of swampy woods and potentially waterfowl-filled marsh. But it also includes the view of a huge factory, the backside of a landfill, and a decaying neighborhood. Your other choice is to put in on the lake at the amphitheater and paddle out of the right corner of the lake into the old millrace. This leads you through Bridgeton's 1,200-acre city park and past a zoo and the Lenni Lenape village. But it also runs by park roads and past the other side of that landfill. In summer, the raceway is a popular destination for rental canoes. A short carry at the old mill site gets you down to the tidal Cohansey in downtown Bridgeton.

The passage through Bridgeton is basically ugly, but mercifully short. On down to Mill Creek, there are some steep bluffs on the east side and marsh or swamp on the west. The shores are mostly wooded. A golf course and some scattered homes also occupy part of your vista.

After Mill Creek the Cohansey changes its general direction to the west, but assumes a serpentine course in doing so. The marshes widen dramatically, and the population density on the high ground beyond decreases. Those houses that remain are often quite attractive.

The next major landmark is Greenwich (pronounced "green witch"). Greenwich was once a bustling colonial port whose historical claim to fame is being the site of a Boston-style tea party held by local activists back in 1774. Only here they burned the stuff rather than throw it into the harbor. The town's colonial prosperity, however, never carried through to modern times. So today one finds a wonderful collection of colonial era houses strung out along a mile of road in this remote rural landscape.

Below Greenwich, the ever-widening Cohansey marshes merge with the vast marshes of the Delaware Bay. One enjoys here a feeling of elbow room. And if that is not enough to relieve your claustrophobia, the exit out into Delaware Bay will surely satisfy you.

The Cohansey's potential as a canoe stream suffers from poor access. Once you pass below the city park in Bridgeton, there is no public access to the river. If you are energetic, it is possible to get in or out via Mill Creek by using the Clarks Pond Fish and Wildlife Management Area. To reach this, turn south off of Fairton Gouldtown Road (Rte. 533) onto a dirt road just a few yards east of the railroad crossing (there should be a sign for the management area). Follow this to its end, bearing right. A short walk to the railroad grade followed by about a hundred-yard walk along the tracks gets you to the head of Mill Creek and the outlet of Clarks Pond. Also note that if you traverse Mill Creek, you must make a short carry over Rte. 553 at Fairton.

The best point of access in Greenwich is a commercial ramp at Hancock Harbor, about 1.5 miles southwest of town. As for the mouth, it is in the middle of nowhere. You can either paddle two and a quarter miles straight across open waters to Sea Breeze, where you can probably obtain permission to cross private property for access, you can double back to Hancock Harbor, or you can paddle northwest along the bay for almost four miles to Caviar Tower (public, see Stow Creek description). Wind and tide should dictate which option you choose.

HAZARDS: None

WATER CONDITIONS: Being tidal, most of this is always runnable. The first half mile below Sunset Lake, though, may be too shallow in spots at low tide.

GAUGE: None

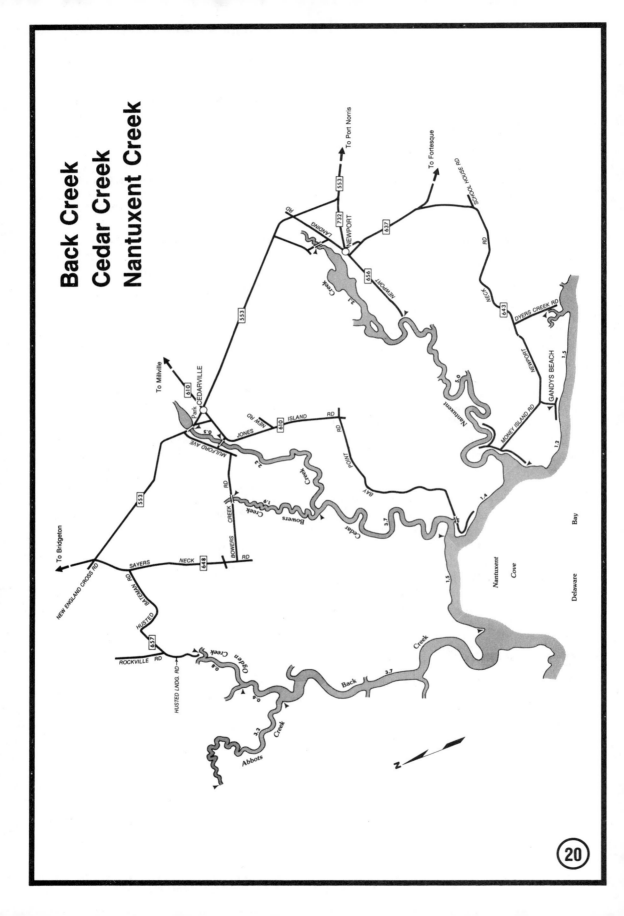

Back Creek
Cedar Creek
Nantuxent Creek

To Port Norris

To Fortesque

553

732

NEWPORT

637

SCHOOL HOUSE RD

LANDING RD

NEWPORT

656

NECK

RD

643

3.1

Creek

DYERS CREEK RD

553

Nantuxent

5.0

NEWPORT

MONEY ISLAND RD

GANDYS BEACH

1.5

To Millville

610

CEDARVILLE

Park

1.2

NEW RD

JONES

0.5

610

ISLAND

RD

MULFORD AVE

2.2

RD

POINT

BAY

1.4

553

CREEK RD

1.9

Bowers

Creek

Creek

Cedar

3.7

To Bridgeton

SAYERS

NECK

648

BOWERS

RD

1.1

Nantuxent

Cove

NEW ENGLAND CROSS RD

BATEMAN RD

1.5

Delaware

Bay

HUSTED

657

ROCKVILLE RD

0.8

Ogden Creek

HUSTED LNDG. RD

0.6

Back

Creek

3.7

3.2

Creek

Abbots

N

20

Back Creek, Cedar Creek, and Nantuxent Creek

INTRODUCTION: These three Cumberland County estuaries are lumped together because they all feed into a little bulge in Delaware Bay called Nantuxent Cove. With a favorable tide, a fairly energetic paddler can combine a pair of these into a single, nice trip.

Section 1. Back Creek. Husted Landing to mouth					
Gradient	Difficulty	Distance	Time	Scenery	Map
0	A	5.0	2.0	Good	20

TRIP DESCRIPTION: The distinguishing characteristic of Back Creek is its width, which is proportional to a stream that is four or five times as long. The surrounding marsh is also wide, so that at high tide your view extends for four or five miles. The marsh is mostly undisturbed, but the distant skyline is a mix of trees and farms — a civilized but graceful view. You can double or quadruple the length of your itinerary if you add side trips up the creek's several winding tributaries. But remember that such excursions inevitably involve paddling against the tide, so allow extra time.

The put-in is a private landing, so you can expect a launching fee. This landing sits only a few inches above sea level. So if there are strong winds from the south, and the tide is out when you launch, be cautious about where you park, or when you return (as has the tide), you may find that you can paddle right up to your car. When you reach the mouth, you will find nothing but water and marsh. So paddle east a mile and a half to the little resort community at Bay Point where hopefully you can find a take-out (with permission) on private property.

HAZARDS: None

WATER CONDITIONS: This is all tidal and always deep enough.

GAUGE: None

Section 2. Cedar Creek. Cedarville (Rte. 553) to mouth					
Gradient	Difficulty	Distance	Time	Scenery	Map
0	A	6.0	2.0	Fair to Good	20

TRIP DESCRIPTION: At high tide, the put-in is at the outlet from Cedar Lake. You can park at the little park across the street. If the tide is out, this upper reach may be too mucky, so retreat downstream a half mile to the steel bridge between Rte. 610 and Mulford Avenue.

You can have a pleasant outing on Cedar Creek, but you can do better on many other more attractive nearby waterways. The creek side of Cedarville is ugly. Moving downstream gets you into a mix of marsh and abutting high and dry ground that is occupied by farms. Where the creek hits the high ground, unfortunately, the banks are shored up by ugly piles of rubble for erosion control. With a high tide, you can bypass a lot of this by starting your cruise on more scenic Bowers Creek at Bowers Creek Road. Below the confluence with Bowers Creek, the path

Oranoaken Creek
Dividing Creek

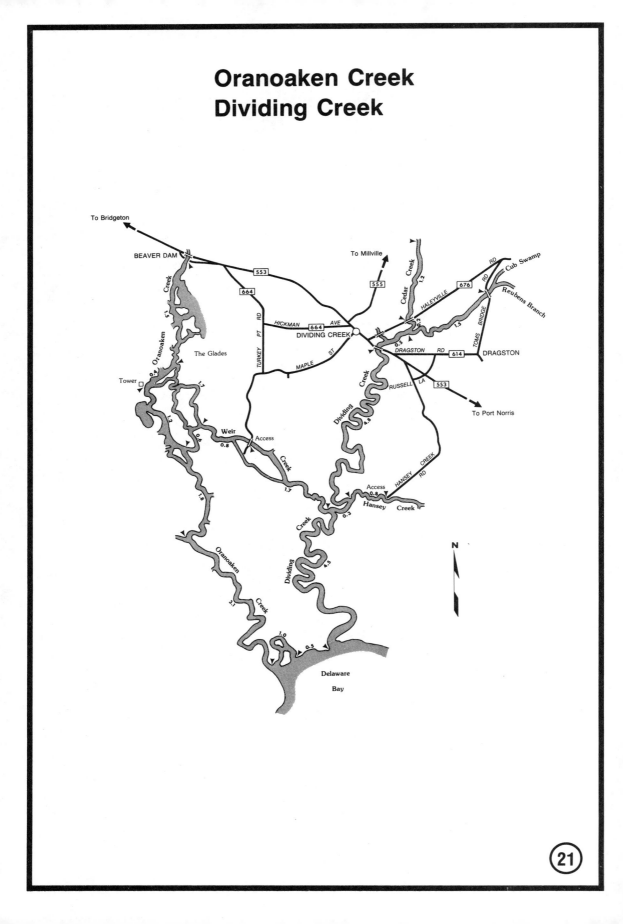

winds entirely through marsh until the resort community at the mouth. Take out there where you can on private property (ask permission).

HAZARDS: None

WATER CONDITIONS: This route is all tidal and always runnable, except for maybe the first quarter mile, which is more mud than water at low tide.

GAUGE: None

Section 3. Nantuxent Creek. Newport (Rte. 629) to mouth					
Gradient	Difficulty	Distance	Time	Scenery	Map
0	A	7.1	2.5	Good to Poor	20

TRIP DESCRIPTION: This section starts off with a lake-like expanse of about a mile and a half that is just inches deep at low tide. There is a shallow channel though, marked by sticks. Happy navigating. The route passes mostly through a natural setting of marsh and cedar-covered hummocks. In contrast, the last mile is an ugly sprawl of docks and second homes. There is no public access here, but you should be able to arrange an exit on somebody's waterfront. You can also push on east down the bay to Gandy Beach, another mile and a quarter, where a public road hits the shoreline. Or you can go two and a half miles down the bay to Dyers Creek, where a gut connects Dyers Creek with Dyers Creek Road.

HAZARDS: None

WATER CONDITIONS: This is tidal and always passable, though it gets pretty marginal at low tide on the uppermost mile.

GAUGE: None

Oranoaken Creek and Dividing Creek

INTRODUCTION: Oranoaken and Dividing creeks are two almost entirely tidal tributaries to Delaware Bay. They start about 10 miles southeast of Millville. They are described here together because, for the energetic, they combine well into a common trip.

There are few marshy places in the state where a canoeist can so get away from it all. If you stand on the banks of these creeks and look in any direction other than towards the village of Fortesque, there is nothing to spoil the view. You gaze upon just miles and miles of marsh and maybe a distant skyline of forest. You have arrived in New Jersey's "big sky country."

Section 1. Oranoaken Creek. Rte. 553 to mouth					
Gradient	Difficulty	Distance	Time	Scenery	Map
0	A	9.0	4.5	Very Good	21

TRIP DESCRIPTION: Put in off Old Beaverdam Road, just downstream of Rte. 553. If you start at low tide, look forward to mud paddling through tediously shallow water for at least the first quarter mile. You then enter a vast network of ponds, crooked channels, and marsh called The Glades. While nice enough from the canoe, you can really appreciate this area from a wooden observation tower on the west bank about a mile and a half into the trip. Take heart in that much of the beautiful view that you enjoy from this tower is protected, thanks to the efforts of the Natural Lands Trust. And in the distance, to the south, much of those wetlands are within a public fish and wildlife area. Except at the beginning, this trip is all out in the marsh. Most of the cover here is short spartina grass so, at least at high tide, your view is expansive. There is nothing resembling a tree nearby, and a few fishing shacks are the only interruptions to this pleasant monotony.

If you make it to the observation tower, you are doing well. For the numerous channels and bays make wrong turns an easy fate. Generally speaking, the channels are obvious because they are deep, while most ponds are shallow. But your best insurance for staying in control of your itinerary is to bring along good maps. First choice would be the Cedarville, Fortesque, and Port Norris 7½-minute USGS quadrangle sheets. Second and cheaper choice would be Sheets 57 and 60 of New Jersey Department of Transportation's General Highway Map series.

As on many Delaware Bay tributaries, there is no access at the mouth. So some of your possibilities are as follows: You can double back up Oranoaken to Rte. 553. You can paddle a half mile down the bay and ascend Dividing Creek to Hansey Creek Road or even up to the town of Dividing Creek. On a calm day you could follow the bay shore westward, around Egg Island Point, to finish at Raybins Beach or Fortesque. You can also form circuit trips by connecting Dividing Creek to Oranoaken Creek by way of Weir Creek. Or you can connect Fortesque with Oranoaken by way of Fortesque and Lone Tree creeks. As you can see, the opportunities for getting tired and lost are endless.

HAZARDS: Wind, tide, and disorientation can combine to a disastrous conclusion. If you are a novice at tidal paddling, plan a conservative itinerary, watch the weather, and allow lots of time for error.

WATER CONDITIONS: Oranoaken Creek is always passable, even at low tide. Tidal currents here seem relatively mild, compared to streams farther up the bay.

GAUGE: None

	Section 2. Dividing Creek. Toms Bridge Road to mouth				
Gradient	Difficulty	Distance	Time	Scenery	Map
0	A	11.6	5.5	Very Good	21

TRIP DESCRIPTION: The headwaters of Dividing Creek are perhaps the most interesting. The surrounding marsh here is narrow and contrasts boldly with the piney and holly-filled woods that bracket it. Also this is freshwater marsh with cattails, bulrush, and other noticeably different plant life. The Toms Bridge Road put-in is not quite the head of navigation. So a short paddle up to the head of Dividing Creek and even up its forks, Reubens Branch and Cub Swamp, is recommended. And if you like this section, you can also ascend a mile of the tributary Cedar Creek, which offers more of the same undisturbed scenery. In fact, you could spend your whole day just poking around upstream of Rte. 553.

Once the creek bends south from Rte. 553, it enters seemingly endless marsh. There are no structures along the creek, though some minor earthmoving activity has disrupted about two miles of the right bank above Weir Creek. The lower creek is a good place for watching birds and, in mild weather, an even better place for watching the incredible swarms of fiddler crabs that scurry up the banks as you approach. If you have phobias about creepy, crawly critters, you will suffer nightmares the night after a trip through these marshes.

Like Oranoaken Creek, Dividing Creek has no roads at or near its mouth. But unlike Oranoaken, it has good intermediate points of access, via Hansey Creek Road on Hansey Creek or via Maple Street on Weir Creek. So you can enjoy lower Dividing Creek without paddling a marathon.

HAZARDS: There are none, unless it is windy.

WATER CONDITIONS: Dividing Creek is tidal, so it is always passable.

GAUGE: None

Maurice River and Its Terrible Tributaries

INTRODUCTION: The Maurice River is the longest and largest tributary to Delaware Bay, not counting the Delaware River, of course. It starts just east of Glassboro and finishes, like most other bay feeders, near nowhere. The name Maurice, incidentally, is pronounced "Morris." The nontidal upper Maurice is a pleasant and frequently traveled canoe route while the tidal lower river is only lightly used by paddle craft. Together, they offer about 38 miles of paddling. Additionally, the Maurice has five marginally canoeable tributaries. Most of these are also beautiful routes, but their potential is locked up behind a barely penetrable cellulose curtain. Nevertheless, they too are described below, for the "enjoyment" of the occasional masochistically inclined explorer or in hopes that some day some paddling Paul Bunyans will make it their lifetime project to clear a path through these jungles.

Section 1. Maurice River. Rte. 690 to Union Lake Dam					
Gradient	Difficulty	Distance	Time	Scenery	Map
4	A to 1	13.7	5.0	Good	22

TRIP DESCRIPTION: The Maurice is born at the confluence of Still Run and Scotland Run, beneath the waters of Willow Grove Lake. So the put-in is at the foot of the spillway of that lake, near its southeastern corner. Best parking, however, is near its southwestern corner, so you may want to first launch into the lake and then make the short carry across Rte. 690 at the spillway. Watch out for fast traffic on this road.

This is an always pleasant, often beautiful run. Most of the route above Union Lake is set back in a deep hardwood swamp, with only occasional contact with high ground. The stretch from Rte. 552 to the lake is particularly pretty, being lined by thick, green stands of cedar and pine, which contrast strikingly with the marshes along the riverside. The lake offers a lightly developed left shore and an undisturbed, relatively high, wooded right shore. Most of the streamside from Almond Road (Rte. 540) to the lake and the right shore of the lake is public land. This setting should not be construed, however, as wilderness. A few power line and road crossings, short stretches of houses visible below Garden Road and Almond Road, and a few torn-up patches of high ground

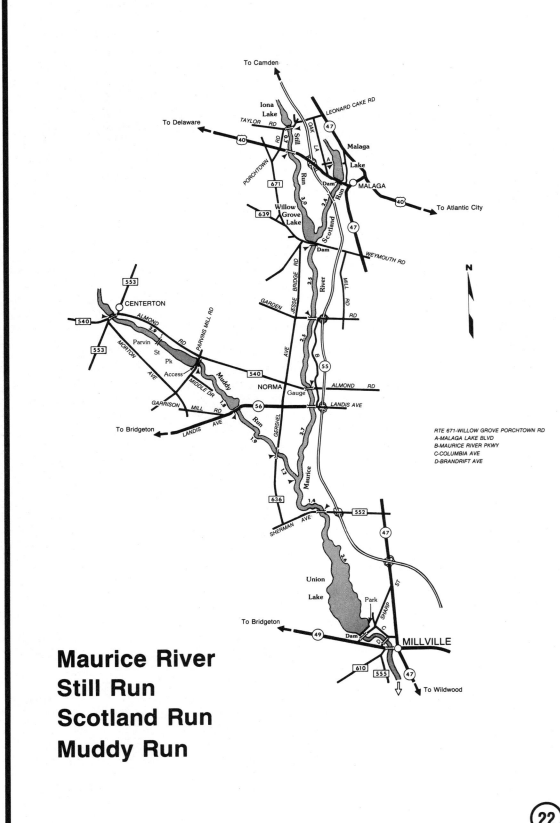

Maurice River
Still Run
Scotland Run
Muddy Run

To Camden

Iona
Lake

To Delaware

LEONARD CAKE RD

47

TAYLOR RD

Malaga
Lake

40

Still Run

OAK LA

PORCHTOWN

671

Willow
Grove
Lake

639

MALAGA

3.0

Dam

2.4

A

Scotland Run

47

Dam

WEYMOUTH RD

40

To Atlantic City

N

553

CENTERTON

540

ALMOND RD

2.9

553

Parvin
St
Pk

MORTON AVE

PARVINS MILL RD

2.5

JESSE BRIDGE RD

River

GARDEN RD

MILL RD

Access

MIDDLE DR

Muddy

540

GERSHEL

GARRISON MILL RD

1.6

56

NORMA

Gauge

ALMOND RD

B

55

LANDIS AVE

To Bridgeton

LANDIS AVE

Run

1.9

3.7

RTE 671-WILLOW GROVE PORCHTOWN RD
A-MALAGA LAKE BLVD
B-MAURICE RIVER PKWY
C-COLUMBIA AVE
D-BRANDRIFT AVE

1.2

636

Maurice

1.4

552

SHERMAN AVE

47

3.6

Union
Lake

Park

SHARP ST

To Bridgeton

49

Dam

C

D

MILLVILLE

610

555

47

To Wildwood

22

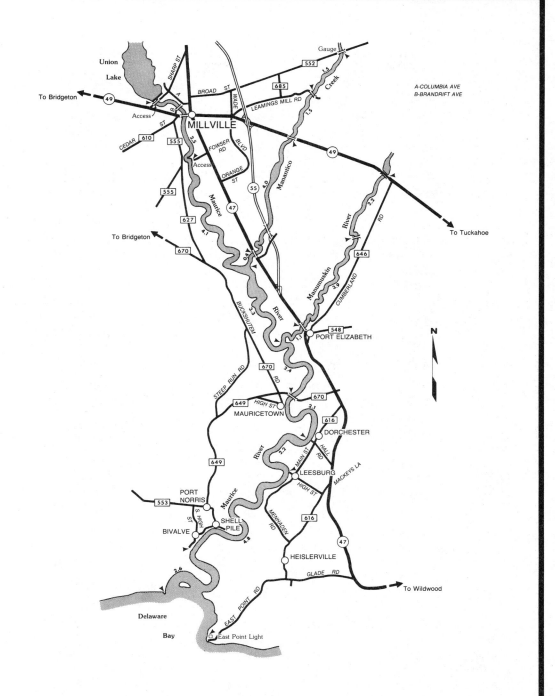

Union Lake

To Bridgeton

MILLVILLE

Gauge

A-COLUMBIA AVE
B-BRANDRIFT AVE

To Tuckahoe

Manantico Creek

Manumuskin River

To Bridgeton

PORT ELIZABETH

MAURICETOWN

DORCHESTER

LEESBURG

PORT NORRIS

SHELL PILE

BIVALVE

HEISLERVILLE

To Wildwood

Delaware Bay

East Point Light

N

Maurice River
Manantico Creek
Manumuskin River

23

interrupt the serenity. But this section's only serious fault is that it is difficult to escape the road noise from nearby and parallel Rte. 55. While this freeway gives the paddlers of the Maurice one of the fastest shuttles per river mile in New Jersey, its noise certainly contradicts the seeming remoteness of the setting that one's eyes witness.

Navigating the Maurice is easy. Though it is a small and twisting route whose natural fate would be to be fairly choked with deadfalls, some of the most energetic of sawyers have blazed a sumptuous path through all obstacles. As would be expected, this is mostly a smoothwater run, though there is actually a sporting series of riffles and very fast current below Sherman Avenue (Rte. 552). There is a sharp, two-foot gauging station weir beneath the downstream edge of the Almond Road bridge. You can clunk over the middle at moderate levels, though it may be rough on your boat.

Union Lake entails about two and a half miles of flatwater paddling, usually with the winds at your back. The take-out is at the recreation area near its southeast corner, just off of Sharp Street in Millville. If for some reason you desire to carry the dam and continue onto the tidal section below, the spillway is on the right, as is the only portage.

The author has had the interesting experience of traversing Union Lake when it was drawn down several feet. At such times, about half of the lake bottom is exposed as a surrealistic mudscape peppered by the macabre forms of ancient, black tree stumps. You can pick you way through this maze via an incredibly serpentine but subtle channel with swift current and even riffles. There is also an old earthen dam exposed with a steep and rocky chute on the right (Class 1 but watch out for chunks of sheet piling in your path). Odds are slim that you will ever confront this condition.

HAZARDS: The weir beneath Almond Road is runnable, but also easily portaged on the right. If the water is high, strainers are potentially dangerous. If the water is really up, there may be difficulty passing underneath Almond Road.

WATER CONDITIONS: Other than during a drought or deep winter freeze, this stream is always runnable.

GAUGE: There is a USGS gauge near Norma on the right and upstream end of Almond Road bridge (call Philadelphia or inspect on site). Flows rarely dip below 2.4 feet (late summer), and high flows seldom exceed 3.2 feet.

Section 2. Maurice River. Millville (Sharp Street) to mouth					
Gradient	Difficulty	Distance	Time	Scenery	Map
0	A	24.0	9.5	Poor to Good	23

TRIP DESCRIPTION: The tidal Maurice is not a prime canoeing destination. It lacks the isolation that so many other bay estuaries possess. Points of public access are few. And being relatively large seems to aggravate the effects of unfavorable winds or tides. Nevertheless, some paddlers do enjoy this river, especially when they concentrate on its nicer reaches.

You can put in at a public dock at Sharp Street or from public parks below Brandrift Avenue and below Main Street. Or better yet, since the passage through Millville offers mainly an ugly view of factories, trailer parks, and bulkheads, start at the public ramp by the municipal sewage treatment plant at the end of Fowser Road. This puts you right into some attractive swampy surroundings that quickly change to marsh. The high ground that lies beyond is wooded, but often built upon. The marshy band soon grows to about a mile wide. Scattered houses are almost always in view, but the landscape is hardly crowded. Just past the midway point is Mauricetown with a small but pretty riverside face. The Rte. 670 bridge there offers easy access, particularly at its east end.

On the lower half of the tidal Maurice, you are always within sight of some waterside villages — Mauricetown, Dorchester, Leesburg, Shellpile, or Bivalve. The last two are particularly interesting. As their names hint, these are seafood harvesting ports for clams and oysters. Strung out along over a mile of the right bank are a line of docks, packing houses, and specialized shellfish dredging boats. Pleasure boats are few. This is a real working port, though it has known better times before MSX killed off so much of the oyster population.

With permission, you can get out at the lower end of Bivalve along High Street. This is the last place to exit. The mouth at Elder Point is over two and a half miles farther, a roadless area where there are many miles of empty coast to the west and a sparsely developed shore to the east. The next point of access is at the pretty, old lighthouse at East Point, about a mile and a half to the southeast across the open waters of Maurice Cove.

HAZARDS: Watch out for motorboats.

WATER CONDITIONS: Being deep, commercially navigable waters, this section is always runnable by your dinky canoe.

GAUGE: None

Section 3. Still Run. Porchtown (Rte. 613) to Rte. 690					
Gradient	Difficulty	Distance	Time	Scenery	Map
4	A	3.7	3.5	Very Good	22

TRIP DESCRIPTION: The start is at the spillway from Iona Lake. This is but a tiny passage that nature never designed for easy canoe navigation. So countless deadfalls and repeated corridors of crowding or overhanging vegetation conspire to slow any paddler to a crawl. Though there has been some effort to saw through the mess, it is generally rough going until Willow Grove Lake.

But this is a beautiful passage. Except for some houses near U.S. Rte. 40, Still Run hides back in a wild and scenic swamp. It is especially nice as it works its way into Willow Grove Lake, where rich, green stands of pine and cedar rise behind the shrubbery of the swamp. Even the lake is undeveloped until its lower end. You can conclude this run at the lower right corner of the lake or portage the spillway, which is at the left corner of the lake, and continue on down the Maurice.

HAZARDS: The water is seldom high and hence powerful enough to make all the strainers a hazard to life. But keep in mind that fighting through such tangles can take its toll in scratches, cuts, poison ivy, poked eyes, and frayed nerves, not to mention twisted ankles and broken bones sustained when slipping off of logs during liftovers.

WATER CONDITIONS: This tiny trail is usually passable in all but the driest months of summer or early fall.

GAUGE: There are none on this stream, so use the USGS gauge on the Maurice at Almond Road (call Philadelphia or inspect on site). A level of 2.6 feet is just fine, zero is unknown.

Section 4. Scotland Run. Malaga (U.S. Rte. 40) to Rte. 690					
Gradient	Difficulty	Distance	Time	Scenery	Map
4	A	1.8	1.0	Good	22

TRIP DESCRIPTION: Scotland Run is a traditional approach to running the upper Maurice River. So it has been mostly sawed out. With its tannin-stained water speeding down a narrow channel over a sand and gravel bottom, it quickly delivers you into the cedar-lined head of Willow Grove Lake. The setting is pretty, though for awhile the noise from N.J. Rte. 55 is distracting.

There is no parking allowed along Rte. 40. So the best idea is to put in on Malaga Lake about a half mile upstream, and portage at the spillway. There is good access on the west shore at the end of Malaga Lake Boulevard and on the east shore from a township park along Rte. 615.

HAZARDS: Possible strainers

WATER CONDITIONS: Same as for Still Run

GAUGE: Same as for Still Run

Section 5. Muddy Run. Centerton (Rte. 553) to mouth					
Gradient	Difficulty	Distance	Time	Scenery	Map
5	A	7.8	6.0	Good	22

TRIP DESCRIPTION: Muddy Run is a generally pretty route, but if you try to follow it all the way to the Maurice, you will think you have detoured to Hell after the Devil had developed a green thumb. The suggested put-in is at Rte. 553, on the right, just below the spillway from Centerton Pond. Most of the following three miles to Parvins Mill Road (Rte. 645) is within Parvin State Park. To the head of Parvin Lake, the tiny stream maintains a single channel in a seemingly remote, woodsy setting. Fallen trees are an annoyance, though many have been sawed out. The water is hazy brown, which relative to most South Jersey streams, makes it seem muddy and worthy of its name. Parvin Lake, of course, offers some easy and unobstructed paddling. It is an attractive pool with cedar-lined shores. There is an easy take-out at Parvins Mill Road, above the dam, on the right. You would be wise to use it.

Below Parvin, the channel begins to braid, and the path is often choked with deadfalls and live brush. Relief comes in about a half mile as the stream slips into the head of Rainbow Lake. While easy to paddle, this lake displays bland, mostly developed shores — hardly one's image of what a Rainbow Lake should look like. You will have to get out to portage the dam at Landis Avenue, so you will have another chance to quit while you are ahead. Below here the channel really gets into serious braiding, especially below Gershel Avenue. It is all swampy and the challenges of dealing with repeated blockages will qualify you for a Ph.D. in creative canoe lifting by the end of your ordeal. On the bright side, the surrounding swamp is certainly pretty and seemingly undisturbed. When you finally reach the mouth, the Maurice will really seem like a river.

HAZARDS: There are two dams to portage. As for strainers, heed the same admonition as given for Still Run.

WATER CONDITIONS: The lake portions are always passable except when frozen. The stream segments are most often passable from late fall to early summer.

GAUGE: None on this stream, but the USGS gauge on the Maurice at Almond Road (call Philadelphia or inspect on site) should be around 2.8 or 2.9 feet for a good level. It can be done lower (zero unknown), but having marginal water levels on such swamp runs usually means fewer bypass options around strainers and many more snags.

Section 6. Manantico Creek. Rte. 552 to N.J. Rte. 47					
Gradient	Difficulty	Distance	Time	Scenery	Map
6	A to 1—	7.0	5.0	Fair to Good	23

TRIP DESCRIPTION: Manantico Creek flows down the eastern side of Vineland to join the tidal Maurice a few miles downstream of Millville. Most of the run on Manantico is nontidal. The clear, tannin-stained brook at the Rte. 552 put-in is certainly large enough to float a canoe. But much of the path is jammed with deadfalls, brush, overhanging branches, vines, thorns, and anything else that can grow out and get you. The current is usually swift, and there are even riffles over the sand and gravel bottom and at the remains of the dam at Leamings Mill. There are also two, long, pond-like stretches below N.J. Rte. 49 (keep right in the first pond to stay with stream). And finally, somewhere around N.J. Rte. 55, tidewater begins.

The settling is basically attractive, being way back in the wild woods and swamp. A few houses only encroach around Rte. 49 and Rte. 47. But the locals know enough points of access to the creek via sand roads and trails, unfortunately, to have left a horrifying amount of dumped trash and scattered litter along this creek's banks. This significantly lowers this stream's aesthetic rating.

The mouth of the Manantico is about a half mile below Rte. 47, down a marshy corridor. There is no access to that point, so you must either double back to the highway or continue down the Maurice to Mauricetown, the latter option adding almost six more miles.

HAZARDS: Follow the same admonition as given for Still Run.

WATER CONDITIONS: Except after a long dry spell, this is usually high enough in late fall, winter, and spring.

GAUGE: There is an abandoned USGS gauging station on the upstream right at Rte. 552. You want at least 1.0 feet to avoid scraping in some of the riffles.

Section 7. Manumuskin River. N.J. Rte. 49 to Port Elizabeth (N.J. Rte. 47)					
Gradient	Difficulty	Distance	Time	Scenery	Map
10	A	6.1	4.0	Fair to Very Good	23

TRIP DESCRIPTION: About the first half of this run is nontidal, wild, and unspoiled. The aesthetics seem assured as The Nature Conservancy has purchased over 2,000 acres in this watershed. Too bad it is so difficult to appreciate. The dark but clear water speeds over a sand and gravel bed through an almost continuous strainer of overhanging and often interlocking branches. Only Houdini could enjoy wriggling through this mess.

Relief comes only at the start of tidewater, so most people would probably choose to explore this creek by starting at Rte. 47, paddling up and back. The head of tidewater is beautiful; it is still a wild swamp. Farther down, marshes develop, but the high ground beyond is often occupied by houses. A mile of marsh-bound creek continues below Rte. 47. If you choose to cover that stretch, the next take-out downstream is at the bridge over the Maurice above Mauricetown.

HAZARDS: They are the same as on the other tangled tributaries.

WATER CONDITIONS: Except after long dry spell, the nontidal section is usually high enough from late fall through mid-spring.

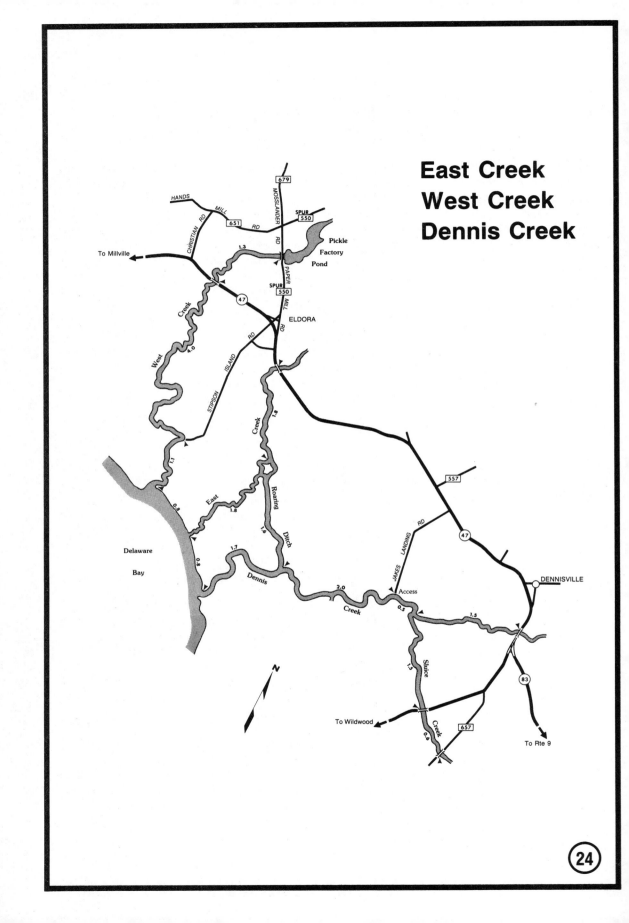

East Creek
West Creek
Dennis Creek

24

GAUGE: There are none on this creek. Use the USGS gauge on Manantico Creek at Rte. 552. Zero is unknown, but anything over 1.0 feet should be adequate.

West Creek, East Creek, and Dennis Creek

INTRODUCTION: These three little Cape May County tidal streams feed into Delaware Bay at its distinctive northeast corner, the point where the Cape May Peninsula juts out like New Jersey's tail. They are lumped together here because their mouths are all within a mile of each other, so a trip down one creek easily combines with a trip up another. Offering short runs within an almost unspoiled setting, these are some of the most appealing canoe trails on the bay.

Section 1. West Creek. Paper Mill Road to mouth					
Gradient	Difficulty	Distance	Time	Scenery	Map
0	A	6.4	2.5	Very Good	24

TRIP DESCRIPTION: West Creek forms part of the boundary between Cape May and Cumberland counties. If the tide is on the high side, you can start your trip at Paper Mill Road, just below beautiful Pickle Factory Pond. This point is the head of tidewater. The swampy woods that frame the channel at the put-in quickly recede, and from here on this is a marsh tour. West Creek is always narrow, and its marsh is always wide. With high tide, views out across the spartina meadows are pretty and uncluttered. With low tide, you may see only a corridor of grass and pungent mud. This may sound monotonous, but surprised waterfowl, swarms of scurrying fiddler crabs, diving muskrats, and maybe even a curious otter should keep you occupied.

The last chance to take out on West Creek is at the landing at the end of Stipson Island Road. If you continue the last mile to the bay, well worthwhile if only for the stunning contrast of emerging from this narrow channel to completely open water, you have two options. If you want a short trip, you can double back to Stipson Island Road. If tacking on several more miles of paddling is acceptable and if the bay is calm enough, the wind is slight, and the tide is with you, then you can continue over to and up either East Creek or Dennis Creek.

HAZARDS: None

WATER CONDITIONS: At low tide, the upper half to quarter mile may be impassably shallow.

GAUGE: None

Section 2. East Creek. N.J. Rte. 47 to mouth					
Gradient	Difficulty	Distance	Time	Scenery	Map
0	A	3.6	1.5	Very Good	24

TRIP DESCRIPTION: The uppermost point of access is Rte. 47. But with a high tide, you can ascend another three quarters of a mile, and it is worthwhile. The open marsh narrows, spartina yields to freshwater reeds and other odd plants, and by the finish, the path winds through the charred remains of a cedar swamp. Surprisingly, the fire damage adds a stark beauty to this final reach.

The trip from the highway to the bay is through a vast marsh. When you turn your back to the few buildings at Rte. 47, the view across the marsh is unspoiled, with a mixed forest of pine and hardwood trees forming the distant skyline. Much of what you behold is public land, a state fish and wildlife management area.

Another pleasant aspect of East Creek is that you can make somewhat of a circuit tour out of it. If you look at the map, you will see that about halfway down from Rte. 47, East Creek splits. One channel, which is lower East Creek, heads directly to the bay. The other channel, called Roaring Ditch, heads to Dennis Creek. So you can follow East Creek to its mouth, head down the bay to Dennis Creek, go up Dennis Creek to Roaring Ditch, and then ascend Roaring Ditch back to the forks (or do this in the clockwise direction). Navigators, take note that most of East Creek flows into Roaring Ditch. So lower East Creek is initially just a narrow outlet, an almost negligible channel at low tide and easy to miss. Other options, needing a shuttle of course, are to tie an East Creek trip with West Creek or Dennis Creek.

HAZARDS: None

WATER CONDITIONS: All of this is tidal. But at low tide, the first few hundred yards of lower East Creek, where it splits from Roaring Ditch, can be shallow, as can be the farthest upper reaches above Rte. 47.

GAUGE: None

Section 3. Dennis Creek. Rte. 47 to mouth					
Gradient	Difficulty	Distance	Time	Scenery	Map
0	A	5.7	2.0	Very Good	24

TRIP DESCRIPTION: Dennis Creek is almost the same as East Creek. In fact, for much of the way, you are just viewing the same good scenery from a different angle. Like East Creek, much of the surrounding land is preserved within the fish and wildlife management area. Also, you could easily incorporate the lower East Creek-Roaring Ditch circuit into this tour. One other nice variation would be to start the trip on Sluice Creek. With a high tide, you can start on this branch at Rte. 657.

HAZARDS: None

WATER CONDITIONS: This is tidal and always passable. But if you try Sluice Creek, it is too shallow at low tide above Rte. 47.

GAUGE: None

It Ain't Easy Writing A Guidebook or
Shuttles, You Can't Live with 'em, You Can't Live Without 'em

I do a lot of my paddling alone, and enjoy it that way. It is not that I dislike company. It is just that when I go alone, I can cover more territory, spend more time, go where I please, pay more attention to my surroundings, and meet more of the locals. And those are the things that make canoeing fun for me.

Lone paddling has its price though. I sacrifice some of my safety margin by having nobody there to help me, if trouble comes. But trouble on a carefully run trip is rare. What is not rare is the need to shuttle. When I paddle alone, getting back to my car after a trip can be a challenge. My success at dealing with this challenge can make or break my day.

Sometimes I think I would sell my soul for a ride. I do what the situation calls for. I have chartered airplanes; ridden trains, buses, and taxis; bicycled, walked, and run; and most important of all, hitchhiked. When these methods work, they are wonderful. When they do not, I suffer.

When I hitchhike, I wear my life jacket, display my paddle, wave my thumb, and look pathetic. You have probably seen me standing by the roadside. Why didn't you stop?

On some days, fortune smiles, and someone stops within minutes. On bad days, I stand there for hours. Bad days usually coincide with cold, wind, rain, snow, plagues of frogs and locusts, or all of these. Perhaps the icicles hanging from my beard turns those potential chauffeurs off.

Things can be bad even when you get rides. One slow day in South Jersey, I was checked out by police twice. I must add, however, they were also kind enough to give me a lift, after some hesitation. You see, one officer told me that he thought my paddle was a weapon. Considering how poorly I paddle, I have also thought that myself at times.

Then there was the time in Connecticut where part way to our destination the driver stopped the car, pulled out a gun, and left me with his car and keys while he went into a store intending to shoot his partner, who he was convinced had embezzled $17,000 (1972 dollars) from their business. Fortunately, his partner was not there. And then there was the driver in Montana who, upon seeing me by the roadside, stopped, staggered out of the car, asked me if I had a valid driver's license, tossed me the keys, and told me to drive because he was too drunk. And then there were all the drivers who did not give me the keys, though they also were too drunk to drive.

So as you can see, even a trooper like myself sometimes longs for a trip that is free of the stresses of hustling a shuttle. However, even a shuttleless outing can be rough. Consider my ill-fated exploration of the Salem River.

When I first studied the map of Salem County, I thought that I had found the ideal trip, in other words, one not needing a shuttle. The Salem River flows within two miles of the Delaware River, and then runs parallel for about 19 miles before joining it. At that first point of proximity, up near Deepwater, a canal links the two rivers. The prospect of a 30-mile circuit paddle with no portages or backtracking and most importantly, no shuttle to hitchhike, just seemed too good to be true. It was.

One frigid, overcast February morning, I launched from a grassy bank by Rte. 540. I was doing a counterclockwise itinerary that took me immediately into the canal. The canal, in turn, led me beneath the busy interchange of the Turnpike, I-295, and U.S. Rte. 40 and then into DuPont's sprawling chemical plant. The plant was a dazzling sight. If ever there was a living monument to the toil of this nation's pipe fitters, this was it. I gazed in awe at this technological masterpiece and sucked up a deep, hearty breath of diesel fumes and essence of organic solvents and knew I had really arrived in New Jersey. I bumped over an oil boom, the bow of my canoe parting the thin rainbow slick trapped behind it, and continued until a strange dam of concrete and steel blocked my path. It was a tide gate. I looked around for the best portage, but a workman called out and told me that he was headed for the control structure right now to open some of the gates.

What timing I thought. Maybe I can shoot the chute.

But then I heard a whistle, and there on the other shore was a security guard who was waving me over. He informed me in no uncertain terms that I was trespassing on DuPont property and that both portaging and shooting the tide gate were out of the question. I also learned that I was not the first visitor to this canal. It seems that a week or two earlier, a flotilla from Greenpeace had invaded by sea, hung disparaging banners, and done who-knows-what other nasty things. So I guess the guard thought I was just another bearded terrorist.

Feeling hurt, my character assassinated, and my plans of circumnavigation dashed, I retreated, debating whether to abort the trip or attempt a three-quarters-of-a-mile-long portage over unfamiliar territory beneath the Delaware Memorial Bridge to the Delaware River. I decided it was not my nature to quit, even when to quit would make good sense. So when I reached the property line, at a little railroad bridge, I landed and prepared to hike. But just then, a slow train rumbled over the bridge. I waved it down and asked the engineer whether I could follow the rail right of way to the river, since a power plant and the resulting potential for more trespass lay in my path. He said that he would be back out shortly and would scout for me. Surprisingly, the train returned in only 10 minutes and he told me to go for it. So I did.

Do you know how long three quarters of a mile is with a heavy canoe on your shoulders? Have your ever seen the soft underbelly of the Delaware Memorial Bridge? Do you know how many dirty, smelly pigeons live under there? I now know the answer to all of these questions. I also know that there is nothing wrong with my heart.

The trip down the Delaware was uneventful. I even had calm weather and a favorable tide. There were no more vindictive security guards. And the air no longer smelled carcinogenic. The trip up the Salem should also have been simple. If only it did not get dark so early in February. I paddled for several miles after dusk, luckily with the assistance of the moon, whose light made the ice that was forming all over my boat sparkle like diamonds. But then the river got so shallow that I ran aground. I thought that maybe I had taken a wrong turn. But search as I might, I could find no channel. I later learned that I had made no navigation error (other than undertake this stupid trip), but that there simply was no channel. It seems that a dike plugs the Salem up where the canal starts. So no water ever flows down the upper Salem, which, as a result, is completely silted in. I had no choice but to retreat a few miles until I found salvation in a isolated public landing.

Climbing out, I slipped on the muddy ramp and dropped my boat. The resonant boom it made as it hit the slimy concrete must have been audible for a mile. It was certainly audible to the couples in the two parked cars at the ramp. They quickly drove off, not even waiting for their windows to defog. It was a cold, lonely night. But the miserable four-mile hike back to my car warmed me up and the circuit was imperfectly completed.

A lot of my plans end up like this. But I do have some great ideas for future trips. Do you want to join me, or should I just plan to go ahead alone?

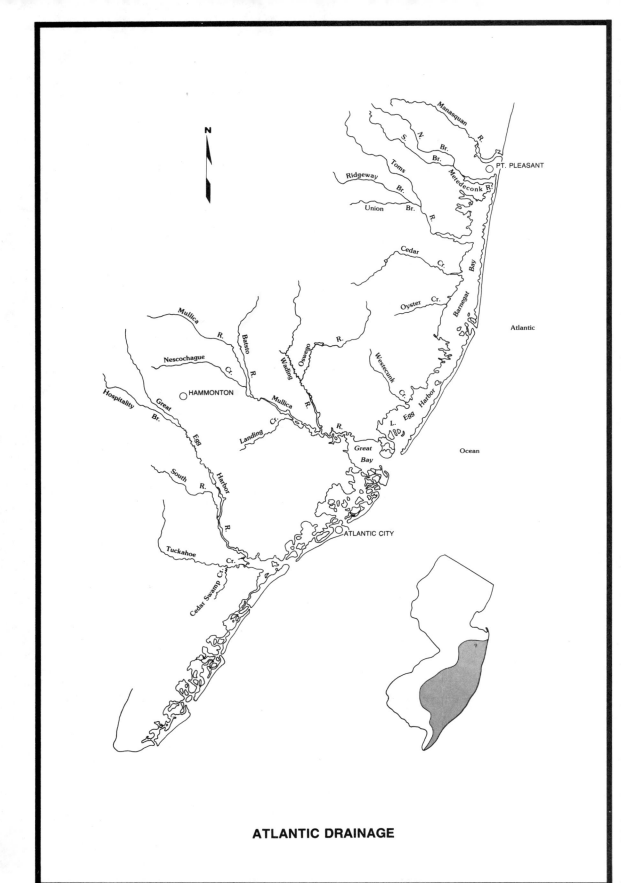

ATLANTIC DRAINAGE

Chapter 3
Atlantic Coast
Drainage

This chapter describes free-flowing streams and tidal waterways that feed directly to the Atlantic Ocean. The waters of this area fit into one of two contrasting categories — diminutive swamp runs and huge marsh-bound tidal estuaries and bays. Both can be exceptional destinations.

Much of the area drained by these streams is part of the famed Pine Barrens. This sandy "wasteland" provides Jersey's most beautiful, most remote, and most unique canoeing. I emphasize the last attribute. Arizona has its Grand Canyon of the Colorado, Idaho its Middle Fork Salmon, West Virginia its Gauley, and New Jersey it Oswego or Mullica or Batsto. I have no hesitation to mention all of these jewels of American rivers in the same breath. While each so different, I would travel thousands of miles to enjoy any of these. Understandably, the Pine Barrens runs are immensely popular, often inundated by a tide of rental canoes and smaller pods of private boaters. If you desire solitude, you will have to resort to creative timing or settle for some of this chapter's alternative routes. Whether you are a veteran whitewater paddler or a timid beginner, you will probably have a delightful time on a trip down one of these rivers.

Much of New Jersey's tideland area is a garish, developed mess. It has been a sad fate for what was once a wonderful world of marsh, woods, and water. Fortunately, some pockets of the real thing remain. So if you have the energy and understanding of how to coexist with the less than idyllic realities of wind, tide, and bugs, you will be treated to some truly great outdoors.

The following waterways are described in this chapter:

Coastal Bays
  Great Egg Harbor River
    Hospitality Branch
    South River
    Tuckahoe River
      Cedar Swamp Creek
    Mullica River
      Nescochague Creek
      Batsto River
      Landing Creek
      Wading River

    Oswego River
  Westecunk Creek
  Oyster Creek
  Cedar Creek
  Toms River
    Ridgeway Branch and Union Branch
  Metedeconk River
    North Branch Metedeconk River
    South Branch Metedeconk River
  Manasquan River

Coastal Bays

To most of us, the Jersey Shore is synonymous with boardwalks, condos, cottages, suntans, and even casinos. And that sums it up pretty well, from Sandy Hook to Cape May — a playground and resort by the sea. Most of this development is perched upon a chain of big sand bars called barrier islands. These islands are thrown up by the stormy seas and are periodically leveled by the same forces. They get the name barrier island because in absorbing the violence of the ocean, they guard the mainland from destruction.

Between the barrier islands and the mainland is a chain of shallow lagoons. They bear names like Barnegat Bay, Little Egg Harbor, Great Bay, and Richardson Sound. Sometimes they are wide open expanses of water, and sometimes they are mazes of serpentine channels between marshy islets. As you might suspect, these might just be canoeable waters.

From the aesthetic standpoint, these waters have seen better days. Once this was a world of lawn-like salt meadows and blue water, fringed by dunes on one side and pine woods on the other. Today, many of those dunes are covered by a string of resort towns. The piney mainland shores are broken by condo clusters, marinas, and Venice-like waterside developments. The Intracoastal Waterway slices down the middle, where swarms of motorboats roar by and fill the air with their acrid fumes.

But some remnants remain to suggest the natural beauty of the past. You cannot completely escape from civilization, but you can experience a pretty good imitation of such. So check out in particular these four areas.

Island Beach State Park

This state park preserves the only significant reach of undeveloped barrier island on Jersey's coast. One can enjoy a scenic journey along its west side on the waters of Barnegat Bay. The bay here ranges from two to nearly four miles wide. The mainland shore is clotted with developments, but they are far enough away to blend in. The view of the barrier island is fairly wild, though you can see several structures, such as the bathhouses for the beach. On the other hand, you also get to see the beautiful Barnegat Lighthouse. For the most part, your view consists of phragmites marsh and vegetated dunes. At the northern end of the park, there is a forest of stunted trees. Further along, only clumps of cedar rise above the bayberry bushes, beach plum, and other hearty dune shrubbery.

Perhaps the most interesting area is the southern end of the island. The island here forms a triangular hook, much of which is an expanse of salt meadows. A particularly pleasant way to enjoy this is via a curving, mile-long channel consisting of a twisting, narrow passage, a lagoon, and another narrow canal. This route is only passable at high tide. The easiest way to find this path is from the south. There is a short line of dunes along the west end of Barnegat Inlet. The first channel west of this dune line is your entrance.

Access to this these waters is limited. No boat launching is allowed in the state park. If you want to start at the north end, the best idea is to launch from South Seaside Park, along the roadside a few blocks north of the park boundary. A little farther north, there is an official public boat launch at 14th Avenue and Bayview in Seaside Park. But during the summertime, you need to first obtain a local permit called a "beach badge." If you want to start from the south, there are public boat launches at 10th Street and Bayview and 25th Street and Bayview in Barnegat Light.

Forsythe National Wildlife Refuge — Barnegat Division

This is a large chunk of soggy real estate on the west side of Barnegat and Manahawkin bays between Barnegat and Manahawkin. The bays here are only about a mile and a half wide. So the string of resorts on Long Beach Island are noticeable. A communications complex at the southern end of the refuge is also difficult to ignore. But if you just look the other way, you can enjoy vast unspoiled vistas of marsh, ponds, creeks, and big sky. Most of this area is characterized by a smooth, green meadow of low spartina grass. Only a few wooded hummocks punctuate the flatness. Farther inland, extensive patches of low shrubbery colonize the marsh. Then over on the west side, high ground supports an unbroken facade of forest.

Creeks, ponds, and little bays make this a ragged coastline. The simplest introduction to this area is to just skirt the coast. But if the tide is on the high side, you can best enjoy the refuge by poking up the various creeks and connecting passages. Perhaps the nicest of these possibilities is to ascend the Gunning River, a passage that takes you up far enough from the bay to get into cattails, cedar, and black swamp water.

The Barnegat Division of the refuge is small enough that getting seriously lost should not be a problem for most people. Still, a good set of maps would give you better control of your fate. The applicable USGS 7½-minute topographic map is the Ship Bottom Sheet. Almost as useful is the New Jersey Department of Transportation General Highway Map No. 47. Even the Department's Ocean County highway map has enough detail to keep a good navigator on course.

The two most convenient points of access are at each end. On the south, in Bayside, put in at the little bridge over Manahawkin Creek on Heron Street. On the north, use the municipal ramp off East Bay Avenue, about a mile and a half east of downtown Barnegat. If crossing open water is not a problem, the public launch sites in Barnegat Light on Long Beach Island, along Bayview at either 10th Street or 25th Street, are just fine. They are advantageous for exploring Clam and High Bar islands, which also are within the refuge.

It is difficult to forget that you are in a national wildlife refuge, as scores of the refuge's obnoxious, white signs litter the scenery. Aesthetics is apparently not a priority in managing a refuge. But these should serve to remind you that the refuge is for the wildlife. While you are entitled to ply these waters, you are not permitted to land anywhere, much less picnic or camp. Also, be prepared to share this area with waterfowl hunters during the late autumn.

Great Bay Fish and Wildlife Management Area

This is a big neck of wetlands that protrudes almost to the Atlantic, between Great Bay and Little Egg Harbor, south of Tuckerton. While wild, it is by no means wilderness. Utility lines span the peninsula, and there are some small marinas out there and a road. Though almost 10 miles away, the glittering skyline of Atlantic City erupts from the southern horizon and makes one wonder whether there really is such a city as Oz. On an island off the west side of the peninsula, a huge, weathered, and crumbling monolith rises improbably above the lonely marsh. It is an old factory that once converted menhaden into fertilizer. No doubt, back then, one could tell direction by his or her nose. At the tip of the peninsula is a Rutgers University marine research station. Formerly a Coast Guard station, this beautiful white frame structure fulfills the sentimental stereotype of what maritime architecture should be. But when you look beyond these distractions, you will still find satisfying doses of elbow room, marsh, sky, and water.

One particularly nice feature of this area is that it is ideally suited for circuit trips. With four major channels cutting through the peninsula, you can choose your distance. You can reach the water where Great Bay Boulevard, the road that bisects the peninsula, crosses these creeks. The best launch site is on the northernmost of these channels, Big Thorofare, where a county park provides ample parking and easy access to the water. If you start here or on Jimmies Creek, you will find that with an ebbing tide, the water flows from Little Egg Harbor to Great Bay. Plan your trip direction accordingly.

Good maps are mostly a convenience, not a necessity, for this area. The proper USGS topographic maps are Tuckerton and Brigantine Inlet 7½-minute sheets. The New Jersey Department of Transportation General Highway Map No. 50 or the Department's Ocean County Map are also adequate.

Forsythe National Wildlife Refuge — Brigantine Unit

This is the biggest expanse of undeveloped wetlands on Jersey's Atlantic coast. Additionally, you have not only the refuge, but also buffer zones to the northwest and south provided by state fish and wildlife management areas. The nearest significant man-made skylines, those of Atlantic City and Brigantine, are far enough from much of the refuge that, on a hazy day, you can feel as if this really might be a wilderness. If wide open waters are your joy, you have Great Bay, Little Bay, Reeds Bay, and, of course, the Atlantic. If you prefer more sheltered waters, a maze of guts and so-called "thorofares" in the north end and east end will give you days of exploration. There are thousands of acres of velvet marsh meadows, green in summer, golden in autumn, and tan in winter. There is forest on the high ground to the west and there are shrub-covered dunes to the east. One interesting but unnatural sight is in Hammock Cove. Its waters are almost entirely dedicated to aquaculture, that is, raising clams. Here one paddles a slalom through a forest of stakes used to anchor and mark nets that cover the bottom and protect the developing clams from predators.

As is the case with most barrier island paddling, the waterways near their backsides are usually shallow. While the Intracoastal Waterway's channel and Great Bay are reliable, most other waterways become impassable or certainly tedious at low tide. Plan and time your itinerary accordingly.

This being a national wildlife refuge, you may only look, not touch. The Refuge prohibits landing anywhere without a special use permit. In particular, stay off of Little Beach Island. It was once a bombing range, and unexploded ordnance still litters the sands. On the bright side, the mile-long expanse of wild beach between Brigantine and Brigantine Inlet is outside of the refuge, so landing should be acceptable.

Public access points are limited. The best situated point is Scotts Landing off Leeds Point Road (Alt. Rte. 561), about two miles east of Smithville. This is within the refuge. A man-made channel and Landing Creek (not the Mullica tributary) will connect you to Great Bay or Hammock Cove. Second best choice is the municipal ramp at 5th Street and Bayshore Avenue in Brigantine. A two to three-mile paddle will get you from here to the heart of the refuge. And finally, a public ramp at the end of Faunce Landing Road in Absecon gets you into Absecon Creek. It is a three-mile paddle from here to the edge of the refuge, but extensive wetlands in a state fish and wildlife management area may be more than enough to satisfy you.

Good maps can keep you from becoming known as the legendary lost canoeist. The USGS's Oceanville, Brigantine Inlet, and New Gretna 7½-minute sheets cover this area. New Jersey Department of Transportation General Highway Maps 51 and 56 or even its Atlantic County highway map are also adequate.

Great Egg Harbor River

INTRODUCTION: Sure, that is a long name for a river. But this is a long river, at least for South Jersey. You can twist down over 30 miles of it before reaching tidewater and the kingdom of the motorboat. This river got its funny name because its first English-speaking visitors were impressed by the abundance of gull eggs on the flats about its mouth. It is difficult to picture such an abundance of gulls back then. What did they eat back before there were sanitary land-fills? That is a good question to ponder as you float for so many hours down these many miles.

Section 1. New Brooklyn (Rte. 536) to Mays Landing					
Gradient	Difficulty	Distance	Time	Scenery	Map
3	A to 1—	31.0	13.0	Excellent to Fair	25

TRIP DESCRIPTION: This is the freshwater, nontidal portion of the Great Egg and, by most people's standards, the best section for canoeing. The head of navigation is New Brooklyn, which is on the Camden-Gloucester county line, about nine miles due east of Glassboro. Except for the first several tangled miles, it is a fine run for the inexperienced.

The first several miles down to Piney Hollow Road take you through an exceptionally beauti-ful, wild setting, most of which is within the confines of a state fish and wildlife management area. Bordering the river is a seemingly impenetrable maple swamp with a few stands of dark green cedar thrown in for variety. The water is clear and tea colored. The only man-made struc-tures that appear are a power line at the start and one road bridge. Even trash is minimal. Only road noise from the nearby Atlantic City Expressway mars the tranquility.

You will probably have this beautiful stretch all to yourself as it is tough traveling through here. Though there has clearly been an aggressive effort to saw out the deadfalls, there are enough fresh ones along with numerous old snags to turn this into a slalom. Particularly troublesome are a few spots with big clumps of fallen trees, which together with their huge root masses, block your way. A short, light boat is an asset here. All in all, this initial section is worth the extra effort for a skilled boater.

Piney Hollow Road marks the beginning of more reasonable travel, though the first several miles still require energetic paddling to get around the obstacles. This reach has all been sawed out, though you should not be surprised to find some fresh deadfalls. Be prepared for an 18-inch weir a few yards above N.J. Rte. 54. If water is high, its backwash could be dangerous.

To Penny Pot, the river proves an attractive passage, winding more through low but solid ground, rather than swamps. Though this river flows through the Pine Barrens, the paddler beholds, mostly, the face of a thick hardwood forest. Little development or trash spoils this reach, but an oppres-sive level of noise from U.S. Rte. 322 and the Expressway destroys any illusion of wilderness.

At Penny Pot, Hospitality Branch swells the flow, and the creek actually feels roomy now. The crooked course, unfortunately, now becomes infested with streamside houses, though it is still not entirely built up. You would miss little to skip this reach and put in at Weymouth. Here a little park preserves the site and ruins of an old iron furnace and paper mill and provides easy access and parking. This is also where you will find the only whitewater (well, riffles) on the Great Egg.

Leaving Weymouth, the river once again becomes a lonely passage. It twists through more Pine Barrens scenery, including high, sandy bluffs, until it comes to rest in Lake Lenape. The head

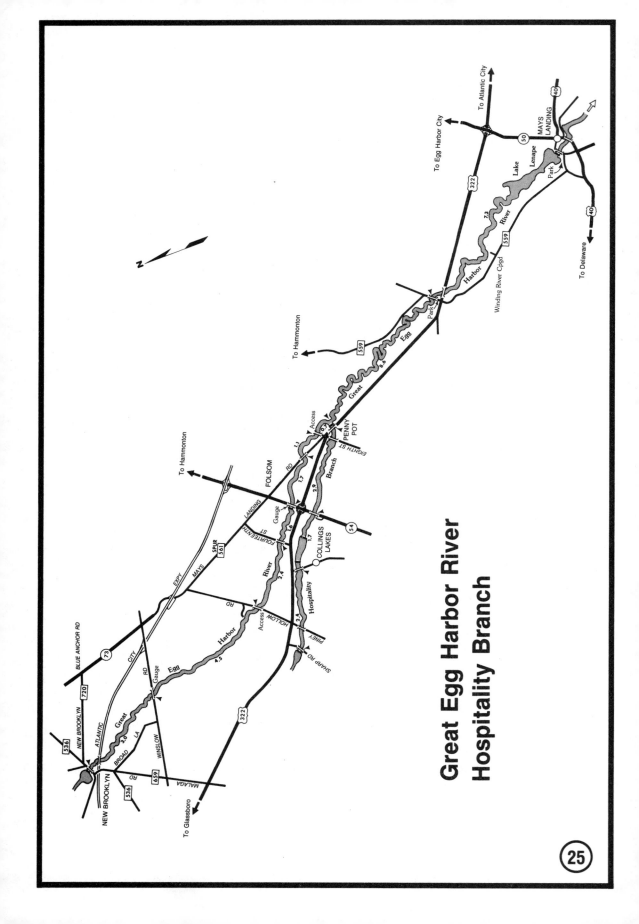

Great Egg Harbor River
Hospitality Branch

25

Great Egg Harbor River
Tuckahoe River
Cedar Swamp Creek

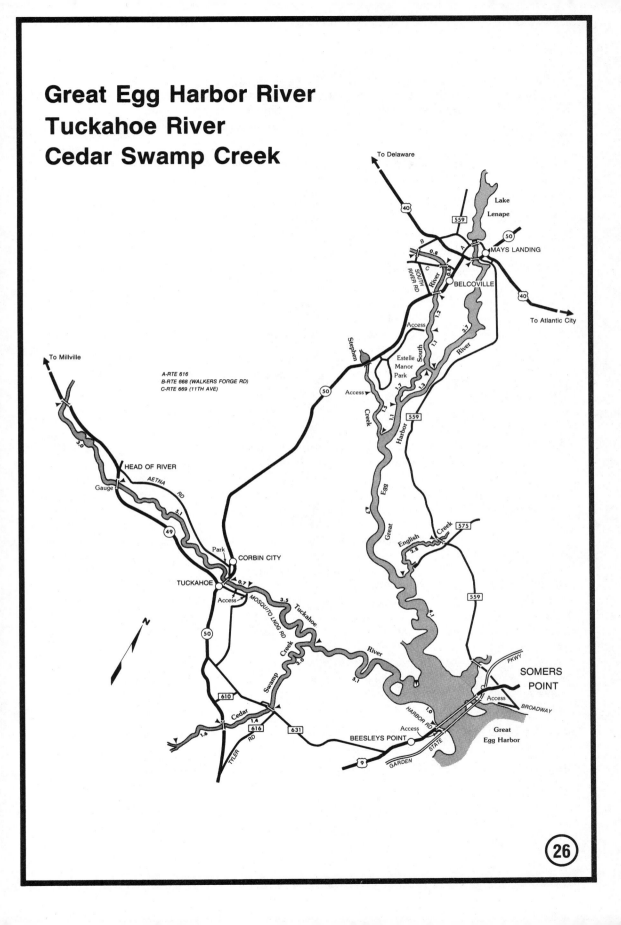

To Delaware

Lake Lenape

40

559

50

MAYS LANDING

B
0.8
A
C
0.4
BELCOVILLE

To Atlantic City

40

SOUTH RIVER RD

South River

1.2

Access

1.1

3.7

River

To Millville

3.0

HEAD OF RIVER

Gauge

AETNA RD

5.1

49

Park

CORBIN CITY

TUCKAHOE

0.7

Access

MOSQUITO LNDG RD

3.5

Tuckahoe

Creek

3.0

Stephen

Access

Creek

1.5

1.1

1.7

1.3

Estelle Manor Park

50

Harbor

559

825

Great

4.7

Egg

English Creek

575

2.8

4.1

River

5.1

Swamp

Creek

50

610

Cedar RD

1.4

616

TYLER RD

631

1.4

9

GARDEN STATE

BEESLEYS POINT

Access

HARBOR RD

1.0

STATE

Access

PKWY

SOMERS POINT

BROADWAY

Great Egg Harbor

A-RTE 616
B-RTE 668 (WALKERS FORGE RD)
C-RTE 669 (11TH AVE)

N

26

of this man-made lake is an unspoiled area of many channels, swamp, and marsh. The lower lake, in contrast, has developed shores, but remains attractive. Finish at the county park on the right. If you would prefer to avoid the lake's still waters, you can get permission to use a private boaters' access at the Winding River Campground (slight charge for use). This gets you out about two and a half miles below Weymouth.

HAZARDS: Treat the weir at Rte. 54 with caution. If you continue on to Section 2, you must portage the dam that forms Lake Lenape, just below the recommended take-out.

WATER CONDITIONS: It takes surprisingly little water to do the Great Egg. Above Piney Hollow Road, the stream is almost always passable from November through June. Except during a drought, the rest of the river is passable throughout the year, with maybe a little scraping in a few riffles.

GAUGE: There is a USGS gauge near Folsom, at N.J. Rte. 54 (upstream left, inspect on site or call Philadelphia). Look for at least 3.8 feet to do the creek above Piney Hollow Road and 3.5 feet for below. There is a staff gauge on the downstream piling of Winslow Road. A level of at least 3.5 feet is desirable for that reach. There is a staff gauge on the downstream left abutment of the Rte. 322 bridge. Probably 1.7 feet is minimal for the shallower spots on that reach.

Section 2. Mays Landing (U.S. Rte. 40) to Beesleys Point					
Gradient	Difficulty	Distance	Time	Scenery	Map
0	A	15.9	6.0	Fair to Good	26

TRIP DESCRIPTION: Tidewater starts at the foot of the Lake Lenape Dam, just above Rte. 559. But there is no good access here. You can launch from a park on the left bank about 200 yards below U.S. Rte. 40/N.J. Rte. 50. Another option is to launch at an abandoned railroad bridge above Rte. 40. The best approach to this spot is from the west via Railroad Avenue (by the fire station). They are poor put-ins, but all the rest of the waterfront around here is private.

The tidal Great Egg Harbor River is disappointing. There is far too much shoreline development and way too much motorboat traffic. The first four miles suffer heaviest from both. Most of the right (west) side of this section, however, is a wild expanse of marsh, largely preserved by a state fish and wildlife management area and a county park. Perhaps the best way to enjoy this part of the river is to probe some of the many winding creeks that penetrate this soggy area. You will get more peace and privacy that way. These little byways are also useful as intermediate points of access. If the tide is in, you can use a few of the tributaries on the east side to connect with Rte. 559. On the west side, the floating dock in Estell Manor Park on Stephen Creek offers access at any tide.

When the river joins the Tuckahoe River, it becomes Great Egg Harbor. If you stay to the right, take out at a public boat ramp along Harbor Road, between U.S. Rte. 9 and the Garden State Parkway. If you follow the left shore, continue a mile past the Parkway's bridge and take out at John F. Kennedy Park (off Broadway, Somers Point).

HAZARDS: Motorboats and wind are persistent annoyances and sometimes hazards. Keeping to the edge helps for both.

WATER CONDITIONS: This section is all tidal and is always passable.

GAUGE: None

Hospitality Branch

INTRODUCTION: Admittedly, one would not expect much of such a dribble. But how could you resist paddling a stream with such a friendly name? Starting several miles east of Glassboro and joining the Great Egg Harbor River at Penny Pot, Hospitality Branch barely manages to stay out of the way of busy U.S. Rte. 322. Something so small should be an unnavigable, strainer-strewn mess. But it is not. Also, something so close to the road should be overdeveloped. But little of it is. And any nice creek in the Pine Barrens should be overrun with other boaters. But you will probably have this stream all to yourself. Now that sure sounds like a hospitable creek to me!

Section 1. Sharp Road to mouth					
Gradient	Difficulty	Distance	Time	Scenery	Map
6	A	7.1	3.0	Fair to Very Good	25

TRIP DESCRIPTION: The easy put-in at Sharp Road is at the base of the spillway of a private lake. From here the tiny creek winds about a mixed cedar and hardwood forest, civilized only by a few houses as it approaches Piney Hollow Road. In spite of its size, there are few obstructions. It is an easy float as the shallow water speeds over a sand and gravel bottom.

From Piney Hollow Road to the head of the first pond, navigation is surprisingly simple for so tiny a stream. The channel seems almost unnatural with its gentle curves and uniform width and bank height. Hemmed in only by a dense and attractive growth of shrubs, there is seldom any blockage here.

The water then opens up into a series of two ponds, each formed by a little dike. Though the shores are developed, the houses are at least well spaced. Carry the first dike on the right, over the emergency spillway. Carry the next on the left.

The lower creek starts unnaturally straight again. Though set in attractive woods, the stream banks are again shrubby. There may be an obstruction or two in here, in addition to a low railroad bridge beneath the high span of N.J. Rte. 54. The channel then returns to a more natural state, with sharp bends and splitting channels. This would normally make for rough going, but some party has sawed out a route. Bring along a saw, too, and keep this path open, for this remaining section is a beauty. The branch winds through a wild cedar swamp, broken by green glades. These are not your usual lawn-like meadows, but rather they are unpaddleable, unwalkable expanses of sedge tussocks. Pine woods stand beyond, so the whole setting is friendly and green, even in mid-winter. This swamp eventually opens into a final pond whose shores seem pristine until you round that final bend and see U.S. Rte. 322.

Rte. 322 is a tenth of a mile above the confluence with the Great Egg Harbor River. Unless you desire to extend the trip onto the Great Egg, take out here. If you go the whole way, you will find that a five-foot wooden weir (about 50 feet below the highway) is why that final pond was there. Carry this on the left.

HAZARDS: There are a few strainers, that low railroad bridge, and the weir below Rte. 322.

WATER CONDITIONS: This usually has enough water anytime from November through mid-May, except during a really dry season.

There are none on this creek. A good rough correlation can be made from the USGS gauge at Rte. 54 (Folsom) on the Great Egg Harbor River. Call Philadelphia or visit. A reading of 3.8 should mean an adequate level.

South River

INTRODUCTION: This South River (there is another that flows to the Raritan) is a small tributary to the Great Egg Harbor River, entering the Great Egg from the west just a few miles downstream of Mays Landing. It offers a small dose of both tidal and nontidal canoeing in the prettiest of settings. One might also be tempted to call this an undisturbed setting. But if you poke about the nearby woods, you will find that it is anything but that, because much of the lower river flows by what was once a major industrial area. Originally there was the glass works that operated from the 1830s through the 1870s, near Stephen Creek and Estellville. It produced window glass. More significantly, there were the loading plants. Built in 1918 to supply munitions for the war in Europe, a complex of plants and access railroads operated by Bethlehem Loading Company sprawled along the South River from Stephen Creek to Belcoville. In fact, Belcoville was constructed specifically to house the thousands of plant employees. The war ended in November 1918, operations ceased in 1919, and as quickly as it was constructed, the plant was dismantled. If you explore the many hiking trails of Atlantic County's Estell Manor Park, you will find old railroad beds, concrete foundations, and bits of steel as evidence of this busy past. You will also marvel at how well the ecosystem has rebounded from this destruction. So be sure not only to paddle the South, but also to wander its banks and visit the fine nature center in the park.

Section 1. Rte. 668, Walkers Forge Road, to N.J. Rte. 50					
Gradient	Difficulty	Distance	Time	Scenery	Map
8	1— to A	1.5	1.5	Very Good	26

TRIP DESCRIPTION: This is the nontidal section of the South. The tiny ribbon of black water burrows into lush, swampy woods. The jungle then yields to the more open swamp of a beaver pond, with its stark skyline of dead, graying trees, as you approach Rte. 669. The twiggy beaver dam is beneath the bridge. Below this bridge, the creek files into a narrow channel confined by two- to four-foot banks. The surrounding woods are mostly high and dry. Some scattered trash, including what appears to be an appliance graveyard (above Rte. 50), and road noise from U.S. Rte. 40 are the only flaws to this section.

While compared to many South Jersey streams, the upper South River is only a moderate challenge to navigation, only swamp enthusiasts should attempt this mile and a half. A short canoe, agility, and lack of claustrophobia are assets. To Rte. 669, the stream is seldom blocked, but it is almost continually confined by an arc of overhanging branches. This tightness is compounded by the frequently splitting channel. You may get away with little carrying, but you will do lots of ducking and squeezing. A swift current pushes you through here, even at low levels, when little gravel riffles appear and further add to the interest. Below Rte. 669, there are plenty of deadfalls, and some liftovers are inevitable. Tidewater starts a few hundred yards above Rte. 50. But if the tide is out, shallow water, current, and snags continue for another few hundred yards past the take-out.

HAZARDS: Strainers

WATER CONDITIONS: Best levels occur from November through early June. Otherwise, if you are willing to put up with some scraping on those riffles, you can get down almost any time.

GAUGE: None

Section 2. N.J. Rte. 50 to mouth.					
Gradient	Difficulty	Distance	Time	Scenery	Map
0	A	4.0	2.0	Very Good	26

TRIP DESCRIPTION: This is an exceptionally beautiful estuary. Most of the right bank is preserved by Estell Manor County Park, while the left bank so far remains undeveloped. A power line crossing is the most significant intrusion on the view. For the first mile, this reach flows between fairly high, wooded banks with only a fringe of marsh. But below there, the high ground abruptly retreats and yields to wide marsh. The marsh is fresh and then brackish, with fairly high reeds limiting your view, though not so high as to prevent glimpses of the houses on the parallel-running Great Egg Harbor River.

There is no access at the mouth. The most interesting option is to continue down the Great Egg a mile to Stephen Creek and then ascend that creek about a mile and a half to the floating dock in the county park. Other options are to double back or to seek other take-outs up or down the Great Egg.

HAZARDS: None

WATER CONDITIONS: This is tidal, so it is always runnable. But the first few hundred yards can be tedious at low tide.

GAUGE: None

Tuckahoe River and Cedar Swamp Creek

INTRODUCTION: The Tuckahoe River is a major tributary to Great Egg Harbor. It forms much of the southern border of Atlantic County, flowing through a thinly populated area of mostly woods and wetlands. At least half of this stream's length is tidal, and that is where most of the paddling can most reasonably be enjoyed. It has one major tributary, Cedar Swamp Creek, also a tidal passage. Together they form a fine canoeing destination in the soggiest of settings.

The name Tuckahoe is common in the middle Atlantic region. Of Native American origin, it describes a wetland plant with edible tubers, probably the arrowhead plant (genus *Sagittaria*). If you paddle in summer, then you have probably seen its distinctive leaves grace the fringes of some pond or swamp. According to Euell Gibbons, in *Stalking The Wild Asparagus,* the plants bear tasty tubers ranging from the size of peas to eggs, ready for harvest in late autumn. So now you can add foraging for supper as another joy of swamp paddling.

Section 1. N.J. Rte. 49 to Head of River (N.J. Rte. 49)					
Gradient	Difficulty	Distance	Time	Scenery	Map
7	A	3.0	3.0	Very Good	26

TRIP DESCRIPTION: This is the only part of the nontidal Tuckahoe that could be considered navigable, and many would dispute even that. For the upper Tuckahoe is a tiny and tangled passage. Particularly the first mile would discourage the faint of heart, for an almost continuous challenge of splitting channels and a relentless sieve of low, overhanging branches make this an exercise in wrestling, not paddling. Following that brutal introduction, the route traverses the remains of a series of ponds. The channels here frequently split and are shallow, but seldom obstructed. It is a beautiful and lonely swamp setting. Only road noise from nearby Rte. 49 dispels the illusion of wilderness. Below the ponds, a relatively wide and deep channel blocked by only occasional deadfalls carries you to the take-out. A gauging station weir at Rte. 49 can provide a final splash.

All of this section is within the bounds of a state fish and wildlife management area. So you will see no development and little litter. Maybe that makes it worth the steep price of admission. But bring along a hand saw, and make it just a bit easier for those who follow.

HAZARDS: Strainers, if they do not endanger you, will tire and strain you. At high water, the weir at the take-out might be dangerous for the inexperienced.

WATER CONDITIONS: Except in a really dry year, there is usually enough water to pass through from November through mid-May.

GAUGE: There is a USGS gauging station on the upstream right corner of the Rte. 49 bridge at the take-out. Zero is unknown, but 4.2 feet on the staff (on the right upstream edge of the bridge abutment, above the weir) should be enough.

Section 2. Head of River (N.J. Rte. 49) to mouth					
Gradient	Difficulty	Distance	Time	Scenery	Map
0	A	14.4	6.5	Fair to Good	26

TRIP DESCRIPTION: Tidewater begins at the foot of the gauging station weir at the put-in. But at low tide, the first quarter mile can be shallow and riffly. With a little more state land continuing on the left, this section starts as an attractive passage through woods and developing marsh. The little river then slowly begins to widen, as do the surrounding marshes. But, all too soon, on the high ground beyond, houses start to dominate the scenery. So the remaining miles down to N.J. Rte. 50 are disappointing. If you care to just skip these first five miles, you can put in at a postage stamp of a park along Main Street in Corbin City, below the town of Tuckahoe at Mosquito Landing, or at a new state access a quarter mile farther downstream.

Below the town of Tuckahoe, the river enters a huge public fish and wildlife management area. Much of this is a vast and beautiful marsh. You can see for a long way out here, giving one an uncommon Jersey experience — elbow room. The open view, unfortunately, is marred by such distant protuberances as communications towers, water towers, the skyline of Somers Point, and, most notably, the power plant at Beesleys Point. So it is a pretty setting, but not exactly a substitute for a trip to the Everglades.

There is no access at the mouth, so continue on down Great Egg Harbor to the public ramp between the Garden State Parkway and U.S. Rte. 9. Or you can combine this with an excursion up Cedar Swamp Creek.

HAZARDS: None

WATER CONDITIONS: If the tide is out, the first quarter mile below Rte. 49 could be too low during summer and early autumn low water. Everything else is always passable.

GAUGE: None

Section 3. Cedar Swamp Creek. Head to mouth					
Gradient	Difficulty	Distance	Time	Scenery	Map
0	A	6.0	2.5	Very Good	26

TRIP DESCRIPTION: Cedar Swamp Creek flows out of Cedar Swamp (of course!). It is unusual in that there is access to neither its head nor its mouth. So one starts near the middle, the best choice being Rte. 631. If you go downstream, you will enjoy big views across the same sprawling spartina meadows that one sees on the Tuckahoe River. If you go upstream, you will find the trip is particularly pretty. The surrounding marsh here is still wide, but not nearly as wide as below. Dense forest forms a backdrop, and the facade is unbroken by development. When you almost reach the top, the now fairly narrow channel splits four ways. There are two large forks. The best choice is the right (west), which quickly takes you to the edge of the marsh and into a cedar-studded swamp. The shallow and clear but dark waters wind for about a quarter mile up into the contrastingly closed-in wetland until deadfalls hopelessly block any further progress. And then it is time to turn around and go back into the sunshine.

HAZARDS: There is nothing dangerous, but a low railroad bridge next to N.J. Rte. 50 will require a short carry.

WATER CONDITIONS: This is tidal, so most of the way is always navigable. The upper fork may not be entirely passable at low tide.

GAUGE: None

Mullica River

INTRODUCTION: The Mullica is a long, lovely waterway that drains the heart of South Jersey. In doing so, it also drains the heart of the Pine Barrens, about 100,000 acres of which now lie protected as Wharton State Forest. We owe this fortune to the misfortune of the forest's namesake, Joseph Wharton, a 19th-century industrialist. Back in the 1870s, Mr. Wharton bought up all those supposedly worthless acres, recognizing the value of the underlying aquifer as a future water supply for Philadelphia. But a parochial New Jersey legislature decided that New Jersey water should stay in New Jersey and thus passed a law quashing this potentially lucrative plan. While Wharton ultimately managed to find agricultural value in the land, his heirs eventually saw fit to sell the tract to the state. So now you can float on that beautiful, clean water rather than (if you are a Philadelphian) water your lawn with it.

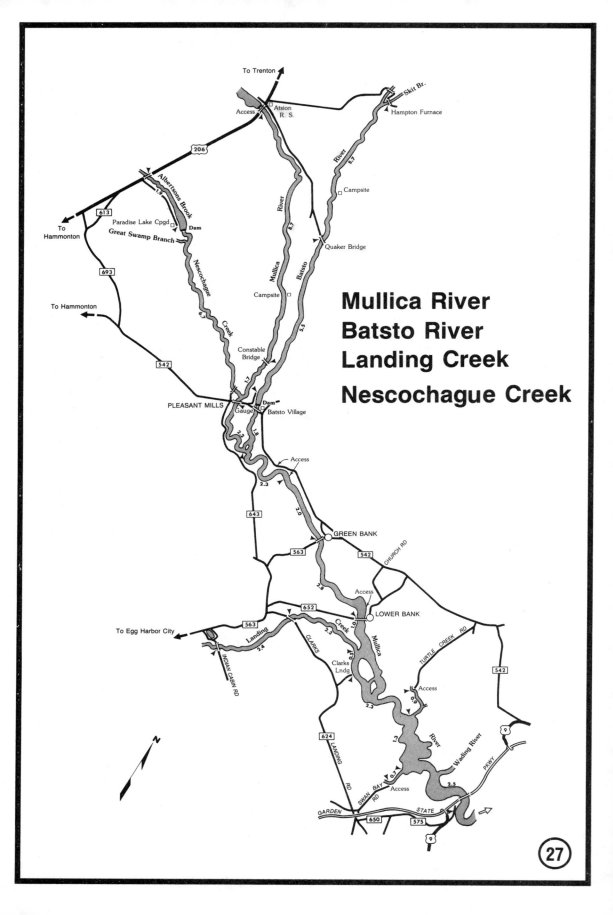

Mullica River
Batsto River
Landing Creek
Nescochague Creek

To Trenton

Skit Br.

Access   Atsion R. S.

Hampton Furnace

206

Albertsons Brook

613

Paradise Lake Cpgd   Dam

Great Swamp Branch

To Hammonton

693

Nescochague Creek

To Hammonton

542

Constable Bridge

PLEASANT MILLS

Gauge   Dam

Batsto Village

Campsite

Quaker Bridge

River

Mullica River

Batsto

Campsite

Access

643

563

GREEN BANK

542   CHURCH RD

Access

563

652

LOWER BANK

To Egg Harbor City

Landing

Creek

CLARKS

Clarks Lndg

INDIAN CABIN RD

624

LANDING RD

SWAN BAY RD

Access

GARDEN

650   575

Mullica

TURTLE CREEK RD

Access

Wading River

542

9

STATE   PKWY

2.5

N

27

Section 1. Atsion (U.S. Rte. 206) to Rte. 542					
Gradient	Difficulty	Distance	Time	Scenery	Map
4	A to 1—	10.4	5.5	Excellent	27

TRIP DESCRIPTION: This is a first-class run. If it seems like a wilderness excursion, that is because it almost is. The only man-made influences are one bridge, a gauging station, and a few sand roads, the latter being seldom evident from water level.

Start your trip at a boaters' access on the south bank about 50 yards downstream of Rte. 206. This makes launching and parking easy and safe (cars move like lightning on Rte. 206). In the classic manner of a Pine Barrens run, the Mullica starts as only an eight-foot-wide ribbon of tea-colored water. Variety keeps this "river" especially interesting. There is a maple swamp, then open tree-studded marsh, the latter caused by beaver flooding. There are cedar-lined corridors and cranberry-covered banks. There are high, sandy banks and bluffs topped by the typical Pine Barrens forest of scrubby pine and oak. Finally, a particularly nice feature of this stream is its glades — lush meadows of grass or sedge, sometimes spotted with cottongrass, and fringed by dark green walls of impenetrable cedar forest. When you behold these scenes, you must repeat to yourself, "I am not in Canada, I am not in Canada. . ." The Mullica loops and loops as if it were reluctant to reach the sea. It also subtly grows, but never gets more than 20 feet wide. The run ends as it began, with the luxury of a formal canoe launch area, this one located on the left about 50 yards below Rte. 542.

As on any wild river, canoe camping is a delightful way to enjoy it, not to mention stretch the trip out. The state insists that you camp only in designated campsites. There is one big site on the Mullica, accommodating 100 campers (both canoeists and hikers), located about six miles below the start. It offers the luxury of privies and drinking water. You need a permit to stay here, and you can get one from the Atsion Ranger Station.

As with other Pine Barrens streams, the Mullica is swift, especially as it gains volume. Generally the water is smooth, but at low levels, towards the end of the run, there are actually some shallow riffles formed by gravel and reefs of bog iron ore. At any level, you get treated to a splash in a few exhilarating drops over surprisingly high beaver dams — the Falls of the Mullica. Strainers are usually sawed out but, especially at low water, snags will keep you busy or bothered. Also, all those sharp turns can make this an exhausting trip for the really green beginner.

HAZARDS: Some deadfalls are possible, mostly in the first few miles.

WATER CONDITIONS: This stream always carries enough water for floating. But in dry summers, August and September levels can be low enough to cause a lot of bumping over normally submerged logs and tangling with more snags than you would like. Autumn cranberry harvesting diversions can supposedly also diminish the flow.

GAUGE: There are no convenient gauges. The staff gauge on Constable Bridge and a USGS gauge about a mile upstream are out of the way and accessible only by poor sand roads. For the record though, minimal but adequate levels are 0.45 feet on the USGS gauge and 0.0 feet at Constable Bridge. The best idea is to inquire at the Atsion Ranger Station.

Section 2. Rte. 542 to mouth					
Gradient	Difficulty	Distance	Time	Scenery	Map
0	A	23.9	10.0	Fair to Very Good	27

TRIP DESCRIPTION: The remainder of the Mullica is tidal. After about two miles, it widens considerably from the diminutive ribbon that you have come to expect. It often reaches a half mile across, even a mile near its mouth. The initial reach, down to Green Bank, is the least attractive portion as much of its shoreline is developed, even up in the woods near Pleasant Mills. After that, except around the village of Lower Bank, the edges are wild. Your world becomes one of open water, vast marshes, and a distant skyline of pine and cedar. There are enough intermediate access points to avoid a marathon cruise, especially if you are a good enough navigator to locate obscure, little sidestreams that have landings on them. If you go all the way to Great Bay, you can take out a third of a mile past the north side of the mouth at the end of Radio Road. Radio Road (Rte. 601) branches off of U.S. Rte. 9 on the west side of Tuckerton. The closest access to the south side of the mouth is three long miles down the bay and up a side channel to Scotts Landing in Forsythe National Wildlife Refuge.

HAZARDS: Motorboaters and wind

WATER CONDITIONS: This is tidal, so it is always deep enough.

GAUGE: None

Nescochague Creek

INTRODUCTION: Nescochague Creek starts just northwest of Hammonton and then arcs along the southern boundary of Wharton State Forest, finally sneaking into the Mullica just above Rte. 572. The upper creek is named Albertson Brook and only assumes the name Nescochague after the confluence with Great Swamp Brook. Nescochague is a relatively unknown canoe stream in this popular canoeing region. This is not for lack of quality though. Most likely, its low profile is attributable to limited access, a short season, and no present use by commercial outfitters. So this isolated route sits there just waiting for you.

Section 1. Paradise Lake Campground to mouth					
Gradient	Difficulty	Distance	Time	Scenery	Map
6	A	6.5	3.5	Excellent	27

TRIP DESCRIPTION: The energetic can actually start this trip on Albertson Brook at U.S. Rte. 206. If you can survive the first half mile, which entails clawing your way through thickets and logjams on a few braided spots, the rest is easy. Only experienced jungle paddlers should start at the highway. After the tough start, Albertson opens into a beautiful marsh at the head of a narrow lake, the site of an old cranberry bog. The lake is also undeveloped, except for Paradise Lake Campground.

Most paddlers choose to start at the campground. This is private, and the owners charge a token fee to launch a canoe. But there are the advantages of having a secure spot to leave your car, missing that tough section, and tapping into the owner's knowledge of the current condition of the lower river and adequacy of the water level. And if you are still interested in the upper section, you can see most of it by putting in at Paradise and just paddling upstream. A short paddle down the lake brings you to the dam. Carry on the right.

The remaining miles to the Mullica pass through wilderness, except for a brief brush by another campground. The stream is regularly sawed out, though many stretches look as though they are naturally clear. Initially, the channel is strangely straight, with often grassy banks. But eventually the creek assumes a more normal, crooked path with cranberry vines covering the banks instead of grass. The surroundings are all forest, a mixture of hardwoods and evergreens. These evolve into thick stands of cedar. The Nescochague finally slinks into the Mullica only about 300 yards above Rte. 572. So finish at the boater's access on the Mullica just below that bridge.

HAZARDS: Strainers are always a possibility.

WATER CONDITIONS: This is usually continually canoeable from November through June.

GAUGE: None. Inquire at the Paradise Lake Campground.

Batsto River

INTRODUCTION: The Batsto takes you down the heart of wild Wharton State Forest, thus offering you the most remote run in New Jersey. To tell the truth, you really cannot tell that this stream is any more remote than several other gems in this area. But it is certainly nice to know that you are paddling through more than just an illusion. The energetic can enjoy the entire river as a day trip. The less energetic can use a midway access point at Quaker Bridge to do either of two more leisurely trips. And those who desire to stretch it out can spend the night on the river, using the state forest campsite at Lower Forge. Whatever your decision, any size dose should please you.

Section 1. Hampton Road to Batsto Village					
Gradient	Difficulty	Distance	Time	Scenery	Map
4	A	11.2	5.5	Excellent	27

TRIP DESCRIPTION: The adventure of running the Batsto starts with locating your put-ins and take-outs. To find Hampton Road, go about 300 yards north on U.S. Rte. 206 from the Atsion Ranger Station. Where the guardrail ends, turn right onto a sand road. Initially the narrow road strikes off straight as an arrow, but often rough as a toad's back. It then takes a few potentially confusing bends. If you take no wrong turns, at the three and three-quarter-mile mark you will reach the second of three bridges and the ruins of Hampton Furnace. This is the first of two alternate upper put-ins. The other one, at the third bridge (which is over a tributary called Skit Branch), is reached by pushing on about another 500 yards, in the process, making a sharp right and then a sharp left. The choice of put-ins is a toss-up.

For those wishing to start or finish at Quaker Bridge, the approach is from the west, thus making a long shuttle for those putting in at Quaker Bridge. The sandy access road starts on the south side of the Atsion Ranger Station and follows the edge of the Mullica's swamp for part way. When you reach a fork at about the three-mile point, bear left to reach the bridge.

Finally, the preferred Batsto Village take-out is on the west side of the old millpond. To get there, go about a quarter mile west on Rte. 542 from its bridge over the river and turn right onto a diagonally intersecting road. Take the first left off of this onto a sand road and follow three tenths of a mile up the pond to a parking area. Do not try to go any farther or they will need a metal detector to find your car beneath the sand.

The Batsto is a beautiful stream. It offers you intimacy on its forks, which are so tiny that you can reach out and touch both banks. But it also offers you space, such as where it spreads out as the serene pool of Batsto's millpond or in its tidal finish. In between it offers the standard range of Pine Barrens scenery, maple swamp, cedar-bound banks, and high, sandy bluffs topped with pines, oaks, and their blueberry understory. This is a good stream for finding cranberries and, down towards the end, for finding those carnivorous pitcher plants. Needless to say, the Batsto's tea-colored waters are pure, and they are clear enough to expose the luxuriant stands of aquatic grasses that carpet the sandy bottom. Litter and other user damage are less evident here than on other popular Pine Barrens streams.

If you care to spend the night amongst all this splendor, there is a state forest campsite set aside exclusively for canoeists and hikers. Camping in Wharton outside of campgrounds is prohibited. Located about a mile and a half above Quaker Bridge, this site accomodates up to 50 souls. It has privies, but you must bring your own water. To stay here you will need a camping permit, which you get at the ranger station at Atsion.

No trip would be complete without a stop at Batsto Village. This is a restored iron-making (and later glass-making) settlement that thrived back in the late 18th and early 19th centuries. For starters, explore the fine visitor center and rustic little nature center. Then wandering about, you can tour the elegant iron-master's mansion, observe an operating water-powered sawmill, and watch the artisans (who occupy several old workers cabins) as they demonstrate the crafts of the era.

Though the Batsto is a gentle stream, its twisting and narrow channel can easily tire and frustrate the inexperienced. So if you are a beginner or out of shape, it is easiest to start your trip at Quaker Bridge. All of this stream has been sawed out. Still, snags can surprise you at low levels, as can overhanging vegetation at any level. When you enter the pond above Batsto, follow the winding channel. Short-cutting across the water weeds and shallows seldom pays off. If you continue through Batsto Village to the mouth, you will need to get around the milldam; there is an easy carry on the right. The minor gauging station weir below Rte. 572 should present no diffculty. After that weir, you are on tidewater. There is no access at the mouth, so continue down the Mullica about two miles to a state forest access on the left.

HAZARDS: There is a milldam at Batsto, but it is below most people's take-out.

WATER CONDITIONS: Most of this river is always passable, but that shallow first mile may get marginal during August and September of a dry year.

GAUGE: There is a USGS gauge about 30 feet below Rte. 572 on the right. A level of 2.0 feet is about as low as this creek usually gets, and this is still adequate for most of the river.

Landing Creek

INTRODUCTION: Landing Creek is a swampy tributary to the Mullica that starts near Egg Harbor City and joins the big river just below Lower Bank. Most South Jersey streams this small would be too choked with wood to consider. But by some stroke of fortune, this beautiful passage has only minimally suffered such a fate. For the veteran swamp pilot, it is worth a visit.

Gradient	Difficulty	Distance	Time	Scenery	Map
5*	A to 1—	4.7	2.5	Very Good	27

*above tidewater

TRIP DESCRIPTION: The put-in is a bit obscure. Starting from U.S. Rte. 30 in downtown Egg Harbor City, go north on Rte. 563 three miles. You will come to a lake. On the north side of the lake, turn right onto a sand road. Follow this around the lake and, at the T-intersection, turn left. Your bridge is about 200 yards down this rough road.

The nontidal portion of Landing Creek is unusual. The route is set in a deep forest, mostly hardwood. But rather than this being a typical jungle, there is relatively light undergrowth when viewed from the creek. In fact, the forest floor is often grassy. At moderate levels, this stream's banks are about two feet high. They are sandy and carpeted with moss. The channel is relatively wide and shallow, its dark but clear waters flowing swiftly over a sandy bottom and forming little riffles over beds of pea gravel. There are many snags, but relatively few strainers that would require portages. After about a mile and a half of this honeymoon, there is a power line crossing. After this, the channel narrows and unnaturally straightens, now flowing between five-foot-high banks. The banks are overgrown, and the dominant flora seems to be thorn bushes. You can expect at least several big trees to block this stretch, creating challenging and sticky liftovers or carries.

Tidewater starts at Clarks Landing Road, though if the tide is out, riffles extend for another quarter mile. The creek meanders through a beautiful swamp jungle. At low tide, snags and strainers are abundant. Any carries or liftovers will be slippery and muddy. So try to time this reach to high tide. The swamp soon parts, and an undisturbed freshwater marsh backed by forests of cedar and pine spreads before you. This in turn evolves to a brackish marsh where your field of vision is confined by a wall of tall reeds. When you reach the mouth, depending on the direction of the tide, turn left and ascend the Mullica a mile and a quarter to the village ramp at Lower Bank or turn right and descend the Mullica a half mile to Clarks Landing.

HAZARDS: The strainers on the last mile above Clarks Landing Road can be nasty.

WATER CONDITIONS: Except during a prolonged dry spell, you should find this passable almost any time from November through the beginning of May.

GAUGE: There is no gauge on this creek. For a rough substitute, check the USGS gauge at Folsom (N.J. Rte. 54) on the Great Egg Harbor River. Call Philadelphia or visit. A level of 3.9 feet should assure you good water.

Wading River

INTRODUCTION: Draining the southeast end of Burlington County and the heart of the Pine Barrens, the Wading River is possibly the most popular canoe stream in South Jersey. And well it should be. The Wading is a beautiful stream that suggests wilderness, though it is never more than a mile and a half from good highway. All of its nontidal miles are protected within Wharton State Forest. It has relatively plentiful access and reliable water, and it is mostly easy to negotiate. Convenient to the Garden State Parkway and N.J. Rte. 70, it is no wonder that this waterway is so used.

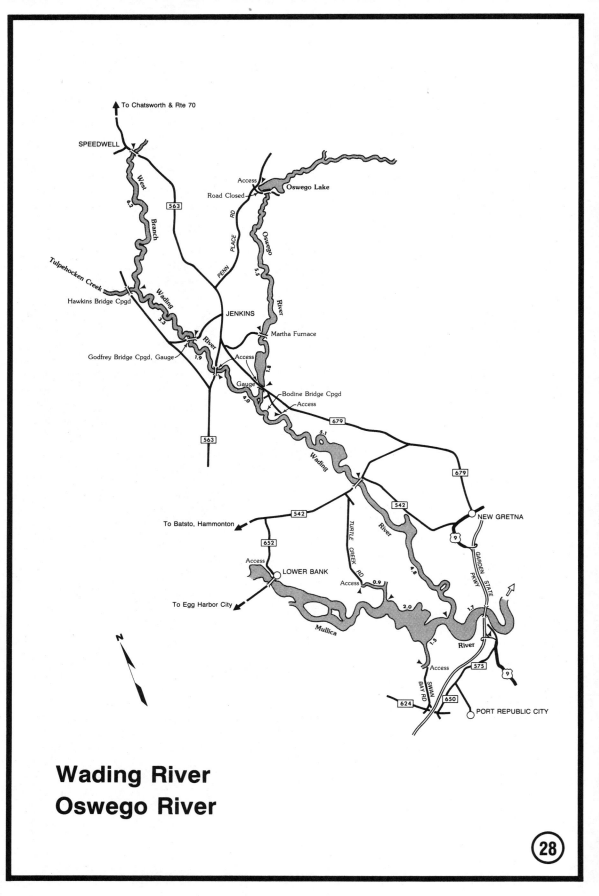

To Chatsworth & Rte 70

SPEEDWELL

West

Branch

6.2

563

Tulpehocken Creek

Hawkins Bridge Cpgd

Wading

3.3

River

Godfrey Bridge Cpgd, Gauge

1.9

JENKINS

PENN PLACE RD

Access

Road Closed

Oswego Lake

Oswego

5.5

River

Martha Furnace

Access

1.8

Gauge

4.0

Bodine Bridge Cpgd

Access

679

5.1

Wading

679

542

563

542

To Batsto, Hammonton

652

TURTLE CREEK RD

River

4.6

NEW GRETNA

9

GARDEN STATE PRKWY

Access

LOWER BANK

To Egg Harbor City

Access

0.9

2.0

1.7

Mullica

1.5

River

Access

575

9

SWAN BAY RD

624

650

PORT REPUBLIC CITY

N

Wading River
Oswego River

28

The Wading, unfortunately, is also abused. Do not come here on a summer weekend with illusions of seeking solitude. Paddling the river at such times is a watery version of rush-hour traffic jam crawl. But the most obnoxious aftereffect of overuse is the copious amount of litter strewn along the banks. For some real human scum also shows up to paddle the Wading. And not all litter is deliberate. Judging from all the unopened cans and bottles that one finds in the water, a portion of the mess is the debris of a lot of inept or alcohol-impaired paddling and the resulting unscheduled baptisms. A more subtle effect of overuse is that the banks and bottom of the Wading are noticeably more chewed up than on less popular streams. There is not much we can do about the bad actors, but maybe you could pick up a can or bottle along the way, and help to restore this creek to its proper glory.

Section 1. Speedwell (Rte. 563) to Bodine Field Campground					
Gradient	Difficulty	Distance	Time	Scenery	Map
4	A	15.4*	6.0	Excellent	28

*to launch site at lower end of Bodine Field

TRIP DESCRIPTION: This is the nontidal section of the Wading. Actually, most of this section, specifically the river above the confluence with the Oswego, is officially called the West Branch Wading River. What you see at the put-in may hit you as less than a branch. More like a twig. Yet, this 10-foot-wide channel represents the final consolidation of an extensive labyrinth of ditches, bogs, ponds, and swamps. A viable canoe trail is born at this point.

The first part of the Wading passes mostly through red maple swamp. With such a small channel, allow for the possibility of a liftover or two, even on such a well-maintained waterway. Except for where it swings by the edge of some cranberry bogs, the setting is all wild. Fugitive cranberry vines from these bogs grace much of the bank for many miles to come.

The inflow of Tulpehocken Creek opens things up a bit, and the current quickens. Cedars begin to become part of the flora, and their numbers increase with each mile. Occasionally the forest walls recede a bit to frame some soggy glades. At spots like these, it is easy to pretend that you are in Canada, not New Jersey. The only permanent signs of civilization here are Evans Bridge (the second Rte. 563 bridge) and two campgrounds at Godfrey Bridge. When you get to Bodine Field, take out at its lower end to avoid tramping through someone's campsite. To reach this point by land, when the sand road from Rte. 679 forks right to the campground, you go straight until it hits the river.

HAZARDS: None

WATER CONDITIONS: The Wading is almost always passable below Tulpehocken Creek. The upper section usually has enjoyable levels from November through late May. Flow changes are relatively gradual in this sandy area, so watch for wet spells rather than just a single storm to give you high water. Diversions in October or November to flood cranberry bogs can also reduce flow in the river.

GAUGE: There is a USGS gauging station at Godfrey Bridge Campground on the right bank about a hundred yards downstream of the bridge. To reach it, find Campsite 36, walk directly towards the river, and then turn upstream. If cranberry diversions are not influencing the stream above the Tulpehocken, 10.8 feet represents a low but adequate level for the first few critical miles. Expect levels to drop to around 10.3 feet in the driest parts of late summer and fall. This level is still adequate for floating below the Tulpehocken.

Section 2. Bodine Field Campground to mouth					
Gradient	Difficulty	Distance	Time	Scenery	Map
0	A	8.5	4.0	Good to Excellent	28

TRIP DESCRIPTION: The transition to tidewater occurs at some vague point below Bodine Field. Fast water and a cedar-bound corridor last for about another mile. The current then slackens, and marsh meadows appear and quickly widen. Backed by a thick green wall of cedar and pine, these are possibly the prettiest and least disturbed marshland vistas in the state. So the appearance of the first houses is almost painful. But on down to the Rte. 542 bridge development remains light, though the presence of numerous "No Trespassing" signs really trash the riverside. They should, however, serve as a reminder that you have now passed beyond state forest land, and the banks are thus all privately owned. Local landowners have voiced numerous complaints of abuses by paddlers who thought otherwise.

Below Rte. 542, the marshes really expand, and changing types of grasses and reeds reflect the growing salinity of the river. This is a pretty enough stretch to canoe, but possibly the best spot from which to appreciate it is from the elevated perspective of the Rte. 542 bridge. With so little development along its banks, motorboat traffic on the lower Wading is relatively light for a Jersey Shore river. The path is mostly simple, except for a point about five miles below the bridge where there is a hairpin loop and a bypass channel. If you bear right, you can take the shortcut. If you bear left, you add a half mile to your trip.

There is no access at the mouth. You can continue another mile and a half down the Mullica (past the Garden State Parkway Bridge) to a private ramp on the right bank (fee charged). Or if you have a good sense of direction, it is possible to paddle a mile up the Mullica and ascend an obscure little gut (if you are facing upstream, it is on your left) for a half mile. It leads to a forgotten landing at the end of Swan Bay Road.

HAZARDS: None

WATER CONDITIONS: Being mostly tidal, this is always passable.

GAUGE: None

Oswego River

INTRODUCTION: Mile for mile, the Oswego is as beautiful as any canoe stream in the Pine Barrens. Alas, the Oswego is but a short run. It starts back up in Ocean County, north of Warren Grove, in some of the wildest recesses of the Barrens. It becomes navigable somewhere above the popular put-in, but all roads leading both to this stream and to the vast network of commercial cranberry bogs that surround it are gated. So the only way to enjoy the upper reaches is to paddle upstream. Since most people prefer to go with the flow, most people only experience the final six miles below Oswego Lake. Unobstructed and largely protected by state forest, either part will delight you.

Section 1. Oswego Lake Access upstream					
Gradient	Difficulty	Distance	Time	Scenery	Map
5	A	about 3.5	3.0 up 1.5 down	Excellent	28

TRIP DESCRIPTION: For the newcomer, finding the put-in is the biggest challenge of the trip. Penn Place Road, the road to the start, is hardtop and branches unmarked northeast off Rte. 563 about 1.5 miles north of the intersection of Rte. 563 and Rte. 679. Follow Penn Place Road about three miles. You will come upon a four-way sand road intersection followed by a bridge over an arm of Oswego Lake. Just past the rusty guardrail on your right is a state forest access area on the lake.

Oswego Lake is about a mile long. Its cedar- and pine-bound shores are completely undeveloped. Its waters are clear and clean. Traveling uplake, you come to a fork. Bear to the left (north) to ascend the stream. People have sawed out the upper Oswego to slightly above the confluence with Papoose Branch, which is about two and a quarter miles above the put-in. But you should be able to probe at least another mile with little difficulty. The route is tiny and twisting, and the current is fairly stiff. Initially it is a cedar-fringed corridor that is as pretty as any spot on the lower river. As you progress farther though, deciduous trees and shrubs take over. Some evidence of logging slightly mars the uppermost reaches. But generally, since visitors have yet to trash this section, the setting seems pristine.

HAZARDS: None

WATER CONDITIONS: Runnable levels are generally reliable during late fall, winter, and spring through May.

GAUGE: You can use the USGS gauge on the right side of the river below Harrisville Pond. Levels for Section 2 apply to this section.

Section 2. Oswego Lake to Rte. 679					
Gradient	Difficulty	Distance	Time	Scenery	Map
5	A	6.3	3.0	Excellent	28

TRIP DESCRIPTION: You start this trip at the same place as for Section 1. Until 1990, you could turn right onto the sand road (now gated) at the four-way intersection and drive to the lake's spillway. But now you must start with a quarter-mile paddle across the lake and a short but steep scramble over the dike to the foot of the spillway.

By every measure, this is a first-class, blue-ribbon, five-star canoe stream. Its water is as clear (but tea colored) and pure as any mountain brook. Take a little taste. It is better than anything that you can import from France. In past centuries, seafarers would send their crews up these types of rivers to fill their casks. The tannic acid acted as a preservative for the long voyage ahead. The stream is bounded by a wonderful forest of fragrant white cedar. They give the Oswego a North Woods atmosphere. You will find water lilies in some eddies, cranberry vines clinging to the banks, and, particularly around Martha Furnace, that carnivorous curiosity, the pitcher plant. The stream bottom varies from sand or pea gravel to rocky bog iron deposits. The water is often shallow and swift, with little riffles appearing at low levels. At a little more than the halfway point, the Oswego spreads out into a marshy, multichanneled, pond-like expanse. The water consolidates again, but in the last mile it slows as Harrisville Pond. So there is variety, too.

Most people end their trip at the roadside park by Rte. 679. If you want to finish the river, head for the southeast corner of the lake and carry the spillway. There is a tiny gauging station weir and even a riffle down below. A half mile of easy paddling through more cedar scenery gets you to the Wading River. Continue from there a mile and a half down to Bodine Field Access.

HAZARDS: None

WATER CONDITIONS: Floatable levels are usually reliable during late fall, winter, and spring through June. In dry summers this can get too low, resulting in much dragging over gravel shallows. Sometimes cranberry bog diversions can create these low conditions in October.

GAUGE: There is a USGS gauge on the right bank below Harrisville Pond. This gauge is less than ideal as discharge from Harrisville Pond may not accurately reflect inflow. Also this gauge is on a wide spot where only a few tenths of a foot make a big difference. But it is all that we have. There are two staffs on the concrete abutment of the station's weir — one above and one below. Minimum level is about 2.9 feet on the upper staff and 2.4 feet on the lower staff.

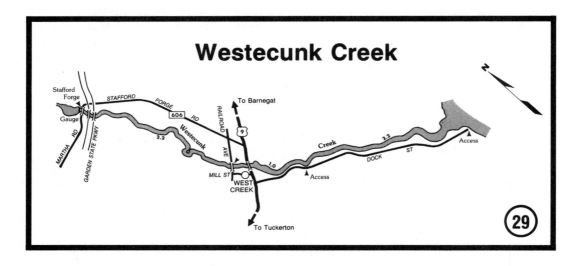

Westecunk Creek

INTRODUCTION: Westecunk Creek flows out of the Pine Barrens into Little Egg Harbor a few miles north of Tuckerton. Only a few miles of this diminutive ribbon of tea-colored water is canoeable, or even accessible. It would hardly be worth the trouble of taking your boat off the racks were it not so beautiful. But paddlers who still insist on some quantity with their quality can easily combine this with a run down nearby and equally beautiful Oyster Creek for an outstanding day.

Section 1. Stafford Forge (Martha Road) to West Creek (Public Ramp)					
Gradient	Difficulty	Distance	Time	Scenery	Map
9	A	3.2	1.5	Excellent	29

TRIP DESCRIPTION: The put-in is at the foot of the spillway of the fish and wildlife management area lake at Martha Road. A flooded former cranberry bog, this is a beautiful pool of water worth exploring. Much of the run down to U.S. Rte. 9 is through cedar swamp. The channel is, of course, narrow and crooked, but it has been sawed out. Though houses along Martha Road are only a short distance away, they are invisible through the thick cedar facade. Then houses on the right, the piers of an old dam, and a bridge announce the village called West Creek. After the creek rushes through those piers, it has reached tidewater. From Rte. 9, a three-quarter-mile paddle past pretty marshes will bring you to a public boat ramp along Dock Street.

HAZARDS: Possible deadfalls, and the old dam piers in West Creek are potential hazards.

WATER CONDITIONS: You can usually find consistently runnable levels from November through early June in a dry year. In a wet or even average year, it usually stays up through late July.

GAUGE: There is a staff gauge on the right abutment of the put-in bridge. Minimum is unknown, but probably around 10.4 feet would be on the low side.

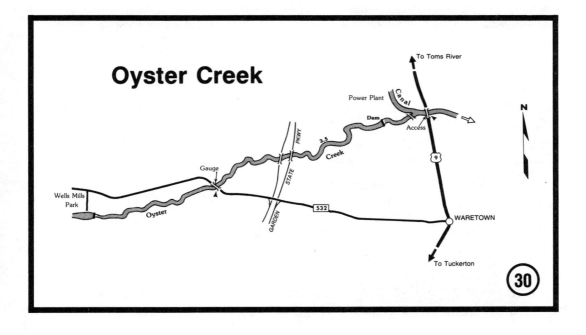

Oyster Creek

INTRODUCTION: Oyster Creek is a pearl. And like a pearl, it is tiny. It has only one major flaw — it is so short a run. Even if you just drift with the current, you will be at the finish all too soon.

The creek is located about two miles south of the town of Forked River, in southern Ocean County, and is easily reached via the Garden State Parkway. It combines well with a trip on nearby and even shorter Westecunk Creek.

Gradient	Difficulty	Distance	Time	Scenery	Map
8	A to 1—	3.5	2.0	Excellent to Poor	30

TRIP DESCRIPTION: Much of this passage is through a cedar swamp. The denseness and homogeneity of this forest is remarkable, and one gets the feeling of being confined by an impenetrable green wall. It is also remarkable that this narrow channel is passable. While we can thank anonymous sawyers for part of this luxury, much of the going seems to be just naturally open. The water is pure, clear brown. It reveals a grassy bottom. In fact, big grass-bound clumps of sand combined with this stream's relatively steep gradient form many easy riffles. And how many grass riffles can you say you have ever seen? The current, of course, is very swift.

The good times end before you reach Rte. 9, as you approach the grounds of Jersey Central Power & Light's Oyster Creek Power Plant. The land to the left is cleared, and the cedars are all gone. There is a short pond formed by a three-foot weir, easiest carry being on the left. Below here, the stream returns to the cedar woods, but the channel presents a shallow, tedious slalom down a cedar log-strewn bed. Cedar logs are particularly nasty as they are rot resistant, thus leaving intact many sharp nubs that can hurt you or your boat. They also get as slippery as grease when wet. So take it slow, especially when lifting over a log. This stretch ends with a passage through a culvert that spits you out into the huge U-shaped cooling canal of the power plant. Rte. 9 is just a short paddle below.

HAZARDS: There is the three-foot weir at the power plant. Deadfalls below will require some slippery liftovers. Be careful on these sharp tangles.

WATER CONDITIONS: In a year of average or above average precipitation, good levels prevail in winter and spring. The more minimal levels described below persist into July.

GAUGE: There are three staff gauges, all at the put-in. One is at the USGS gauging station just upstream of Rte. 532, and two are attached to the right downstream abutment of that bridge. The USGS gauge should probably read at least 4.0 feet, and the staff on the downstream edge of the abutment should be about 3.0 feet for getting down to the weir. But to minimize your liftovers below the weir, you would be happier with about 4.7 feet and 3.7 feet respectively.

Cedar Creek

INTRODUCTION: Located in Ocean County just a few miles south of the busy town of Toms River, the Cedar blazes a crooked trail through a prime portion of the Pine Barrens. It certainly lives up to its name, though at times Cranberry Creek or Maple Creek might seem just as fitting a title. Though of average length for a Pine Barrens canoe stream, all of its turns and complexity make it seem much longer. But intermediate access points at Dover and Double Trouble allow you to tailor the trip length to your ability. For some reason this fine creek has traditionally seen much less use than the streams of Wharton Forest. But traffic has been increasing, a fact that is unfortunately best evidenced by the massive increase in litter and bank erosion. So go enjoy what is natural, and perhaps pick up a bottle or can on the way.

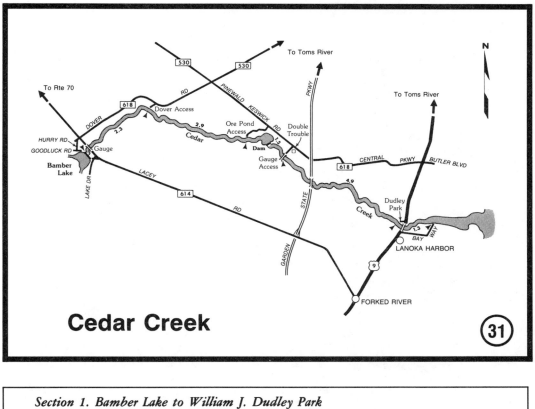

Cedar Creek

31

Section 1. Bamber Lake to William J. Dudley Park					
Gradient	Difficulty	Distance	Time	Scenery	Map
6	A	11.6	6.0	Excellent	31

TRIP DESCRIPTION: It would be nice to be able to put in as we used to at Lacy Road, but that prime spot is currently posted against parking. So start at Bamber Lake Dam, at the foot of the spillway. The first quarter mile is a narrow, tangled mess, definitely in need of some pruning. After that initial challenge, the next few miles unfold as tight, crooked ribbons of clean, tea-colored water through a jungle of maple, alder, berry bushes, and other often shrubby swamp vegetation. Though sawed out, tight turns, strong current, and splitting channels make this a bit of a slalom. There is then a welcome interlude (at least for claustrophobic types) at Dover, where the Cedar meanders for about a half mile through a pond — the site of some old cranberry bogs. A short sand road off of Dover Road, 2.2 miles east of Lacy Road, reaches a state canoe access near the head of this pond, not far above the old dam site. This marks the end of this first particularly tortuous stretch. If you are a beginner, this canoe access would be a much more suitable put-in than Bamber.

The creek stays confined now to what is usually an easier, roomier channel through a swampy forest with some cedar. The next landmarks are a short pond and its concrete dam. The dam is easily portaged on the right. This is in the heart of Double Trouble State Park, which now protects Cedar Creek between Lacy Road and the Garden State Parkway. Below this dam are some extensive old cranberry bogs that still bear a lot of fruit. The banks are typically higher now and support dense stands of cedar. There are also some high sandy banks that expose the face of the pine and oak scrub forest that really dominates this area.

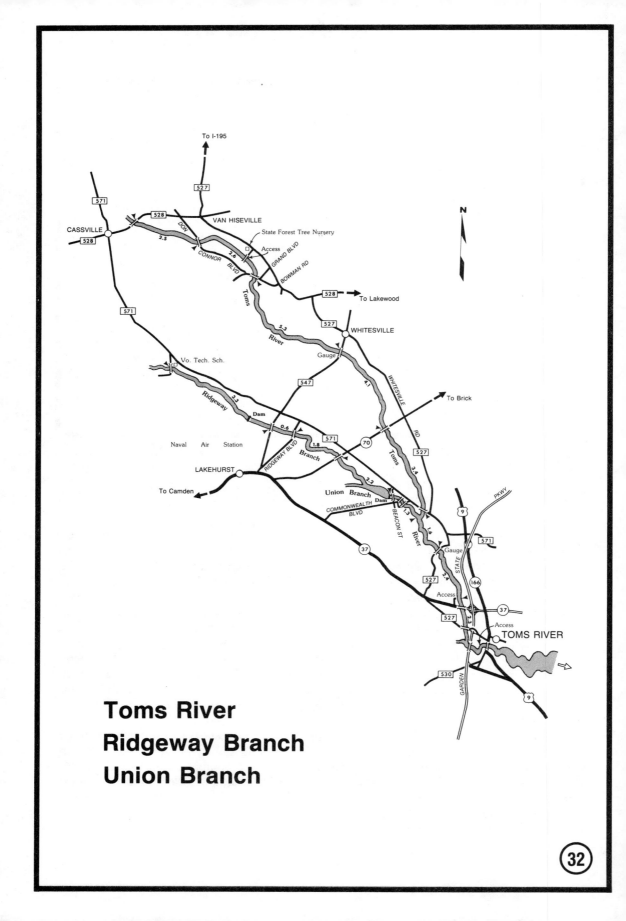

Toms River
Ridgeway Branch
Union Branch

The best place to finish your trip is at the township park a half mile above U.S. Rte. 9. Tidewater and motorboat territory begin shortly below, after a final drop over a two-foot weir of an abandoned gauging station at Rte. 9. If you choose to paddle down to tidewater, the next public access is at the end of Bay Way in Lanoka Harbor.

Anyone who paddles the Cedar will probably wonder about that name, Double Trouble. Double Trouble was a little settlement of the late 19th and early 20th centuries that supported itself by milling timber, making charcoal, and growing cranberries. Its few remaining structures are preserved in the state park. The origin of its strange name is a matter of dispute, but the most common explanation relates to a bad day long ago when burrowing muskrats poked two leaks in an earthen dam. A more contemporary theory, espoused only by the author, is that the name describes the all too common paddling scenario — a husband and wife novice canoe team trying to struggle through five miles of a twisting, snag-strewn Pine Barrens canoe trail. Now that is double trouble.

HAZARDS: You must portage the dam at Double Trouble. The weir at Rte. 9 is runnable, but treat it with caution.

WATER CONDITIONS: Cedar Creek is usually canoeable anytime.

GAUGE: There is a staff gauge on the upstream side of the right abutment of Lacy Road. Zero level is unknown, but expect some bumping over normally submerged logs and scraping in shallow riffles when levels drop below 3.7 feet. There is also a staff gauge on the white bridge at Double Trouble (left abutment, upstream side). Roughly, 1.8 feet means the water is on the low side, but it is still passable.

Toms River

INTRODUCTION: The Toms River drains the Pine Barrens of northern Ocean County, finishing up in Barnegat Bay. Located near the northern limits of the Pine Barrens, this stream has scenery that is subtly different from that of streams to the south. But it is still quite pretty. And considering that the Toms does not enjoy the protection of any state or county forest, park, or wildlife management area, it is amazing just how much of the natural riverscape remains intact. This is one of the longer nontidal runs of South Jersey, so you can really get your fill of it.

Section 1. Don Connor Boulevard to Toms River (N.J. Rte. 166)					
Gradient	Difficulty	Distance	Time	Scenery	Map
5	A	21.7	12.0	Very Good to Good	32

TRIP DESCRIPTION: The Toms is large enough to carry a canoe at Rte. 528, east of Cassville. But this extra two and a half miles is a tangled mess that would quickly sap your energy and enthusiasm. Even by starting at Don Connor Boulevard, you will have to battle much wood. Bring a hand saw.

The reach of river from Don Connor to Rte. 547, south of Whitesville, may offer you the finest trip on the Toms. Sure it has strainers, but many have been sawed out, and you plan to remove one or two more of them yourself. Right? The compensation for your extra effort is getting to enjoy what is, at least visually, a wilderness atmosphere. The setting is a deep, dense maple swamp.

Sometimes you can peer through the trees and appreciate the extent of these soggy woods. Sometimes you cannot, for your world is hemmed in by a dense corridor of streamside shrubbery. This is nice too, for in fall many of these bushes bear a cheery display of red berries (a form of holly, I think) in profusion matched by no other stream in New Jersey. The water, of course, is the typical clean Pine Barrens tea flowing over a sand and gravel bottom. The only significant civilization that you will encounter are two small clusters of houses and some road crossings. And if the local urchins are not out terrorizing the sandy high ground beyond on their ATVs, the silence of the swamp will round out the experience.

Paddlers preferring an easier route can start at Rte, 547. Outside of the possibility of one or two fresh deadfalls, the problems have all been well sawed out. The stream by now has gathered a good volume of water and is swift, so you may find that you must scurry to make it through the slots cut through some of those deadfalls. The surrounding sandy ground is often higher now, supporting stands of pine (often big ones) and American holly, with some cedar appearing along the banks. But while the scenery can be pretty, it comes in smaller chunks now as road crossings come more frequently. Also, you will spot more scattered houses, a campground, and big housing tracts crowding the edge of the swamp. The real coup comes below Rte. 571 as the path of the Toms converges with that of the Garden State Parkway. The road's dull roar will nullify some of the visual pleasure of this final and otherwise attractive stretch. And after N.J. Rte. 37, the forest yields to either marsh or open high ground, giving a clear view of the Parkway, power lines, office buildings, etc. Tidewater takes over only in the last mile. If you insist on paddling into town, there is a good take-out on the left, at the old railroad bridge about a hundred yards above Rte. 166. There is a launching ramp and a municipal parking lot here.

HAZARDS: As the river grows, the current becomes fast and strong enough to make strainers hazardous.

WATER CONDITIONS: On the average, the section starting at Don Connor Boulevard is up anytime from November through June. Generally, the section downstream of Rte. 547 is passable all year. In exceptionally dry years, even the lower reach may be too low in July, August, or September.

GAUGE: There is a staff gauge on the upstream end of the left pier of Rte. 547. Anything over 3.15 feet is enough to cruise anywhere downstream of Rte. 547. Zero for the upper river is unknown. There is a USGS gauging station about a hundred yards below Rte. 527. To reach it, park at the lot for the equestrian center, at the northwest end of the bridge. Cross the highway to a bicycle trail, follow the trail about 100 yards, and then take the first sandy footpath to the right. A level of 3.2 feet is adequate for anywhere below Whitesville. Zero is unknown.

Ridgeway Branch and Union Branch

INTRODUCTION: The Ridgeway and Union branches in series form a vile little tributary to Toms River and on the map appear as a deceptively significant-looking blue line that could be irresistible to the adventurous canoeist. Do not be deceived, as the author was. For this is the type of stream only a termite could love. It is enmeshed in the perfect sieve, whose intricate cellulose structure allows only water to pass through, not boaters. Some obstructed streams can be sawed into canoeability. This one would have to be nuked. But if you are still dumb enough to ignore good advice, this description is for you.

Section 1. Ocean County Vo-Tech School to mouth					
Gradient	Difficulty	Distance	Time	Scenery	Map
7	A	9.2	10.0	Very Good to Fair	32

TRIP DESCRIPTION: Ocean County Vocational Technical School is located three miles west of Rte. 547 on Rte. 571. If you continue west about a half mile past the school, you will find a sand road cutting back diagonally on your left. If you follow this a half mile, you will come to a nice, new wooden bridge and your put-in.

What follows is a beautiful, wild reach of cedar swamp. This place is particularly pleasant in late April when the streamside shrubbery puts on a handsome floral display. Sometimes the path through here is reasonably straight and easy to negotiate. Sometimes fallen cedars make each inch forward a victory. But all succumbs to hopelessness somewhere inside the boundary of the Naval Air Station when suddenly your trusty channel spreads out and disappears into the shrubs. The author, upon finding himself totally stymied by this challenge, just got out on the right and portaged a quarter mile through a residential corner of the Naval Air Station (a detour of questionable legality) and launched again in a lovely pool formed by a seven-foot rubble dam. An easy portage is then followed by a nearly straight (obviously channelized), unobstructed run down to Rte. 547.

Things get no better below Rte. 547, only different. The channel braids, but never disperses. So while there is always a floatable route, deadfalls and brush will repeatedly interfere. You will need an accountant to keep track of all the times you must carry or lift over.

Ridgeway Boulevard marks the beginning of a plausible canoe path. The channel consolidates now and has gained more of the volume of flow necessary to flush out strainers. But there are, no doubt, still more obstructions than most people would care to deal with. As for aesthetic compensation, one enjoys the sense of isolation at first, but around N.J. Rte. 70, housing tracts begin to crowd the edge of the floodplain. Below Rte. 70, Ridgeway slows in the backwater of Pine Lake and merges with Union Branch. The upper reaches of this pond are pretty and natural. The lower reaches are lined by houses. Portage the dam responsible for this lake on the left.

The final passage to the Toms River, on Union Branch, is actually easy. It suffers, unfortunately, from development and massive littering. There is no access to the mouth, so continue down the Toms River 1.4 miles to Rte. 527.

HAZARDS: You must carry two dams, and if the level is high, strainers will become dangerous.

WATER CONDITIONS: The best time to catch this is between early November and early May, within a week of hard rain.

GAUGE: There are none. Roughly, the gauge on Toms River should be around 4.5 feet. Zero is unknown.

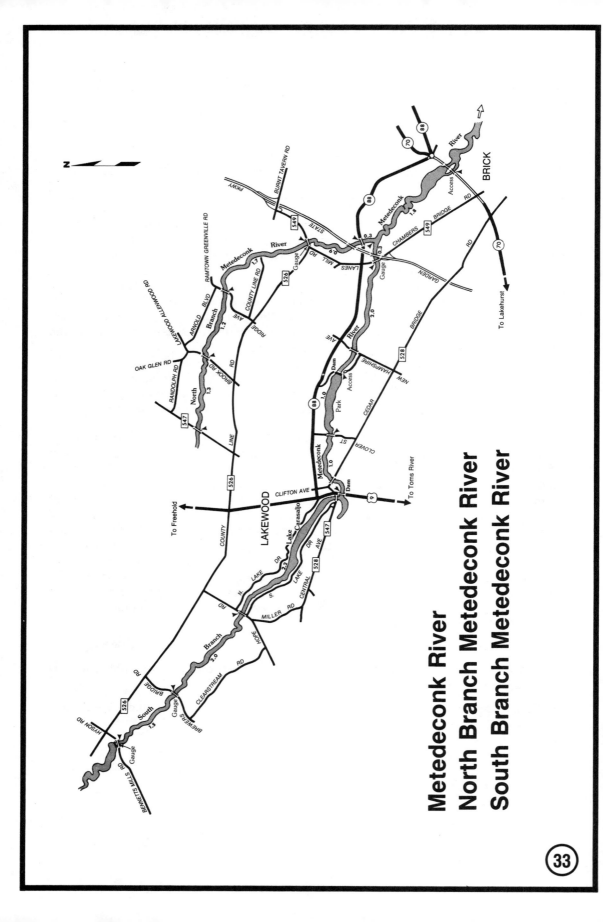

Metedeconk River
North Branch Metedeconk River
South Branch Metedeconk River

Metedeconk River and Branches

INTRODUCTION: The Metedeconk is mostly a brackish tidal estuary that branches off the extreme northern end of Barnegat Bay, at Point Pleasant. Possessing shores that are totally lined with houses, docks, marinas, and those Venice-like waterside developments with a canal in everybody's backyard, this would probably only be sought as a canoeing destination for one who lives along these waters. But luckily it also has a short nontidal stretch and two considerably longer branches that offer some good microstream paddling, or at least the potential for such. These streams have their origins on the northernmost fringe of what could be considered the Pine Barrens. But outside of their tannin-stained waters, they bear little resemblance to the streams of that area. With sprawling Lakewood filling much of the land in between them, they almost qualify as urban waterways. So their potential value as an island of open space grows with each new subdivision.

Section 1. North Branch. Rte. 547 to mouth					
Gradient	Difficulty	Distance	Time	Scenery	Map
7	A to 1-	5.4	5.0	Fair to Good	33

TRIP DESCRIPTION: As this stream stands right now, it will appeal to few paddlers because its path is blocked by just too many deadfalls. Although obstructions decrease significantly with each mile downstream, we can only hope that some good Samaritans, wielding chain saws, will someday blaze a path through all that cellulose.

The North Branch offers some attractive and potentially enjoyable canoeing. Though houses are sometimes nearby, the stream usually stays well hidden in the woods. The surrounding ground is relatively high and dry, at least at normal water levels. Its forest seems to have been left alone for a long time, as there are many big, healthy-looking trees back there. The dark water carries you along swiftly and even accelerates through some riffles. These riffles usually run over gravel bars, but a rock garden beneath a railroad bridge and a small rubble weir provide some variety. There is no easy access to the mouth, so plan on combining this trip with the main stem (Section 3).

There are many more miles of North Branch above the suggested put-in. But do not even think about trying to canoe there, for the headwaters section makes the stretch just described look like the Mississippi River. The author was foolish enough to put in once at Aldrich Road, about six miles above Rte. 547. Several hours of battling through poison ivy, thorn bushes, logs, trash jams, low overhanging and interlocking branches, and vertical sapling filters advanced him more quickly to the brink of insanity than to the take-out. If there is a wet and wooded version of purgatory, it would look like the upper North Branch Metedeconk. It was the toughest swamp paddling that the author had ever undertaken. Stay away.

HAZARDS: Strainers

WATER CONDITIONS: Minimal levels generally prevail from early November through the middle of May. Good levels generally last for at least a week after a hard rain during that same season.

GAUGE: There is a staff gauge on the upstream face of the right abutment of Rte. 549 (difficult to read). You need at least 3.3 feet to totally avoid scraping in the shallowest riffles, but over most of this reach 3.0 feet would be enough.

Section 2. South Branch. Bennett Mill Road to mouth					
Gradient	Difficulty	Distance	Time	Scenery	Map
6	A to 1−	10.0	9.0	Good	33

TRIP DESCRIPTION: Overall, the South Branch is fraught with far fewer obstacles than the North Branch, but it still has its tough sections. So most paddlers will choose to do only select pieces of the following miles.

To the first bridge, Brewers Bridge Road, navigation is a struggle. Though the stream winds through an attractive, rolling, and wooded parcel of land, few will find it worth fighting through the clumps of dense overhanging vegetation and fallen trees. If you do it, bring a saw.

From Brewers Bridge Road to Hope Road, the challenge is more worthwhile. There are still many fallen trees, but they are usually clean logs that you can often slip under or bump over, or at least easily lift over. This is a pretty segment through old forest. Medium high sandy banks are carpeted with soft green moss or clothed in stands of mountain laurel. The clear water is shallow, passing over a sand and gravel bottom with frequent gravel riffles.

Below Hope Road, the South Branch meanders through a pretty swamp, which signals the beginning of Lake Carasaljo. The open waters of the lake lead you through Lakewood, which displays a handsome facade of well-kept houses and lake-side park land. Access is plentiful all along South Lake Drive. The dam is at U.S. Rte. 9, but you must follow the lake to the right to find the spillway, where the relatively long portage is on the right. Trying to cross Rte. 9 will be the most dangerous part of your trip.

The short stretch to Clover Road is often clogged by a mass of logs, fallen trees, and bushes. It is worth skipping except for an attractive bit of swamp near the end, which you could best enjoy by just paddling upstream from Clover Road.

Another lake starts at Clover Road. It stretches for about a mile, enveloped by a large county park. The pretty shores are mostly wooded. The lake is formed by a low dam that is easily portaged on the right, up and down steps put there for that purpose.

The remaining miles to the North Branch are easy because, thanks to the efforts of a local outfitter, most deadfalls have been sawed out. The water flows mostly smooth. Except for brief passages by an asphalt plant and a few buildings, this final section seems wild and remote. If you are only doing this last stretch, there is an official canoe launch area on the right bank about 50 yards below the dam. You reach it from the park entrance on New Hampshire Avenue. There is no access to the mouth, so continue down the main stem.

HAZARDS: There are lots of strainers. Stay away from the spillways of the two dams. Be careful crossing Rte. 9 if you have to portage the Lake Carasaljo Dam.

WATER CONDITIONS: There are usually adequate water levels from early November through the middle of May. In drier than average years, catch within two weeks of hard rain.

GAUGE: There are staff gauges on the downstream end of the pier of Bennetts Mill Road, on the downstream end of the right abutment of Brewers Bridge Road, and on the downstream end of the right abutment of Rte. 549. For paddling the part above Lake Carasaljo, you probably want at least 2.3 feet, 1.6 feet, and 4.2 feet respectively. Below the lake, probably any reading you see will be enough to float you.

Section 3. Main Stem. Confluence of North and South branches to N.J. Rte. 70					
Gradient	Difficulty	Distance	Time	Scenery	Map
0	A	1.8	1.0	Good	33

TRIP DESCRIPTION: This is a short, easy passage that would usually be the final part of a trip on one of the forks. Or, lacking a shuttle, you could just put in at Rte. 70 and paddle up to the forks and back. The first few bends of this reach remain a narrow stream, but they are free of any woody obstacles. There is still a current, but usually not too much to paddle against (if you started at Rte. 70). The rest is backwater of a long pond, which is really the head of the tidewater section. Groping through the head of the pond for the narrow and twisting channel can be tedious. But such shallows can be a good spot to find wading birds and other waterfowl. The preferred take-out is a roadside access on the upstream side of Rte.70 between the two little bridges that cross the river. Second choice, also on the upstream side of the highway, is approached by a steep and rutted road down from a store parking lot to the north side of the north bridge.

HAZARDS: There are none on the river. But pulling out from the take-out into busy Rte. 70 can be a thrill.

WATER CONDITIONS: There is always enough water to float here.

GAUGE: None

Manasquan River

INTRODUCTION: The Manasquan is a southern Monmouth County stream, starting just south of Freehold and flowing directly into the Atlantic via Manasquan Inlet, between Briele and Point Pleasant. Probably the best known part of this river is its estuary. Bisecting a densely populated strip city by the sea, the lower Manasquan has banks that are totally developed, bulkheaded, and bristling with marinas. It is a great place to moor your cabin cruiser or to depart for deep sea fishing or diving excursions, but not so great for canoeing or communing with nature. So this book concerns itself only with the diminutive, wild upper reaches.

Section 1. U.S. Rte. 9 to Allenwood Road					
Gradient	Difficulty	Distance	Time	Scenery	Map
6	A to 1—	12.6	6.0	Good	34

TRIP DESCRIPTION: You would think that if you had seen one Jersey Coastal Plain stream, you would have seen them all. But the Manasquan proves that this is not so. Unlike the Pine Barrens streams just to the south, the surrounding forest is of big hardwoods, not pine or cedar. The bordering land is usually high and dry, rather than swamp. And the land is composed of all sorts of soils and even rock, not just sand. The water runs clear or hazy, rather than tannin-stained. And the bottom sediments and snags are often lightly coated with a yellowish substance. This last characteristic, reminiscent of what one sees on acid coal mine drainage streams in Pennsylvania or West Virginia, is a similar chemical phenomenon, here caused by iron-bearing ground water and soils. It is a natural form of pollution, though no doubt exacerbated by earth-moving activities in the basin.

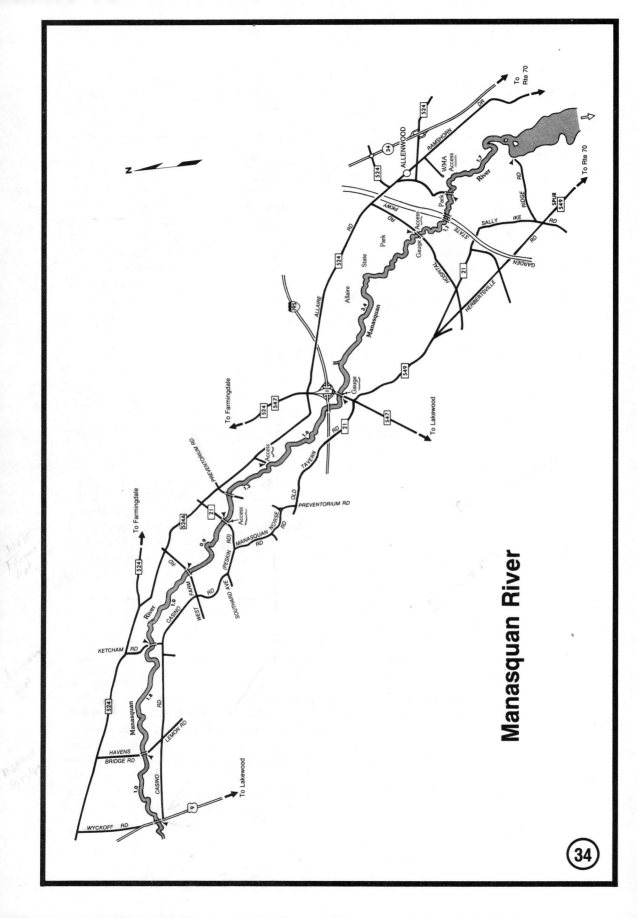

Manasquan River

To Rte 70

To Rte 70

524

ALLENWOOD

34

524

RAMSHORN DR

WMA
Access

River

RIDGE RD

1.7

Park

SALLY IKE RD

SPUR
549
RD

524
RD

PRKWY

Gauge
Access

STATE

21

GARDEN

1.1

HOSPITAL RD

549

Allaire

State

Park

HERBERTSVILLE

I95

ALLAIRE RD

Manasquan

3.4

To Farmingdale

524
547

Gauge

547

To Lakewood

To Lakewood

Access

1.4

OLD TAVERN RD

RD

21

PREVENTORIUM RD

1.3

PREVENTORIUM RD

524A

21

Access

MANASQUAN (PESKIN RD)
NORSE RD
RD

To Farmingdale

524

0.9

SOUTHARD AVE

River

RD

FARM RD

WEST RD

CASINO 1.0

KETCHAM RD

524

Manasquan

1.8

RD

LEMON RD

HAVENS
BRIDGE RD

CASINO

1.0

To Lakewood

9

WYCKOFF RD

N

34

In paddling the Manasquan, one typically looks at high mud banks. These banks are wooded, as is at least a narrow strip of land beyond. Along some reaches, the surrounding woodlands extend back for almost a mile, particularly in Allaire State Park, where a large, rich swamp forest stands preserved. An unusual exception to the continuous line of mud banks occurs above West Farm Road where the waters are lined by sloping, smooth walls of solid rock. Glistening from ground water seepage, at first glance they resemble the freshly exposed mud banks one sees along a tidal stream at low tide. But they are indeed solid (though slimy). As the miles go by, the surrounding land rises and assumes an increasingly rolling nature, yielding some high bluffs in the last few miles through Allaire. You will see a few houses in the first few miles below Rte. 9. After that, there are few structures other than bridges until just above Hospital Road, where you pass the intakes of a huge pumping station. This plant conveys water to a large reservoir built on a little tributary near Southard Avenue. This arrangement spared the Manasquan from being plugged by a major dam and allowed a larger reservoir at a higher elevation (good for distribution) than would otherwise be possible.

The Manasquan flows over a bottom of sand, gravel, and rock with enough gradient to regularly form simple riffles. Strainers present a more significant challenge. Though passages have been sawed through many an obstacle, you should still expect several portages evenly spread over the length of this section. There is a vertical, two-foot weir at the USGS gauge in the median strip of Rte. 547. It can form a strong reversal at high water, so most should carry this. There is another two-foot weir at the pumping station, but it has a usually safe chute in the middle. Tidewater begins around the Garden State Parkway.

There is still about a mile and a half of wild stream left below Allenwood Road. It first passes through dense, tangled woods, then through a marsh of tall phragmites reeds. This ends where the estuary suddenly broadens, and development starts in earnest.

Here are a few comments and suggestions on access to the Manasquan. Access at Rte. 547 is well hidden. The lanes diverge as the highway crosses over the creek and I-195. Between these two crossings is a little paved road connecting the northbound and southbound lanes. Turn into this road to reach the river's edge or an old Quaker cemetery. As for access at Allenwood Road, there is a large, tempting township park (Brice Park). But use of this park for boat launching or landing is prohibited. So use the old, abandoned bridge of Allenwood Road instead. As for paddling below Allenwood Road, your options are to go down and paddle back (not so bad), to ask to use one of the private marinas at the end of Ridge Road (anticipate a charge), or to paddle two additional miles down to N.J. Rte. 35. The old highway approach on the northwest side is probably functional. But ask permission.

Finally, if time allows, include a side trip to Allaire State Park. The park features another well-preserved old iron-making town, a steam railroad, and some nice trails on which to stretch your boat-worn legs.

HAZARDS: Anticipate strainers, and treat the gauging station weir at Rte. 547 with caution.

WATER CONDITIONS: Except in a really dry year, you can usually count on adequate levels for canoeing anytime from early November through late May. In a wet year, June is also often good, and any hard summer rain can often produce canoeable water levels for two or three days.

GAUGE: There is a USGS gauge in the median strip of Rte. 547, south side of the creek. It has two staffs, one above and one below the weir. The upper should be over 2.7 feet and the lower over 0.9 feet to avoid scraping in the shallowest riffles. There is a staff gauge on the downstream end of the left pier of Hospital Road. A level of 0.5 feet corresponds to the above readings for Rte. 547. For the creek below Hospital Road, you can float without difficulty as low as 0.2 feet.

It Ain't Easy Writing A Guidebook or
The Joy of Swamping

There may be glory in being an explorer, but it can also be humbling. For example, one thing that I could once proudly claim about my paddling career was that I had always finished any stream that I had started. Goodness knows it had been rough sometimes. There had been waterfalls and deadfalls, low water and high water, storms, too few hours of daylight for too many miles, and so on. Yet, no matter what obstacles Mother Nature or my own incompetence could hurl in my path, I had always reached my designated take-out — that is, until one lovely autumn day in the Pine Barrens.

It was a routine self-assignment. Go explore an off-the-beaten-path creek that one just never heard anybody talking about. So that morning I stood in the Wharton State Forest Visitor Center in Batsto with Roger Corbett, a fellow guidebook author and similarly compulsive explorer. Our meeting was purely by chance. Roger was running his own trip that day on one of the traditional local runs.

But he took time out to join me in studying an intriguing blue squiggle on the topographic map. It bore the name Sleeper Branch. Roger's attention, however, seemed to focus on the several dozen apparent side channels and extensive swath of swamp symbols that surrounded them. He just kept shaking his head and had the nerve to question whether I would ever find my way out of that wilderness. He agreed, nevertheless, to drive me and my trusty canoe to the put-in. I ignored his barrage of irreverent and pessimistic remarks, my confidence as solid as the Rock of Gibraltar.

At the U.S. Rte. 206 bridge, my intended put-in, we found what some people might regard as only a damp spot — an eight-foot-wide ribbon of clean, cool, tea-colored water burrowing into the glory of the autumn woods. "Oh boy," I thought, "Let me at it," while Roger was no doubt thinking, "My gosh, this guy's a lunatic."

Wasting little time, I eased my boat into the water. Soon strong, rhythmic strokes propelled the sleek craft into the unknown, about 40 feet, where I crashed into my first log. Lifting over that first log, I observed that one good stroke would get me to log number two. I heard Roger's car start and rumble down the highway. Lifting over log number two, I observed that it did not even pay to get back into the boat for log number three. And from there things seemed to rapidly deteriorate. I began wonder whether I was trying to paddle down the remains of an old corduroy road. I also (perish the thought) considered turning back. But I rationalized that I should not, because you cannot turn around a 13-foot boat on an eight-foot-wide stream, and because the surrounding impenetrable jungle precluded walking out. Besides, Mrs. Sawyer, my third-grade teacher, taught us that if one perseveres, then one will be rewarded.

Mrs. Sawyer sure knew what she was talking about, for a little bit farther, things finally opened up and canoeing was fun again. But success proved to be short-lived (about a half mile), as my pretty little stream pulled a stunt that I had never witnessed before. It completely vanished into the swamp. Now, not only were deadfalls a problem, but so were overhanging vegetation and densely packed live trees and shrubs that protruded right out of the water. There was just a plain absence of anywhere to go.

But, by golly, I was determined to fight onward.

Stream cruising now degenerated to the equivalent of puddle jumping as the water repeatedly emerged downstream of one barrier and then quickly disappeared into the next. One particularly frustrating instance occurred when, to advance any farther, I had to get out and shove my boat *over* an impenetrable clump of overhanging limbs that rose several feet above the water. This was a cow-jump-over-the-moon maneuver in which I shoved a little too hard and lost my grip. The boat lurched forward and upward, but not over and down. This left me standing there, on a slippery log, with my canoe stranded up in a tree. It took a lot of violent shaking — and my language may have wilted a few of the leaves on the tree — but I finally got the boat down and forged onward.

Time crept by slowly. Finally, as abruptly as it had disappeared, the channel materialized again, delivering me to a big cranberry bog, just carpeted with the plump, red fruit. I munched and pondered my situation, which, like those cranberries, seemed very sour.

Like an idiot, I decided to proceed onward.

Once again, I got my just reward as the stream disappeared into more tangles. After several hundred yards of trying to sniff out a channel, I saw light through the trees and just charged across the swamp to that light in the straightest line possible. This brought me to a good, well-watered channel, which carried me to a large, shallow lake — an old, flooded cranberry bog. Remembering this point from my morning studies of the topographic map, I now knew exactly how far I had progressed — one mile in three hours. I also remembered that there was a sand road from this pond out to the main highway. And with at least six more river miles to the finish, I knew that I should seriously consider making use of that road.

But, on the other hand, there was this really nice outlet from the pond, all deep, strongly flowing, and tempting, and, besides, Mrs. Sawyer would never approve of a quitter. So, again, onward I forged, and I was glad.

The going was relatively easy now as the stream meandered lazily through a big, beautiful marsh and open swamp. I passed a party of duck hunters (with a canoe), who assured me that it would be easy going for the rest of the way. But a little farther along, I spoke to a more cynical hunter who told me that I had better turn back now, because this river gets lost in a terrible, endless cedar swamp. I informed him that this conflicted with the other hunters' testimony. He was not impressed.

Sure enough, about a quarter of a mile downstream, Sleeper Branch vanished into a cedar swamp. It was at that time that I hatched my most brilliant strategy of this most brilliant trip. Dimly recollecting from my earlier map studies that about a mile to the east flowed the unquestionably navigable Mullica River (to which Sleeper Branch ultimately feeds), I decided that I could just switch to the easier stream. It was easy, I would simply drag straight through the swamp until I reached high ground and from there carry or drag across relatively open pine/oak forest to the Mullica. All that was my fantasy, and I was not even carrying a compass.

If you have never seen a cedar swamp, then you may not fully appreciate my predicament. A cedar swamp can best be described as a densely-packed cedar forest whose floor is not only flooded, but also thickly littered with fallen cedars that do not rot, but just get black and slimy. Now I do not like to get my feet wet in cool weather, much less sink up to my armpits in muck and slime. So to traverse this navigational nightmare, I was attempting to tiptoe and fox-trot across this giant, cellulose spiderweb while dragging my 50-pound canoe. Believe it or not, it took more than an hour of pushing and pulling, slipping and falling, and being cut, stabbed, and bludgeoned by this unforgiving obstacle course before it occurred to me, "this is stupid." Besides, I was getting lost. And so, summoning long-unused, primitive, reptilian homing instincts, I proceeded to fight my way back to the point where I had last enjoyed open waters and daylight. It took even longer to find my way back out of the swamp than it did to get lost. And having to backtrack past that one gloating hunter was almost more than I could bear.

Upon reaching the lake, I took up a position by another duck hunter and stood there shivering pathetically in the gathering dusk until, taking pity, he volunteered to give me and my canoe a ride back to my car, to complete my humiliating retreat.

So now you know why Sleeper Branch is absent from this scholarly text.

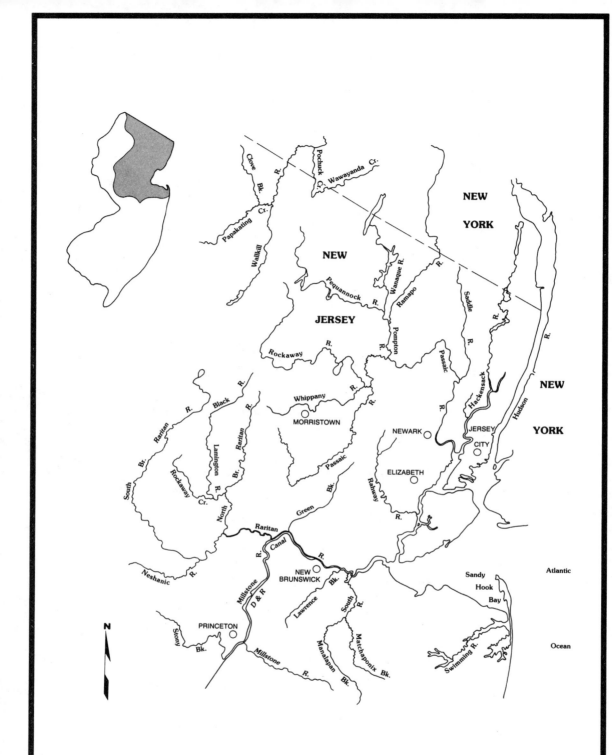

NEW YORK BAY DRAINAGE

Chapter 4
New York Bay Drainage

Strictly speaking, New York Bay is a vaguely defined water area just south of the Verrazano Narrows. I have stretched it to mean the collection of bays that make up the arrowhead-shaped indentation of the Atlantic behind a line from Sandy Hook to Long Island's Rockaway Point. One could most easily describe the bulk of this basin as the New Jersey portion of the New York metropolitan area. It reaches from the state's highest peak (High Point) to the sandy Atlantic seashore. It encompasses the stereotypical New Jersey that so many travelers only know — the refineries, tank farms, factories, The Turnpike, smells, noise, and incredible congestion. But it also includes the lesser-known side of North Jersey — the many beautiful towns, open rural areas, mountain ridges, and beautiful, sparkling rivers.

The greatest value of the paddling possibilities in this area is that they are nearby to many people. Most of the streams around here are not the sort of destination for which one travels great distances. But for the paddler who lives in the neighborhood, but has neither the time nor resources for a four-hour drive out to the hinterlands, there are plenty of opportunities for a nice day in the outdoors. They include traditional favorites like the Ramapo or South Branch Raritan. They also include rivers that deserve more attention thanks to recent improvements in water quality, such as the Passaic or Hudson. And they include backyard surprises like the Rahway or Saddle rivers. You can find plenty of little silver linings here.

The following waterways are described in this chapter:

Sandy Hook Bay and Atlantic Ocean
   Swimming River and Navesink River
   Raritan River
      South Branch Raritan River
         Neshanic River
      North Branch Raritan River
        Black and Lamington rivers
          Rockaway Creek
   Millstone River
      Stony Brook
   Green Brook
   Lawrence Brook
   South River
      Matchaponix Brook
      Manalapan Brook
  Rahway River

Passaic River
   Rockaway River
      Whippany River
   Pompton River
      Pequannock River
        Wanaque River
      Ramapo River
  Saddle River
Hackensack River
   Overpeck Creek
Hudson River
   Wallkill River
      Papakating Creek
        Clove Brook
      Wawayanda and Pochuck creeks

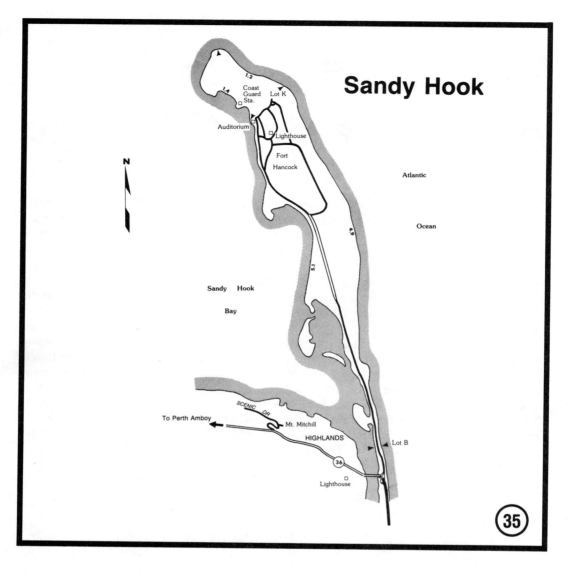

Sandy Hook

INTRODUCTION: Sandy Hook is not a waterway, but rather a spit of sand that juts out from the northeast corner of Monmouth County to define the southern entrance to New York Bay. On its west is Sandy Hook Bay and on its east is the Atlantic Ocean. The peninsula is part of Gateway National Recreation Area. Since it is surrounded by water, it is only reasonable that one way to enjoy it is by paddling along its shores. This is a particularly good destination for sea kayakers.

Section 1. Parking Lot B to Parking Lot B					
Gradient	Difficulty	Distance	Time	Scenery	Map
0	A	12.6	6.0	Good	35

TRIP DESCRIPTION: The suggested tour is essentially a circuit, starting at the southern end of the first parking lot inside the recreation area, where the peninsula is only about a hundred yards wide, and paddling up one side, around the point, and down the other. If this is too long a trip, you can make a one-way trip starting or finishing within a mile of the point. For this one-way trip, the bay side northernmost access is at the Auditorium in Fort Hancock and the ocean side northernmost access is via Parking Lot K.

What should really determine the direction of your itinerary are the tides and wind. This being really open water, wind can be a particular problem. The above trip time is based on a calm day and favorable tide. Adjust accordingly.

Taking this trip clockwise, you start in the shadow of Twin Lights. Built during the 1860's, this unusual landmark is now out of service, but it houses a museum and offers a beautiful view. Back to the water, the bay side of Sandy Hook is a bit different from other barrier islands, as there is relatively little in the way of marsh. Mostly you see barren or shrub-covered sand and some forest. This forest includes an impressive, old stand of holly trees, worth a visit to shore.

The upper half of the Hook is occupied by an old army base, Fort Hancock. Usually military bases are eyesores. But this facility, dating to the 19th century, displays an attractive collection of yellow brick buildings that almost add some elegance to this forlorn peninsula. These structures are visible from the water. So is the ancient octagonal lighthouse, dating back to 1764. This one is still in use, making it the oldest operating lighthouse in the country.

On past the Coast Guard Station and around a curving expanse of barren sand, you are now out in the Atlantic. To the north, the skyline of Manhattan and Brooklyn and the Verrazano Narrows Bridge rise boldly above the water. They seem much closer than they are, and it is impossible to distinguish which feature is closest to you. Directly to the east, about 4,000 miles, is the coast of Portugal. But you will probably only see blue water. And to your right, of course, is the old Hook. With a wide beach backed by low, grassy dunes, this second half of the tour is pleasantly monotonous. But having before you this endless ocean and, during the cold months, even an almost empty beach, can infuse a wonderful spirit of freedom in your soul, especially if you spend the rest of your time in the crowded city or suburbs.

Possibly the most interesting perspective on Sandy Hook can be had from above. If you cannot charter a plane, the next best choice is to drive up to the top of Mount Mitchill, a 250-foot-high bluff between Highlands and Atlantic Highlands. What you see is like looking at a map, but so much prettier.

HAZARDS: Wind is the biggest problem out here. A wrong tide, even in this open water, can add to your miseries. Unless it is a really calm day, a sea kayak is clearly the craft of choice.

WATER CONDITIONS: Low tide can limit your range in the shallow waters close to shore on the bay side.

GAUGE: None

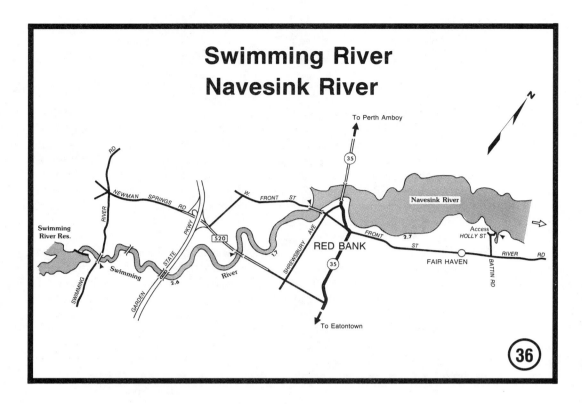

Swimming River
Navesink River

To Perth Amboy

35

NEWMAN SPRINGS RD

W FRONT ST

Navesink River

Swimming
River Res.

RIVER

PKWY

STATE

520

1.7

SHREWSBURY AVE

FRONT

2.7

ST

Access
HOLLY ST

Swimming

2.6

River

RED BANK

35

FAIR HAVEN

RIVER RD

BATTIN RD

GARDEN

SWIMMING

To Eatontown

36

Swimming River and
Navesink River

INTRODUCTION: These names describe the same body of water, the Swimming River being the Navesink above Red Bank. This is a short run featuring a small pocket of still relatively natural riverscape in the heart of the well-populated northeast corner of Monmouth County. The entire run is on tidewater, as the headwaters have been buried beneath a big water supply reservoir.

Section 1. Swimming River Road to Fair Haven (Holly Street)					
Gradient	Difficulty	Distance	Time	Scenery	Map
0	A	7.0	2.5	Fair to Good	36

TRIP DESCRIPTION: The trip begins just downstream of the Swimming River Reservoir Dam. For months at a time, this dam bottles up the entire freshwater flow from the watershed. And herein lies a problem. The absence of scouring action afforded by a perennial flow has left the upper estuary filled with silt and snags. Additionally, at low tide the put-in now lies a few feet above sea level, leaving you without any water to carry you over the stream bed's modest gradient. So it is important that you start this trip with a high, but falling, tide (unless you start at the other end). The high tide will save you from tedious dragging over logs and sand and gravel shoals. The falling tide is not only so that you have a favorable current, but also to assure you clearance through the relatively tight culvert tubes under the government railroad and beneath two low pipe crossings.

This is a surprisingly pretty reach as far as Rte. 520. The river follows broad loops past low, wooded bluffs and past widening marshes. The surrounding towns are initially screened out by those bluffs and trees, but ultimately the towns come into clear view. Most people would chose to end the trip at Front Street, where the river seriously begins to widen. There is no public access there, but the marina on the upstream left has a fee ramp and lots of parking.

Below Front Street, you are completely back in the city. The surrounding towns are pretty, well-kept, and old. Perched on high ground, they present an attractive waterfront, but all private. So the next easily used public access is an obscure ramp at the foot of Holly Street in Fair Haven.

HAZARDS: None. But the culverts and the two pipe crossings could be a hindrance at high tide.

WATER CONDITIONS: These waterways are canoeable year round (unless frozen). In spring, if the winter was wet, there may be enough outflow from the reservoir to provide passage from the put-in even at low tide.

GAUGE: None

Raritan River

INTRODUCTION: The Raritan is the largest river within New Jersey, draining about a thousand square miles of Monmouth, Middlesex, Mercer, Hunterdon, Somerset, Union, and Morris counties. This is a variable area that includes heavy industrial development, major transportation corridors, sprawling suburbs, plush estates, and working farms. You can observe all these facets while canoeing this basin, but only a little bit from paddling the Raritan proper. For this is a short river.

The Raritan forms at the confluence of the North and South branches just west of Somerville. It flows for only about 16 miles before slowing in tidewater at New Brunswick, and its estuary extends only 14 more miles before meeting Raritan Bay at Perth Amboy. Occupying a long-settled and long-exploited corridor, this is not a particularly outstanding or scenic canoe stream. But it is easy to navigate, often floatable, and convenient to many. It also, like its Millstone River tributary, combines well with the Delaware and Raritan Canal to make a simple, shuttle-free trip. So many will still find enjoyment in these waters.

Section 1. Confluence North and South branches to New Brunswick (Donaldson Park)					
Gradient	Difficulty	Distance	Time	Scenery	Map
3	A to 1	19.0	8.0	Fair	37

TRIP DESCRIPTION: This river will mainly be a target for paddlers who live nearby — just some easy outdoor retreat from the megalopolis on which to wet a blade. The river has its nice points. Its fairly high banks are usually wooded and are sometimes backed by big strips of undeveloped, forested bottomlands. You get some brief views of farm country at the start and even a little line of low shale cliffs (across from Duke Island Park). And some long strips of county park land also insulate you from the sea of civilization beyond. But civilization predominates. While

Raritan River

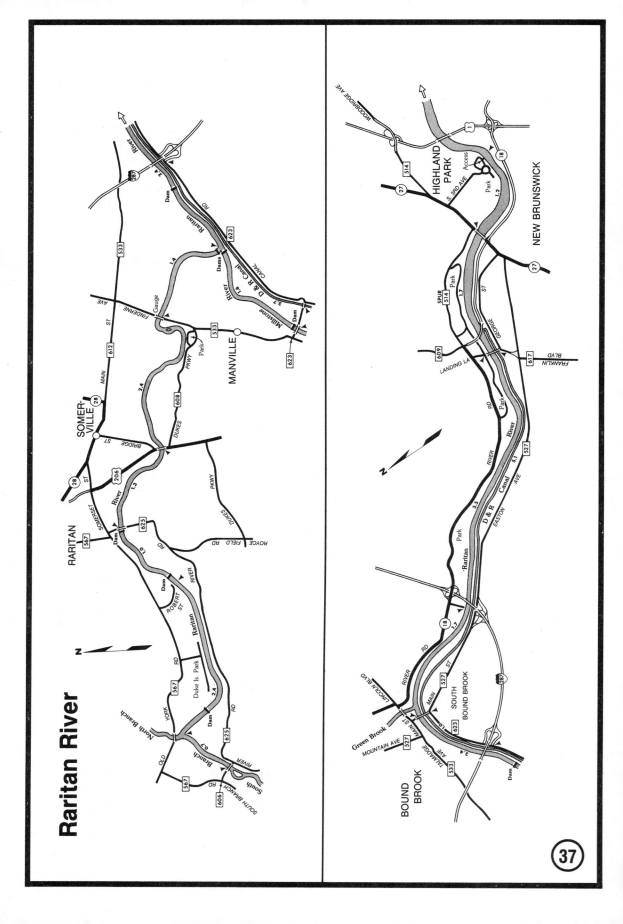

seldom crowding the banks, roads, railroads, radio towers, power lines, houses, and other buildings are usually a part of the scenery. There are also some huge factories, but they are usually set way back from the water and your field of vision. And it is difficult to ignore the drone of highway noise.

You can start just a few yards above the confluence on the North Branch at Rte. 567 (Old York Road). But it is a steep and muddy put-in. Provided one pays attention to the hazards, this is a good beginners' stream. The gentle gradient is expended over many tiny riffles and a few straightforward rapids. These riffles all wash out at more than minimal flows. The first problem spot is a five-foot weir about a half mile below the start, near the head of Duke Island Park. A carry on the right is easy. About three miles below the start, just below a small junkyard perched on the left bank, is a four-foot weir. A strong hydraulic and energy dissipator at its foot make this a death trap. The carry on the left is easy. A two-foot weir just above the bridge at the town of Raritan has a strong hydraulic. For the inexperienced, it may be difficult to spot. But nobody could miss the castle-like building rising above its left abutment. Carry the weir on the right. Next, just above the confluence with the Millstone River, comes a deceptive and hard-to-see one-foot weir or pipe crossing with a powerful hydraulic. Once again, this is difficult to spot and could be dangerous. Carry on either side. About a quarter mile above the first I-287 bridge (look for a yellow pump house on the left bank), you come upon an 18-inch weir. Once again this has a strong hydraulic, and you should carry it (right side). The last potential concern might be the remains of Fieldville Dam, just above the second I-287 bridge. This wooden structure is mostly washed away now on the left, but a low, remaining chunk on the right might form a nasty hole at higher levels. After that, it is clear paddling to and through New Brunswick. Tidewater starts roughly at the N.J. Rte. 18 bridge. There is plenty of park land on the left on which to end your trip, but a boat ramp at Donaldson County Park, within sight of U.S. Rte. 1, makes the easiest take-out. This park is reached via South 3rd Avenue in Highland Park.

HAZARDS: All of the intact weirs mentioned above are extremely dangerous. Do not be deceived by their modest height. Because they usually drop into pools, their reversals have exceptional holding power for such debris as boats and bodies.

WATER CONDITIONS: In an average year, one can usually find at least minimal (that is, no scraping necessary) levels year-round. If the weather has been noticeably dry, the river will probably be too low from mid-July through October.

GAUGE: There is a USGS gauge at Rte. 533 (Finderne Avenue), downstream side, left end. Most people would consider 4.1 feet to be minimal but adequate. But with all the long pools, depending on how much scraping you are willing to put up with, you can probably get down as low as 3.9 feet. The bottom of the staff ends at 6.8 feet, so bring along a tape measure.

South Branch Raritan River

INTRODUCTION: The South Branch is a long-time, crowd-pleasing canoe stream with portions that will delight the advanced, novice, and beginner paddler. Its source is the outflow from Budd Lake, a glacial remnant located a few miles northeast of Hackettstown. Flowing out of Morris County, down the middle of Hunterdon County, and along the western edge of Somerset County, the South Branch ties together a series of exceptionally beautiful villages and traverses

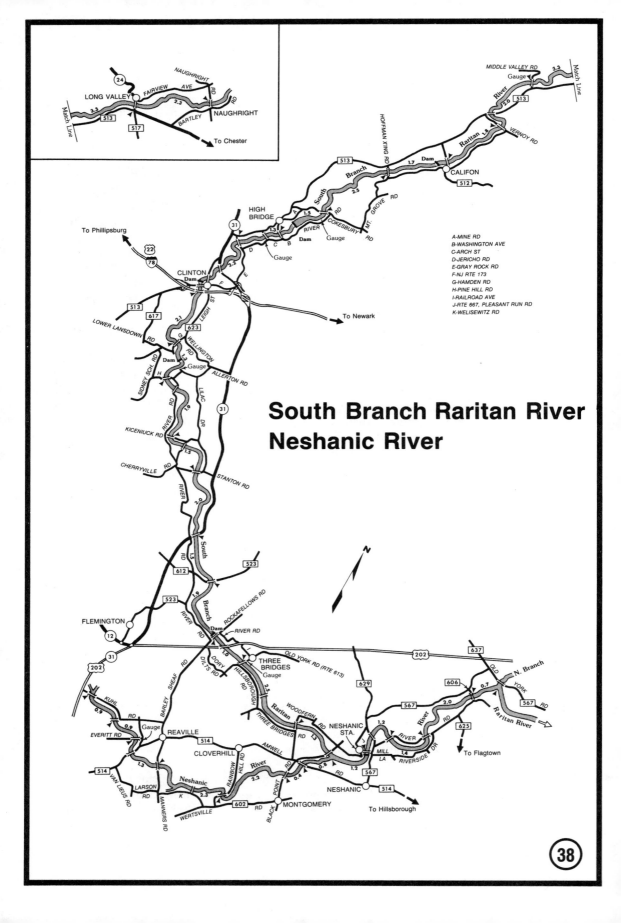

South Branch Raritan River
Neshanic River

Inset (top left):
24
NAUGHRIGHT RD
FAIRVIEW AVE
LONG VALLEY
2.3
3.3
513
517
BARTLEY RD
NAUGHRIGHT
Match Line
To Chester

Main map labels:

MIDDLE VALLEY RD
Gauge
3.3
513
River
2.0
513
Raritan 1.8
VERNOY RD
HOFFMAN X'ING RD
513
1.7
Dam
CALIFON
512
South
Branch
2.5
MT. GROVE RD
GROVE RD

To Phillipsburg
31
HIGH BRIDGE
A
1.5
COKESBURY RD
RIVER
B
1.3
C
B
Dam
Gauge
22
78
D
Gauge
CLINTON
Dam
2.2
E
F
To Newark

513
617
2.1
LEIGH ST
623
LOWER LANSDOWN RD
G
WELLINGTON RD
1.3
Dam
Gauge
ALLERTON RD
SIDNEY SCH. RD
H
RIVER
1.9
LILAC DR
31
KICENIUCK RD
CHERRYVILLE RD
1.5
RIVER
STANTON RD
2.0

South
RD
1.3
612
523
523
Branch
RIVER
1.9
FLEMINGTON
12
31
202
ROCKAFELLOWS RD
Dam
RIVER RD
1.0
THREE BRIDGES
OLD YORK RD (RTE 613)
202
637
Gauge
629
606
0.7
OLD YORK RD
N. Branch
567
KUHL RD
0.9
0.9
Gauge
EVERITT RD
REAVILLE
514
CLOVERHILL
567
2.0
River
RD
625
Raritan River
To Flagtown
BARLEY SHEAF RD
DILTS RD
DORY RD
HILLSBOROUGH RD
2.5
Raritan
WOODFERN RD
1.3
NESHANIC STA.
J
1.2
RIVER
1.4
MILL LA
RIVERSIDE DR
AMWELL RD
514
RAINBOW HILL RD
1.3
Neshanic
K
River
2.2
BLACK POINT RD
0.8
0.4
567
1.2
NESHANIC
514
VAN LIEUS RD
LARSON RD
MANNERS RD
2.3
WERTSVILLE RD
602
MONTGOMERY
To Hillsborough

A-MINE RD
B-WASHINGTON AVE
C-ARCH ST
D-JERICHO RD
E-GRAY ROCK RD
F-NJ RTE 173
G-HAMDEN RD
H-PINE HILL RD
I-RAILROAD AVE
J-RTE 667, PLEASANT RUN RD
K-WELISEWITZ RD

38

a most variable topography. Though located on the frontier of suburbia, most of this stream offers little evidence of such. This is the kind of stream that was just made to be enjoyed.

Section 1. *Naughright Road to Hoffman Crossing Road*					
Gradient	Difficulty	Distance	Time	Scenery	Map
9	A to 1 +	11.1	3.5	Good	38

TRIP DESCRIPTION: This first section of the South Branch is a good novice run. It has enough gradient to offer a healthy allotment of riffles and easy rapids. The drops are usually short and forgiving. Sometimes, they are the ruins of old mill dams, and sometimes, little rock weirs built to enhance the fishing. Particularly interesting are the drop over a crumbling weir less than a quarter mile below the start and some debris-cluttered ruins about a half mile above Main Street in Califon. While the rapids are forgiving, remember that this is a small stream, especially in the first few miles. So plan for some challenge from swift water on brushy bends, some braided passages, and occasional strainers.

The scenery up here is pleasant, but not outstanding. Along the first several miles, a low, wooded mountain follows on the right, but it only has a low-key presence when viewed from the river angle. The valley is rolling and still largely agricultural. A highway follows closely along much of the first several miles. But whenever the stream loops away from the road, the landscape seems passably remote. The frequent proximity of the highway, incidentally, makes this part of the South Branch an extremely popular trout stream. So expect company at least on the banks and in the shallows.

As for the towns, Long Valley is a pretty village, and Califon is straight out of a New England calendar scene, especially with its duck and goose-filled millpond. The latter town is also kind enough to display its best side to the river. Below Califon, the left bank is entirely residential. So that stretch may better serve as a warm-up for doing Section 2 than a conclusion to this section.

HAZARDS: There is a dam at the end of the pond in Califon. Carry on the right. There may be some strainers, or at least some brushy/thorny bends. If you come within two weeks of trout stocking time, add a few cranky fishermen to your troubles.

WATER CONDITIONS: This section is most often runnable in late fall, winter, and spring. If the weather has been dry, it may stay up for about two days after a hard rain. But following a wet spell, it can remain runnable for as long as a week.

GAUGE: There is a staff gauge on the left abutment of the Middle Valley Road bridge. A level of 2.5 feet is about as low as you want to run this. The USGS gauge on Section 2 (visit gauge or call Philadelphia) should be at least 6.5 feet.

Section 2. *Hoffman Crossing Road to High Bridge (Washington Avenue)*					
Gradient	Difficulty	Distance	Time	Scenery	Map
56*	A to 3 +	4.0	2.0	Good to	38
*for 2.5 mi.				Very Good	

TRIP DESCRIPTION: Short though it may be, this is some of Jersey's best whitewater. And it is in a wonderful setting, too. Upon leaving Hoffmans, the South Branch files into the deep and forested recess of the Ken Lockwood Gorge. For the next two and a half miles, the clear waters tumble down a boulder-strewn bed to form almost continuous whitewater. The boulders are seldom large enough to impede visibility, but even so, at moderate levels they challenge you by forming a tortuous course that will keep you busy. Anticipate one or two strainers lodged in here. And with such fast water, they could be particularly hazardous. Most of the gorge is preserved in a state fish and wildlife management area, and this is wild except for a wretched excuse for a dirt road that follows the left bank. The access afforded by this road means plenty of anglers sharing the river throughout the year, not just after stocking.

The whitewater ends less than a half mile below Cokesbury Road. This point is past the last public land, unfortunately, and some paddlers have experienced access difficulties here. So, especially during the height of trout season when landowners are already stirred up by the invasion of fishermen, continue on down to Washington Avenue where a town park protects the right bank. This final stretch leads you across Lake Solitude, a shallow pond that is about a half mile long. With a marshy beginning and hilly, mostly undeveloped surroundings, this is a pretty reach. And if you consider all flatwater odious, just look upon this as an opportunity to recount with your friends the highlights of your upstream adventures. The lake is formed by a 25-foot dam with an easy but steep carry on the left. Washington Avenue soon follows.

HAZARDS: This is still a small stream, so watch for strainers. There is a big dam at the end of Lake Solitude. With so many fishermen, expect a few cranky ones (and please avoid fueling the animosity).

WATER CONDITIONS: This takes just a little bit more water to run than Section 1. But frequency and longevity of runnable flows are about the same as for Section 1.

GAUGE: There is a USGS gauging station located 0.3 miles below Cokesbury Road on the left bank. You can call Philadelphia for a reading (identified as South Branch Raritan at High Bridge) or inspect on site (outside staff only goes down to 7.6 feet, so bring a tape measure). Consider 6.6 feet as a minimum level.

Section 3. High Bridge (Washington Avenue) to mouth					
Gradient	Difficulty	Distance	Time	Scenery	Map
6	A to 1 +	27.0	9.0	Fair to Good	38

TRIP DESCRIPTION: Having had its whitewater fling, the South Branch settles now into a peaceful path of steadily decreasing gradient. Fast and rocky at first, and slow and gentle by the end, this section belongs to the novice and even the beginner boater. There is plenty of beauty left in the rolling countryside, both natural and man-made. The stream will treat you well.

High Bridge is the high point of this section, as far as elevation, but the low point as far as scenery goes. It is a shame that such a pretty town, clinging to the hills above the right bank, displays to the paddler an unappealing facade of industry, drab homes, and commercial buildings. The South Branch shakes free of all this by Gray Rock Road, now flowing by mostly uncrowded, wooded banks and bottomland. Then it enters Clinton.

Clinton is a beautiful village that makes a living off being so. It once was a small industrial center but now is a tourist haven. Two of its beautiful, old mills remain, one of which is now a museum of 18th- and 19th-century life, the other an arts center. Add to this a milldam, a pond full of waterfowl, a park, Main Street's distinctive yellow iron truss bridge, and the old buildings of the town, and you have a spot that begs some of your time to linger. The passage through the town is on a millpond, and the view is pleasant. Carry the eight-foot dam on the left.

Below Clinton, the river widens. It is often shallow and its many riffles are usually short, dropping over cobble bars. The view is initially confined by bottomland jungles of multiflora and saplings, though these do not hide a sprawling housing development on the left. Shortly below I-78, the river flows into a big pond, perhaps an old mining site. Bear left with the current to stay with the stream, though a side trip on the pond may reward you with some good waterfowling. Low banks and fewer streamside thickets reveal an ever prettier countryside. The area is largely pastoral, often occupied by horse farms. It is both hilly and flat. Those houses that are visible are often deluxe. There are also swaths of bottomland woods, often protected by a series of county preserves. You will also see some rock scenery along here. One particularly pretty spot lies below Hamden where low, red cliffs bearing a lush cover of ferns line the right side. The huge New Jersey Water Supply Authority's pumping station at Hamden eventually interrupts the serenity. The plant pulls water out of the South Branch (it has a pumping capacity of 100 million gallons a day) and stores that water up in Round Valley Reservoir. Watch out for a diagonal, sharp, and difficult-to-see three-foot weir at the station. Carry on the right.

This section of river describes a big arc. As the river swings east past Flemington, the immediate valley widens and flattens. The low banks display more farms, woodlots, and only a little more residential development. The pools get longer down here, some of them formed by old weirs or their remains. The two-foot drop over the remains of a weir at Dart's Mills (just below Rte. 523) can be run almost anywhere now. At certain medium levels, this drop creates a fine surfing wave on its left. The weir at Holcombe Mills (about a mile downstream) is gone, but a good riffle remains. The three-and-a-half-foot weir at Rockafellows Mills (a mile farther) is still intact. Carry this. Finally, the old weir at Neshanic Station, by a beautiful old brown mill, is mostly washed out. Run anywhere towards its right side.

There is no good access right at the mouth. But a short paddle up the North Branch to Old York Road, or another mile down the Raritan to Duke Island Park will get you to reasonable take-outs.

HAZARDS: Weirs at Clinton, Hamden (pumping station), and Rockafellows Mills all require carries.

WATER CONDITIONS: Above Flemington, this is most often runnable in late fall, winter, and spring within a week of hard rain. Pumping station withdrawals could definitely eclipse this, but usually they occur around February and March, at high flows. Below Flemington, it is passable just about any time from late fall through midsummer, except after an extended dry period.

GAUGE: There is a staff gauge on the downstream side of the left abutment of Arch Street bridge in High Bridge. A level of 2.0 feet is the minimum to float between High Bridge and the Flemington area, or, if the Authority is pumping, this is the minimum for High Bridge to Hamden. There is a staff gauge on the downstream corner of the left abutment of the Hamden Road bridge site, just below the pumping station. It should read at least 1.2 feet for any paddling upstream of Flemington. These levels correspond roughly to 6.6 feet at the USGS gauge at High Bridge (call Philadelphia) if the Authority is not pulling out water. For the river below Flemington, the only staff gauge is on the left abutment of Rte. 613 at Three Bridges. Minimum is roughly 7.9 feet. There is also a USGS gauging station at Stanton. You can only call Philadelphia for its readings. For the section between the pumping station and Flemington, you want at least 3.3 feet. For below Flemington, you want roughly at least 2.7 feet.

North Branch Raritan River
Rockaway Creek
Lamington River
Black River

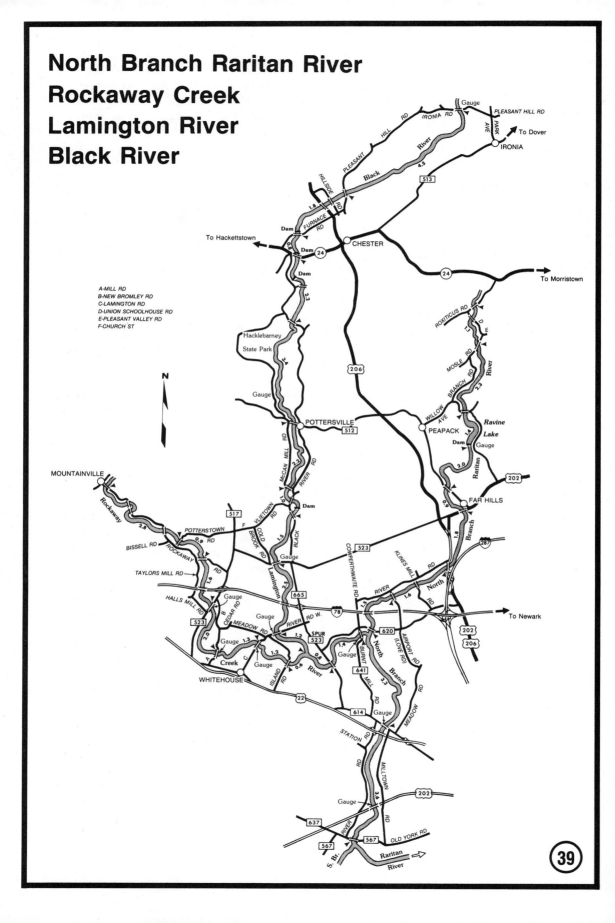

A-MILL RD
B-NEW BROMLEY RD
C-LAMINGTON RD
D-UNION SCHOOLHOUSE RD
E-PLEASANT VALLEY RD
F-CHURCH ST

Neshanic River

INTRODUCTION: The Neshanic is the only reasonably canoeable tributary of the South Branch Raritan. Like so many New Jersey streams, the title of "river" is hardly fitting. It is just a country brook, usually too low to float more than a stick. The countryside through which it passes remains largely unspoiled — a pleasant surprise for a spot so close to the edge of the megalopolis. Let us hope that it remains so, and hope for a hard rain this weekend so that we can go enjoy it.

Section 1. Kuhl Road to mouth					
Gradient	Difficulty	Distance	Time	Scenery	Map
6	A to 1	8.8	3.0	Good	38

TRIP DESCRIPTION: The Neshanic fills the prescription for one who is seeking a quiet, pleasant, no-frills day in the outdoors. While the valley is a beautiful remnant of rural New Jersey, the high mud banks of the creek allow you only a limited opportunity to admire it. Still, it is comforting to float down a river knowing that there are wide-open spaces beyond the confining walls of mud or vegetation. Usually there is a nice wooded strip just beyond these banks. And for variety, the stream hits up against forested hillsides and, down near the water level, some red siltstone outcrops.

The Neshanic is only about 12 feet wide at Kuhl Road. But significant tributaries continually pour in to bolster the volume. Throughout its length, there is little here to menace you at moderate levels. The water is usually smooth, and all riffles are simple. Even beginners should be able to handle this. This being cattle country, however, watch out for one or two barbed wire fences. And maybe a downed tree may block your path. But neither situation is common.

The confluence with the South Branch is only a few feet from the road, but a steep and muddy bank makes disembarking difficult. A better idea would be to continue down the South Branch Raritan a little over a mile to Neshanic Station where there are gentler banks and lots of parking.

HAZARDS: Be alert for possible fences and trees.

WATER CONDITIONS: Runnable late fall, winter (if not frozen), and spring within two days of hard rain.

GAUGE: The is a USGS gauging station at Everitt Road. The staff is attached to the downstream side of the left abutment of the bridge. Zero level would be approximately 3.0 feet.

North Branch Raritan River

INTRODUCTION: The North Branch starts up in the rugged hill country west of Morristown. Much of its watershed is regarded as a prime residential neighborhood, and much is divided into great estates, some with chateau-like mansions. This is horse and hunt country. In between the opulence are spotless little villages, old houses, and even a few working farms.

It is really pleasant paddling through this land of conspicuous consumption. There is little litter, it is quiet, it is uncrowded, and there are even few fishermen. You will find it quite a contrast to the gritty work-a-day Raritan main stem.

Section 1. Roxiticus Road to Lamington River					
Gradient	Difficulty	Distance	Time	Scenery	Map
21	A to 2	12.8	4.5	Good	39
1 mi. @ 44					

TRIP DESCRIPTION: Especially above Far Hills, the North Branch is but the tiniest of brooks, and you will be fortunate to catch it with enough water to float your canoe. The creek starts with a bang. After bending around the back of a pasture, it leaps a crumbling four-foot weir (run on the left) and then rushes down the cool, green corridor of a hemlock-filled ravine. It is a beautiful reach, but the steep gradient and rocky bed will command most of your attention. The ravine then opens to a rolling valley graced with attractive old houses and farms. The stream speeds on through rock gardens and splashes over two little weirs, but drops at a milder rate than that first half mile. It does not pause until reaching the backwaters of Ravine Lake. High, wooded hills hem this short, beautiful man-made pool. A 30-foot dam is the reason for the lake, and it has an easy but steep portage on the left. After the dam, the North Branch snakes through rolling hills occupied by manicured grounds of estates and by horse farms. A gradually diminishing gradient allows you to do much more sightseeing now. And the welcome addition of Peapack Brook's flow provides more elbow room.

Once past Far Hills, the North Branch is a different river. It flows now in a fairly open valley. Its bed and floodplain are often made of loosely consolidated gravel and cobbles, so its banks are often medium high and steeply cut away. Such channels are often prone to having strainers, so be careful. The stream is much flatter through here, but there are still plenty of gravel riffles, and, above Klines Mill Road, you will find a runnable weir. The surroundings are usually woodlands, periodically broken by houses, usually very fancy ones. There is no access to the mouth, so you can take out at the last bridge, Rte. 620, or a hundred yards up the Lamington River at Burnt Mill (Rte. 641).

HAZARDS: Carry the dam at Ravine Lake. The weir just below the start is worth a look before attempting. Other little weirs might form bad holes at exceptionally high water. Strainers can be a problem throughout the run. Finally, this is probably a good stream to avoid in early trout season, not only because of fishermen, but also because of irate landowners who, in looking out for fishermen to chase away, might just vent their territoriality on you.

WATER CONDITIONS: The season is usually from November through the beginning of May. Runnable levels on the uppermost miles are a rare treat — usually happening just a few times a year. Catch within 24 hours of a hard rain. Below Far Hills, the water will stay up as much as a week after a hard rain.

GAUGE: The USGS gauging station at the crest of Ravine Lake Dam (call Philadelphia for "Far Hills Gauge" or inspect on site) should read at least 2.7 feet to start at Roxiticus Road, 2.5 feet to start at Ravine Lake, and 2.4 feet to start at Far Hills. Roughly, the staff gauge on the Lamington River at Burnt Mill should be 3.8 feet to start at the top and 3.5 feet to start at Far Hills.

Section 2. Lamington River to mouth					
Gradient	Difficulty	Distance	Time	Scenery	Map
5	A to 1–	6.8	2.0	Good	39

TRIP DESCRIPTION: The remainder of the North Branch is a beginner run, where smooth water is broken only now and then by riffles that are little more than a quickening of the current. This is a remarkably pretty retreat. In fact, the first few miles down to U.S. Rte. 22 seem absolutely remote, save for the distant drone of traffic on I-78 and I-287. Medium-high to low banks allow you to appreciate the open farmland, classic farm buildings, bottomland woods, and surprising absence of much development. Here and there little red shale cliffs add further variety. Take out on the left, up steep and slippery mud banks at Rte. 567 (Old York Road). This is just a few yards above the confluence with the South Branch.

HAZARDS: There is a runnable gauging station weir of about 18 inches just above U.S. Rte. 202. Carry if there is any doubt.

WATER CONDITIONS: Except during a prolonged dry spell, this section is usually passable from November through mid-May. Even in summer it is often up for a day or two after hard rain.

GAUGE: There is a UGSG gauging station near Raritan on the right bank about 130 yards above Rte. 202 (call Philadelphia). Roughly, 3.0 feet would be zero level. There is a USGS gauging station on the right bank at the Rte. 614 bridge. Its staff is attached to the right side of the center pier of that bridge. Roughly, 3.2 feet would be zero level. Or, even more roughly, the staff gauge on the Burnt Mill Road bridge over the Lamington, just above the confluence with the North Branch, should read over 3.2 feet as a minimum.

⎡ Black River and Lamington River ⎤

INTRODUCTION: These are two names for the same river. It is called the Black River until Pottersville, the Lamington River for the rest of the way. This stream's source is near that of the North Branch Raritan, just several miles west of Morristown. It has only a narrow watershed for much of its length, so it remains mostly just a brook. Yet packed into its modest length is some of Jersey's most exciting whitewater, some excellent novice cruising, and a beautiful swamp that is suitable for beginners. Easily accessible by two interstate highways, this should be on your mind when the next wet spell hits North Jersey.

Section 1. Ironia Pleasant Hill Road to N.J. Rte. 24					
Gradient	Difficulty	Distance	Time	Scenery	Map
1	A,1	7.1	3.0	Good	39

TRIP DESCRIPTION: The run starts just a few miles downstream of the Black's ambiguous source. What follows is a pleasant wetlands tour largely within the bounds of a state fish and wildlife management area. After one floats past the few houses at the start, a stretch of power line on the hillside to the left is the only interruption to this natural setting for many miles. The pond-like pause at the start quickly changes to a narrow, winding channel through weed-filled shallows set in a maple-studded marsh. This eventually evolves to a completely wooded swamp, though there are times when you cannot see the forest for the thickets of alder and other shrubs that crowd the channel. If you visit here in late spring or summer, ferns, water lilies, and arrowhead plants dominate the understory. Eventually the swamp gives way to a more sunlit route through marshes of grass and cattails. As the river's name implies, the water is dark from tannin leached from these sodden surroundings.

While this is mostly a flatwater run, showing up with both fastwater canoeing skills and swamp experience would make this trip more enjoyable. Often one has only a three-foot-wide channel to negotiate through the waterweeds. Sometimes that tiny channel splits, and the correct route can be difficult to determine. The wooded sections are generally unobstructed, and sometimes this can be attributed to someone's sawing effort. The current is usually sluggish until below Furnace Road. Still the tedious route can challenge you like a slalom at times. Low bridges at Hillside and Pleasant Hill roads will require carries at higher levels. Finally, just above Furnace Road, at the defunct railroad bridge, is an old weir with three or four sluices. The debris jam situation du jour determines which chute you can consider running.

Between Furnace Road and N.J. Rte. 24 the valley narrows as the stream turns south. Vegetation also crowds the stream more. There are a few fast natural chutes which, in running through corridors of overhanging alders, could rough up the inexperienced. The water slows again in a short pool behind a five-foot weir immediately above Rte. 24. Whether you are finishing here or portaging, take out on the left.

HAZARDS: There are strainers, though at moderate levels, they are more an inconvenience than a hazard. The sluice weir above Furnace Road has about a three-foot drop into still water. The sluice walls minimize the danger of being caught in its reversal. But beginners should still consider the short but strenuous carry. Carry the weir at Rte. 24.

WATER CONDITIONS: Except in a dry year, this is runnable almost any time between November and mid-May.

GAUGE: There is a USGS gauging station on the upstream left side of Ironia Pleasant Hill Road. The staff is in midstream, visible from the left bank. Minimum level is probably around 2.0 feet.

Section 2. N.J. Rte. 24 to Pottersville (Rte. 512)					
Gradient	Difficulty	Distance	Time	Scenery	Map
90	1 to 3, 4 +	5.6	3.5	Excellent	39

TRIP DESCRIPTION: This is a beautiful and exciting segment. Yet, for all of its aesthetic and whitewater compensations, it is a run that will appeal to relatively few paddlers. There are just too many portages and points of potential danger to provide a relaxing type of whitewater boating. The run starts off with a bang as the narrow waters tumble down a steep rapid that usually ends in a strainer or two. And be assured that there will be many more strainers to come. A short woodland pond follows, ending with a portage on the left around a five-foot weir. The Black then rushes along nicely at the bottom of the first of a series of ravines. Then abruptly the even gradient ends with a plunge over a six-foot ledge. The ledgy bed begins to create some particularly beautiful rock-bound and hemlock-framed scenery, interesting and complex chutes, and one notably long and steep staircase that will probably be impassable for all the strainers. Also plan on portages around an impassable concrete dam and a three-foot stairstep weir.

The passage through Hacklebarney State Park is mostly a reasonable rush down a bed of boulders and ledges, and at times, a slalom through a lot of anglers. This is one of the rare reaches of river where the fishermen actually flock to it in spite of having to walk a long way to get there. The gradient is fairly evenly distributed, but you may have to carry one steep drop whose narrow chutes are often clogged with debris.

Below the park, the Black settles into a relaxing stretch of continuous Class 2+ whitewater. One old three-foot weir has a nice chute through the breakout on the left. Otherwise this is a stretch that lulls one into thinking that all the excitement is over. Believe that if you want, but when you see some summer homes on your right, get out on the left and scout. For here the river twists around a blind curve and roars down a ledgy and difficult rapid (at least Class 4+). Shortly below that is another six-foot ledge. Then you truly can relax.

HAZARDS: Expect lots of strainers, and they are frequently lodged in some of the best whitewater. Watch for all of the four weirs or dams described above. Also, the rapids on this stretch offer many opportunities for nasty pins at low levels and nasty holes at high levels.

WATER CONDITIONS: The Black is most often up between November and May. Catch within two days of hard rain.

GAUGE: There is a UGSG gauging station 0.8 miles up Black River Road from Pottersville. A level of about 2.3 feet is minimal.

Section 3. Pottersville (Rte. 512) to mouth					
Gradient	Difficulty	Distance	Time	Scenery	Map
12	1— to 1+	10.9	3.0	Good	39

TRIP DESCRIPTION: The violence is all behind you now. And the name has changed. You are now on the Lamington River. Until the confluence with Rockaway Creek, the Lamington is not appreciably bigger than the tiny Black. But the surrounding country seems as if it has expanded, having opened up to an either flat or gently rolling terrain. There are no more closed-in ravines, but some red shale cliffs provide some relief. The stream winds through woods and a golf course, and past farms and scattered, plush homesteads. It is an uncrowded landscape. Finally, roads seldom follow the stream bank. As a result, the banks bear little litter.

The river provides an easy ride through this pleasant setting. There are lots of riffles, particularly in the first several miles, but with gradually lessening gradient. Only below Rockaway Creek are the pools very slow. Even though the stream is still small enough for trees to block it, there are usually few such problems. Watch out for a five-foot weir about three miles below Pottersville.

HAZARDS: Look for one weir and possible strainers.

WATER CONDITIONS: Best conditions occur from November through early May. Water sometimes stays up as long as a week after a hard rain.

GAUGE: There is quite a selection. There is a staff gauge on the upstream side of the left abutment of Rte. 523. It should read at least 1.7 feet. The staff gauge on the right abutment of River Road West, below I-78, should read at least 1.0 feet. The staff gauge on the upstream side of the right abutment of Burnt Mill bridge should read at least 3.5 feet to start at Pottersville and 3.3 feet to float below Rte. 523.

Rockaway Creek

INTRODUCTION: You will find this creek hidden away up in the northeast corner of Hunterdon County, near no place big or important. And 99 percent of the time, you will behold only a trickle of clear water seeking a tortuous route down a rock-strewn bed. For one does not catch this tiny creek at a runnable level very often or for very long. But if you can beat the odds, treat yourself to a ride down this exhilarating, little-known run.

Section 1. Mountainville to mouth

Gradient	Difficulty	Distance	Time	Scenery	Map
31*	1 to 3 +	10.4	3.5	Fair to Good	39

*Only an average. Range is from 100 fpm in first mile tapering to less than 8 fpm by end.

TRIP DESCRIPTION: Basically, the quality of the whitewater is inversely proportional to the quality of the scenery, with all of the good whitewater in the first few miles. Put in where Rockaway Road crosses at Mountainville. Flowing around the base of Hell Mountain, Rockaway tumbles down a narrow and bouldery bed to form continuous rapids. The gradient is uneven, thus creating some distinctly steep and blocked drops. Add to this a few fallen trees, some cables, and maybe even a fence, and you should find this a source of some excitement. In addition, this distracts you from the presence of a nearby road and chain of houses that scar what would otherwise be a beautiful ravine. The bouldery rapids gradually subside to gravelly riffles, but look forward to one final splash as the creek bounces over a rubble dam at the stone plant at McCreas Mills (Taylors Mill and Rockaway roads). After that, the creek seeks a more secluded, mostly woodland route. You will pass a few beautiful, deluxe houses and a dairy plant. Without the roar of the rapids now, you will never completely escape the noise from I-78. There is no access at the mouth, so continue down the Lamington almost a mile to Rte. 523 Spur.

HAZARDS: You will encounter various man-made and natural strainers.

WATER CONDITIONS: This is most often up from late fall through early May within 24 hours of a hard rain.

GAUGE: There is plenty of opportunity to assess conditions from Rockaway Road, but if you want gauges, there are also plenty. There are staff gauges on the right abutment, upstream end, of Rte. 523, on the middle of the right abutment of Mill Road, and on the upstream side of the right abutment of Lamington Road (associated with a USGS gauging station). Respectively, they should read over 3.8 feet, 2.5 feet, and 3.0 feet to run the difficult section, 3.3 feet, 2.1 feet, and 2.6 feet to start at McCreas Mills, and 3.2 feet, 2.0 feet, and 2.5 feet to paddle below the South Branch junction (just above Mill Road).

Millstone River

INTRODUCTION: The Millstone is a long-popular novice canoe stream that spans a great arc from western Monmouth County to the Raritan at Manville. This path is unusual in that it flows from the Coastal Plain onto the Piedmont, possibly the only stream on the east coast that does so. This is not to say the Millstone flows uphill. It just seems to have sought an inefficient route to reach the sea.

The Millstone is in Princeton's backyard and is convenient to paddlers from anywhere in the metropolitan corridor. It is not only convenient to reach, but also convenient to paddle. With nearly three quarters of its canoeable length paralleled by the Delaware and Raritan Canal, you need not ever deal with the complexities of organizing a car shuttle. Now that is freedom!

Section 1. Rte. 535 to Princeton (D & R Canal Aqueduct)					
Gradient	Difficulty	Distance	Time	Scenery	Map
4	A	7.5	3.0	Good to Fair	40

TRIP DESCRIPTION: This section could use a better start. For Rte. 535 is a poor put-in, with its inconvenient parking, fast traffic, and lack of shoulder. The next bridge upstream, Old Cranbury Road, is a much easier spot at which to park and launch. But if you start there, you will have to hack your way through the quarter mile of dense swamp that lies just above the confluence with Rocky Brook. Few will care to endure this struggle.

The upper Millstone is a fairly attractive place to paddle, but it could be better. It is mostly a wetland route — sometimes swamp, but usually marsh. We have, unfortunately, come here a few years too late. What once must have felt like a remote canoe trail, is now succumbing to the relentless sprawl of suburban Princeton. The houses that loom on the high ground just beyond are usually big and expensive. But built upon old farm fields, they stick out like a sore thumb. So you will have to focus on the foreground to appreciate this section. Hopefully the beauty of the marsh plants and some sighting of wildlife will justify your presence.

As for ease of navigation, it is just fine. Obstructions are unlikely, the current is slow, the channel is narrow, and only a few simple riffles break the otherwise smooth water.

The backwater of Lake Carnegie starts less than a mile above U.S. Rte. 1. The final third of a mile below Rte. 1 is uninteresting, but it gets you to a good take-out with ample parking at the D & R Canal Access by the north (right) end of the old aqueduct.

HAZARDS: None

WATER CONDITIONS: You can usually find enough water any time from November through late April.

GAUGE: There are staff gauges on Old Cranbury Road (downstream right abutment) and Millstone Road (left abutment, upstream). Respective levels of 1.4 feet and 3.7 feet are just fine. Zero is unknown, but is probably below 1.0 feet and 3.0 feet. The USGS gauge on Section 2 at Blackwells Mills (call Philadelphia) will probably be around 2.7 feet at the just mentioned good levels.

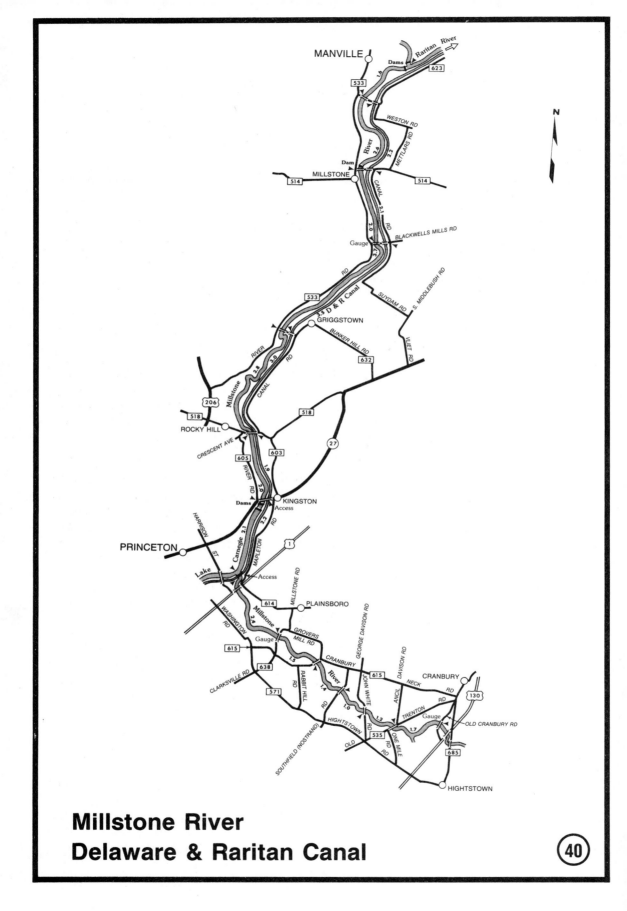

Millstone River
Delaware & Raritan Canal

(40)

Section 2. Princeton (D & R Canal Aqueduct) to mouth					
Gradient	Difficulty	Distance	Time	Scenery	Map
2	A to 1	17.8	7.0	Good	40

TRIP DESCRIPTION: This has long been a popular section — a fact no doubt influenced by its proximity to Princeton, its gentle nature, reliable water, and fairly good scenery. And with several miles of its banks protected by the Delaware & Raritan Canal State Park, we can hopefully look forward to this remaining a nice canoe stream even after development has engulfed the countryside.

A start on Lake Carnegie will not appeal to everybody. The lake, or more specifically the dam that creates it, was a gift from Andrew Carnegie to Princeton University. It is a moderately attractive body of water with the canal right-of-way on the right and attractive houses on the left. On a nice day, you will share this straight stretch with people piloting sailboats, rowing shells, and sailing windsurfers. Portage the dam on either side. The pool below is short, bringing you to another dam, this one associated with a beautiful, old mill. Carry on the right, and launch by the 200-year-old stone arch bridge. This is also a good spot to start your trip, if paddling lakes and portaging are not part of your idea of fun.

You are back on a creek now. It flows between high, wooded banks, meandering gently about a wide and usually wooded floodplain. Because of that width, the canal, which follows high ground, only occasionally runs close to the stream. This wide floodplain also gives the paddler the impression that the surrounding country is relatively flat. One notable exception is the passage by Rocky Hill, where there is indeed a high, rocky (but forested) hill. One other exception is a pretty little cliff by the village of Millstone. On the state park-protected stretch from Rocky Hill to Manville, you see only scattered houses, and they seldom crowd the river. There are only two seriously ugly spots on this run. The first is the rock quarry at Kingston. The other is at Manville, where the backside of the town clings to the high left bank. A few of the residents here are real pigs who have found the bank and river a convenient dumping ground for their garbage.

The Millstone is usually a forgiving stream. It has only a slight gradient and often flows narrow and deep. At moderate levels, the current is slow. There are few riffles, and these are mostly concentrated in the first few miles below Kingston. There is one easy rapid — a straightforward, bouncy chute through the remains of an old dam just below the bridge at Rocky Hill. Fallen trees may occasionally complicate the narrow passage as far as two miles below Rocky Hill where the inflow of Beden Brook widens the Millstone. You should be able to safely enjoy the plunge over the 18-inch weir at the USGS gauging station just below the bridge at Blackwells Mills. The first regular portage comes at Manville, Rte. 623, where there is a five-foot mill weir (easy carry on left). A more subtle danger lurks just a few yards above the confluence with the Raritan. There is a rounded, 18-inch weir or pipe crossing that forms a powerful hydraulic. A pump house on the right serves as an easy landmark. Carry this deceptive drop.

There is no convenient access at the mouth. But it is easy to carry up to the canal here or slightly downstream and paddle back up the canal a mile and a quarter to the canal access at Rte. 623. Or another option would be to continue down the Raritan about two and a half miles to the canal access at Five Mile Lock in South Bound Brook.

HAZARDS: There are weirs at the end of Lake Carnegie, at Kingston (N.J. Rte. 27), at Rte. 623, and just above the mouth. There should be a few strainers between Kingston and confluence Beden Brook.

WATER CONDITIONS: In an average year, you can find adequate water levels anytime from November through mid-May. Summer rains can provide canoeable flows for three or four days.

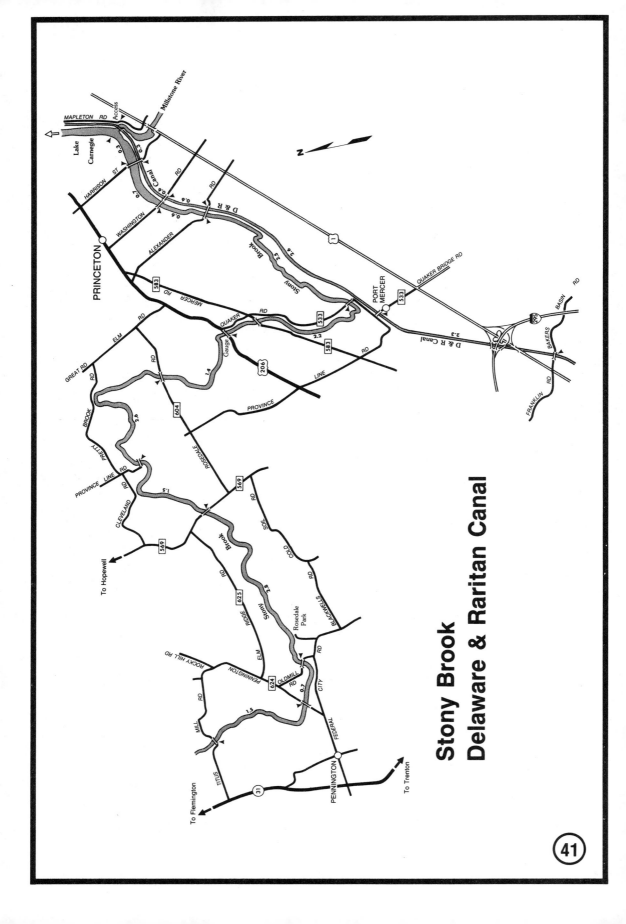

Stony Brook
Delaware & Raritan Canal

41

GAUGE: There is a USGS gauge at Blackwells Mills (call Philadelphia or inspect on site). The staff is attached to the downstream side of the left abutment of the bridge. The level should be at least 1.8 feet to clear the shallowest riffles.

Stony Brook

INTRODUCTION: Stony Brook is indeed just a brook. It follows an erratic path across the rolling countryside of northern Mercer County to join the Millstone River just east of Princeton. Some of this area is remnant rural in nature, though generally it has evolved into low-density, upscale residential real estate. But the stream has benefited by the demographics of the neighborhood, as many of its neighbors seem to regard Stony as a special asset that should be always protected. It appears that they have been good stewards. You will find it a worthy wet weather destination.

Section 1. Titus Mill Road to mouth					
Gradient	Difficulty	Distance	Time	Scenery	Map
5*	A to 1	16.8	5.5	Good	41
*1st 9 mi. @ 9					

TRIP DESCRIPTION: Certainly one of Stony Brook's qualities is its changeability. In its initial miles, it offers you some solitude. With many acres of the surrounding countryside bound within a wildlife management area, a park, and the Amoco Research Center, you see little development, other than when the creek brushes by Pennington. And further isolating you from the fairly level terrain beyond are medium-high mud banks and dense walls of wild multiflora rose. There are also pleasant patches of woods and here, as on most of the creek, there is remarkably little litter.

As the miles pass, the countryside becomes more rolling. Houses begin to appear. Sharecroppers' shacks by no means, their architectural diversity and often attractively landscaped grounds actually add to the appeal of this trip. After passing U.S. Rte. 206, the immediate surroundings flatten out. Some fields, but mostly woods, occupy the land. Judging by the tree size, some of these woods have stood uncut for a long time. The creek is confined by high mud banks, banks which do not subside until approaching the swampy head of Carnegie Lake. This upper lake is a bit smaller and more attractive than that section below the Millstone confluence. A good takeout is at the confluence of the Millstone, on the upstream side of its aqueduct, where there is a canal access area.

This is a simple but lively run. Averaging nearly 10 feet per mile in gradient as far as Rosedale Road, it provides a fast current and steady diet of riffles. The most exciting drops are formed by the rubbly remains of old milldams. There is one just above Old Mill Road, near Pennington, one just above Rte. 569 (right chute best at low water), and an especially rocky surprise between Rte. 583 and Quaker Road. Only one weir remains intact. Located by the USGS gauging station at Rte. 206, it has a chute down its center that should present no problems for you. Though you would expect otherwise, tree problems on Stony Brook are rare. The creek makes up for it, however, just upstream from the head of Carnegie Lake, where it is clogged by possibly the biggest logjam in New Jersey.

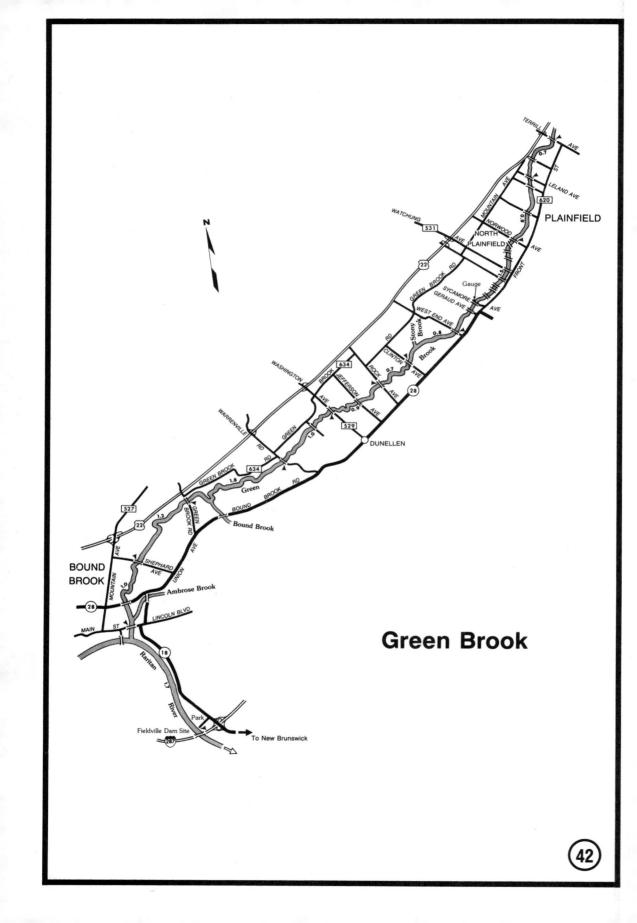

Green Brook

TERRILL AVE
0.7
LELAND AVE
620
PLAINFIELD
0.9
MOUNTAIN AVE
NORWOOD AVE
WATCHUNG
531
NORTH PLAINFIELD
FRONT AVE
22
GREEN BROOK RD
Gauge
SYCAMORE
GERAUD AVE
AVE
WEST END AVE
Stony Brook
0.8
Brook
RD
WASHINGTON
634
CLINTON AVE
0.7
28
JEFFERSON AVE
ROCK AVE
BROOK
AVE
WARRENVILLE RD
GREEN
0.9
AVE
529
1.0
DUNELLEN
GREEN BROOK RD
634
1.8
Green
BROOK RD
527
1.2
GREEN BROOK RD
BOUND BROOK
22
Bound Brook
MOUNTAIN AVE
UNION AVE
SHEPHARD AVE
1.0
BOUND BROOK
Ambrose Brook
28
LINCOLN BLVD
MAIN ST
18
Raritan
1.7
River
Park
Fieldville Dam Site
287
To New Brunswick

42

HAZARDS: No regular dangers, but new strainers in fast water are always a possibility. Be careful lifting over the logjam above Carnegie Lake. It presents an easy opportunity to break a leg.

WATER CONDITIONS: The best time to catch this is from November through early May within two days of hard rain.

GAUGE: There is a USGS gauging station at Rte. 206, by the downstream side of the right abutment. Its staff gauge should read at least 2.8 feet to clear the shallowest riffles. This is also enough to clear two of the three dam-ruin rapids mentioned above. To make it through the rapid at Pennington, you probably need at least 3.1 feet.

Green Brook

INTRODUCTION: Green Brook starts up on Watchung Mountain west of Springfield and flows southwestward and parallel to that ridge for a rendezvous with the Raritan at Bound Brook. We can only imagine that at one time, maybe four centuries ago, Green Brook was a clear rivulet gushing through the twilight of a primeval forest. Subsequent inundation by the tide of civilization has transformed much of that rivulet into an urban ditch. Abused here, neglected there, it seems as if streams like this only get attention when they flood. Still, if there is a little bit of wet weather, this stream is big enough to carry a canoe. And no doubt, some local paddlers may find enjoyment in navigating in, maybe literally, their backyard.

Section 1. Plainfield (Terrill Road) to mouth					
Gradient	Difficulty	Distance	Time	Scenery	Map
10*	A to 1	10.7	4.0	Ugly to Fair	42
*1st 3.5 mi. @ 22, rest @ 5					

TRIP DESCRIPTION: One might expect better of a stream flowing through a town as pretty as Plainfield. This town has been an established bedroom community since back in the 19th century when only the existence of a rail link to New York City could allow one the luxury of such long-distance commuting. So Plainfield is a town of big, old houses and neat, tree-shaded streets. But since the creek back in the early days was the center of industrial activity (hat-making was the big industry here) and no doubt a real sewer, the genteel town long ago turned its back on Green Brook. Today, the industry is gone and the water is only as bad as what washes off of the streets and lawns of the town. Hemmed in by high mud banks, over which cascade a relentless assault of old shopping carts, styrofoam, tires, etc., the creek snakes behind houses, apartments, and the backside of the downtown commercial district. It even tunnels briefly beneath a big building. This portion is endowed, however, with a good gradient, so that lots of little riffles may distract you from being depressed by the dismal surroundings.

Relief comes at Geraud Avenue where an attractive, orderly city park begins. Now joggers and strollers seem to displace litterers. Below the park, the brook acquires some elbow room. The neighborhoods recede from the edge of the creek to provide a comfortable buffer of wooded floodplain. Thus, at the leafy time of year, the paddler sees little of the surrounding community. In May the sight and fragrance of wild azalea further enhances the experience. Only the drone of nearby U.S. Rte. 22 and presence of residual trash discourages the illusion of remoteness. This section of the creek receives major tributaries, first Stony Brook, much later Ambrose and Bound

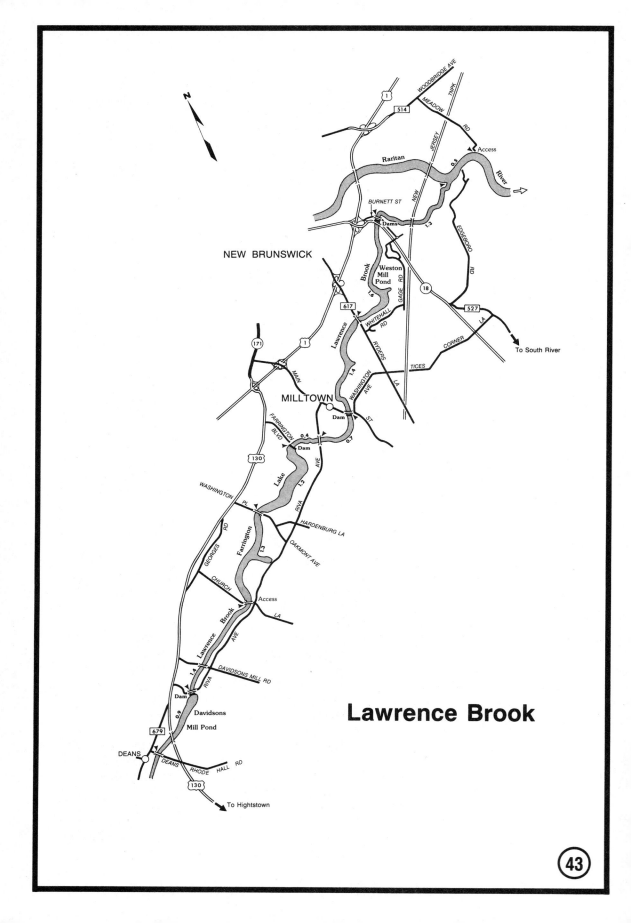

Lawrence Brook

43

brooks. So the stream widens and the gradient moderates considerably. The slower creek flows over a sand and gravel bottom with fewer riffles. An occasional deadfall may block your progress.

The last possible take-out before the Raritan is Main Street in Bound Brook. But finishing here would deny you the pleasure of bouncing down the only rapid on the creek. If you paddle down to the mouth, your choices are two. The longest, but easiest, is to float down the Raritan a mile and a half to I-287 and Fieldville Dam. A park road off of N.J. Rte. 18 goes to the dam site and right to the river bank. A closer but more strenuous option is to take out just below the mouth of Green Brook, at the left end of the railroad bridge over the Raritan, carry up to the tracks, and follow the grade to where it crosses River Road, a 200-yard walk. I recommend the first option.

HAZARDS: Possible strainers

WATER CONDITIONS: Catch this within several hours of a hard rain to start at Terrill Road and within a day of hard rain for that section below Stony Brook.

GAUGE: There is a USGS gauging station on the downstream left side of Sycamore Avenue in North Plainfield. The outside staff should read at least 0.9 feet to start at Terrill Road and 0.6 feet to paddle below the confluence with Stony Brook (roughly, Clinton Avenue).

Lawrence Brook

INTRODUCTION: Lawrence Brook is an insignificant tributary of the lower Raritan, nestled in an unpromising corridor between the New Jersey Turnpike and U.S. Rte. 1. So you may be surprised to learn that here lies an easy, reliable, and attractive canoe route. The explanation for this anomaly is a series of old milldams and water supply dams. They form a nearly continuous chain of pools — dependable water when all other creeks are just trickles. This is a good destination for some quiet paddling in northern Middlesex County.

Section 1. Deans Rhode Hall Road to mouth					
Gradient	Difficulty	Distance	Time	Scenery	Map
8*	A to 1—	10.2	5.0	Fair to Good	43
*above tidewater					

TRIP DESCRIPTION: The start is just outside of the pretty little crossroads of Deans, at the head of a pond. This is an old millpond whose now wooded shores are protected by a county park. Depending on the season, you may share these placid waters with large flocks of geese, ducks, or fishermen (or does one say schools of fishermen?). The carry around the dam is easy, but beware of fast traffic that barrels around the blind curve of Riva Avenue.

The head of the next pool, Farrington Lake, starts immediately below the spillway. It begins as a narrow, twisting passage past wooded hillsides, with the right bank protected as leafy park land as far as Davidsons Mill Road. Below this bridge, the shores diverge and more houses appear. But enough of a screen of trees and patches of undeveloped land remain to keep the setting pleasant. One of the many attributes of this lake is that the only power boats permitted here are those with silent electric motors. Of course, paddling a lake should be simple, but if for some reason the lake is drawn down several feet, the linked wooden piers of an old bridge can form a barrier just below Hardenburg Lane (Washington Place). But this would be a rare instance. The lake is formed by a 20-foot dam with a relatively easy carry on the right.

There is actually a short stretch of free-flowing stream below Farrington Lake. Unless you visit after a hard rain, you will most likely need to get out and drag over a few short gravel riffles and maybe lift over a fallen tree. This is a pretty, jungle-like passage that serves as a welcome change from the open waters of the lake. The creek curves around the backside of Milltown, but a dense screen of swamp shrubbery provides an effective layer of insulation. At this point you have entered another small pool. Be sure to check out the interesting and colorful collection of ducks, geese, swans, peacocks, and pheasants that the Milltown Rescue Squad maintains in some pens along the right bank just above Main Street. You will need to get out near here anyway, just a few yards downstream, to avoid a weir beneath the bridge.

The stretch below Milltown is particularly attractive. A short, twisting passage past wooded hillsides and bottoms evolves into swamp and then marsh as the creek eases into the next pool, this one named Weston Mill Pond. With wooded shores that bear little development, it provides pleasant touring. The lake unfortunately ends with two dams beneath and below N.J. Rte. 18. Carry the first on the left (easy) and the second on the right (more difficult).

Tidewater begins just below the second dam, at Burnett Street. If the tide is out, you may have to scrape over a few riffles at this bridge. This final segment has its merits. It starts with wooded banks and bluffs on both sides. In contrast with the natural stream corridor, the towering glass and glitter of a huge office/hotel complex, Tower Center, will almost shock the paddler rounding the first bend. Then, beyond the tower and the Turnpike, an attractive marshy fringe develops. One unusual sight here, along the side of the creek, are some outcrops of reddish shale that are similar to what one sees farther upstream on the Raritan. This is a rare characteristic for a coastal plain stream. You know that you are approaching the mouth when the marsh to the right gives way to the junk- and equipment-filled yard of a contractor. You know that you have reached the mouth when you paddle into the imposing hulk of a rusting, old ferryboat.

There is no access to the mouth, so you have three options. First, you can double back to Burnett Street. Burnett Street is reached by turning off Rte. 18 at the traffic light at Tower Center and then bearing left and downhill. The second option is to take out about a half mile down the Raritan on the left at the Edison Municipal Boat Basin, a fancy name for a forlorn-looking boat ramp located at the foot of Meadow Road. This adds a few more miles to the shuttle, but is fast and simple to reach. Finally, for the adventurous, you can reach the right bank of the Raritan, slightly upstream and opposite the Edison Boat Basin. To get here, turn off of Rte. 18 about three quarters of a mile south of the Turnpike onto Edgeboro Road (both Edgeboro and Rte. 527 intersect here). Follow Edgeboro 1.5 miles until the hardtop ends. Continue straight ahead following the good gravel road as it curves around a huge landfill mountain (there is a gate on this road, but it should be open). At 0.7 miles from the hardtop, look for a dirt side road on your left that goes steeply uphill. Follow this 0.3 miles and, voila, you are almost at the water's edge. This route is usable in a conventional two-wheel-drive vehicle.

HAZARDS: Five dams and weirs must all be portaged.

WATER CONDITIONS: Most of this is canoeable anytime, other than when frozen. The only way to avoid scraping just below Farrington Lake or at Burnett Street at low tide is to run within 48 hours of a hard rain.

GAUGE: None

South River and Its Forks

INTRODUCTION: The South River is a mostly tidal tributary of the Raritan, joining the big river about midway between New Brunswick and Perth Amboy. Over 200 years of civilization have been rough on the South and, aesthetically speaking, have pretty much worn the old river down. It will appeal to few paddlers.

The South is formed by the confluence of Matchaponix Brook and Manalapan Brook. These streams substitute generally rough going for generally better aesthetics. But all things considered, you probably would make better use of your time on just about any other stream.

Section 1. Matchaponix Brook. Mounts Mills (Rte. 527) to mouth					
Gradient	Difficulty	Distance	Time	Scenery	Map
8	A to 1–	7.4	6.0	Good	44

TRIP DESCRIPTION: A bunch of tiny creeks that start northeast of Freehold, Monmouth County, join together at Englishtown to form the Matchaponix. It is possible to put in where Rte. 527 crosses, by the flea-market grounds, about a mile north of Englishtown. But the ensuing stretch is incredibly trashy — the near equivalent to paddling down the center of a landfill. A fortunate character of trash, however, is that once past its source, the bulk of it snags on vegetation, sinks, silts in, or washes totally away. So if you start another mile north on Rte. 527, at Mounts Mills, inside Middlesex County, conditions vastly improve.

No doubt, the first thing that will catch your attention is the orange/yellow coating on the snags, roots, stream bed, and anything else the water touches. And the water may be colored a hazy green. If you have ever been to the coal fields of Pennsylvania or West Virginia, you will think that you are seeing acid drainage from coal mines. Or perhaps you will imagine some grimy, smoke-belching factory upstream disgorging its vile, toxic liquor into this innocent brook. But it is neither. The condition is of natural origin — the result of an iron-bearing soil formation and aquifer. When the dissolved iron compound is exposed to air, it drops out of solution to coat everything it touches. You will note its iron or sulfur odor. Though this is naturally occurring, the intensity has probably been exacerbated by agriculture, development, or any other soil-disturbing activities that cause exposure to the air. Anyhow, fear not, the stuff will not hurt you.

This is generally a pretty passage that feels more remote than it really is. Except approaching Spotswood, where it starts bumping up against suburbs, the creek wanders through a wide swath of woods, and beyond that, there are farms. These are nice woods too, with some big specimens of trees, particularly silvery groves of beech that cover the steeper slopes. A power line's persistent proximity is the only real disappointment. The stream twists a lot. It has a good gradient, and many little riffles are formed as it speeds over a bottom that varies from solid rock to clay to sand, and even to wood. Between Texas Road and Mundy Avenue (West Greystone Road), there is an 18-inch weir with a powerful hydraulic. It is runnable, but if you are inexperienced with such drops, it would generally be wise to carry. Needless to say, there are plenty of deadfalls on this stream — too many to be tolerated by most paddlers, but not nearly as bad as it could be. This stream would be well worth sawing out and preserving as a park.

HAZARDS: Treat the sharp concrete weir with caution. Strainers are a hazard when the water is high.

South River
Manalapan Brook
Matchaponix Brook

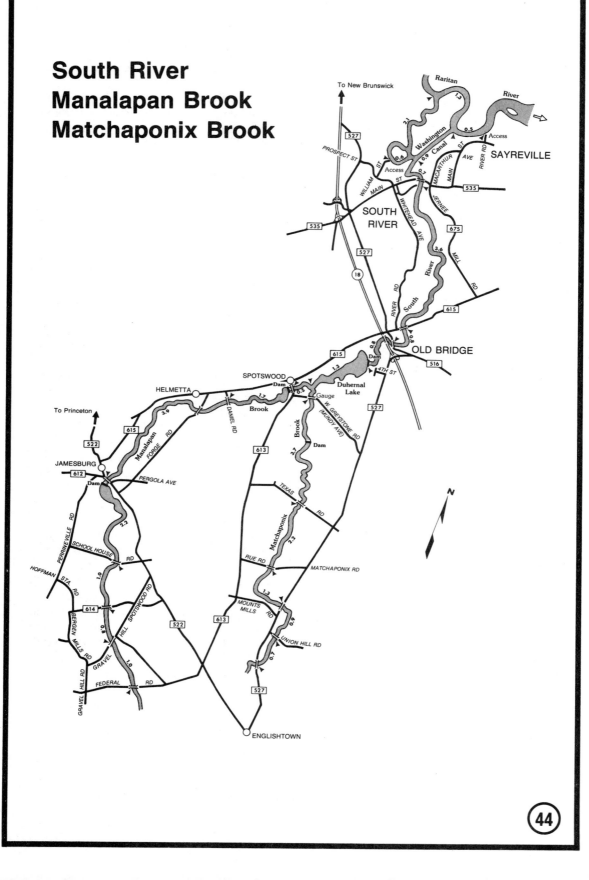

WATER CONDITIONS: Catch between November and early May, within a week of hard rain.

GAUGE: There is a staff gauge on the right abutment, upstream face, of Mundy Avenue (West Greystone Road if you are approaching from Rte. 527). Some riffles start getting too shallow at about 3.6 feet.

Section 2. Manalapan Brook. Federal Road to mouth					
Gradient	Difficulty	Distance	Time	Scenery	Map
6	A to 1−	11.1	10.0	Good to Poor	44

TRIP DESCRIPTION: Manalapan Brook (Native American for "good cultivation" or "good country") starts just a few miles south of Monmouth Battlefield, right next to the Matchaponix's headwaters. You can start paddling it at Federal Road, maybe even higher. As far as Rte. 614 (Hoffman Station Road), the creek has been channelized and straightened, but not recently. So its high mud banks are well vegetated and backed by thick forest. Marred by little litter and free of any significant development, this ditch is surprisingly pleasant to paddle. And best of all, this reach is usually devoid of tree problems. The current is swift, and there are even little riffles. Like the Matchaponix, the water and bottom show iron discoloration.

To Schoolhouse Road, the creek resumes a more natural path, but it continues to appear as if it was once dredged. Otherwise, the scenery is as good as above, and navigation should be almost free of impediments (or impaddlements).

Between Schoolhouse Road and the head of Jamesburg Pond, the channel is at last natural again, meandering through a swamp and bumping against some beechy hillsides. This is the prettiest reach of the Manalapan. Jamesburg Pond, in contrast, displays negligible beauty, in spite of its north shore being protected by a large county park. Carry this pond's dam on the right.

Below Jamesburg, Manalapan returns to the woods. This is a swampy reach that would be pretty, if it were a little farther from civilization. Jamesburg has dumped tons of trash into the stream, and the local youths periodically and generously supplement the load at some obviously popular, sylvan party spots.

Once past Helmetta, houses are usually visible, though the floodplain remains undeveloped. And the trash gets even worse. And to add injury to insult, you have to labor to expose yourself to this mess, for deadfalls plague the whole section from Jamesburg to De Voe Lake. So progress is a grind. Like Jamesburg Pond, De Voe lake is lackluster. Portage its dam on the left. This leaves a slow but fairly attractive final half mile to the mouth. At that point, you can either double back, ascend Matchaponix to Mundy Avenue (easy), or continue down the South River.

HAZARDS: They include two dams, lots of strainers, and the poison ivy that you may get from portaging or lifting over the latter.

WATER CONDITIONS: Manalapan is most often passable between November and early May, within five days of hard rain.

GAUGE: There are none on this stream. Roughly, the staff gauge on Mundy Avenue on the Matchaponix should read over 4.0 feet.

Section 3. South River. confluence of Matchaponix and Manalapan to mouth					
Gradient	Difficulty	Distance	Time	Scenery	Map
0	A to 1−	8.1 or 9.9	4 or 5	Poor	44

Rahway River

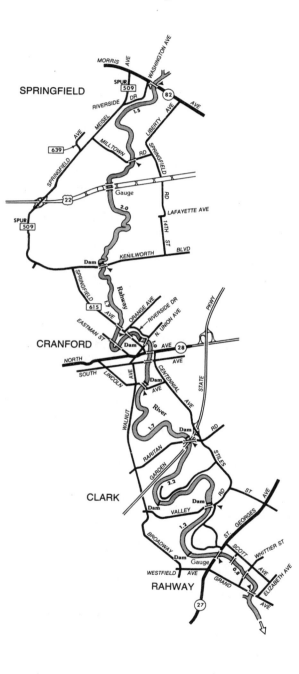

SPRINGFIELD

MORRIS AVE
WASHINGTON AVE
SPUR 509
82
RIVERSIDE DR
MEISEL AVE
1.5
LIBERTY AVE
AVE
639
SPRINGFIELD AVE
MILLTOWN RD
SPRINGFIELD RD
22
Gauge
2.0
LAFAYETTE AVE
SPUR 509
14TH ST
KENILWORTH BLVD
Dam
SPRINGFIELD AVE
Rahway
1.1
615
ORANGE AVE
RIVERSIDE DR
N. UNION AVE
PKWY
EASTMAN ST
CRANFORD
Dam
28
AVE
NORTH AVE
SOUTH
LINCOLN AVE
CENTENNIAL AVE
Dam
AVE
STATE
River
.7
Dam
RD
STILES
RARITAN
GARDEN
CLARK
2.2
ST
AVE
Dam
VALLEY
Dam
RD
ST. GEORGES
SCOTT AVE
WHITTIER ST
1.2
BROADWAY
Dam
Gauge
0.8
ELIZABETH AVE
WESTFIELD AVE
GRAND
RAHWAY
27

45

TRIP DESCRIPTION: The best place to start is at Mundy Avenue on the Matchaponix, there being no access at the confluence. This puts you at the head of Duhernal Lake, an uninteresting pond dominated by two big factories, one of which you may find very smelly. There is an easy portage around the dam on the right. Tidewater starts at the foot of the dam, but if the tide is low, you can enjoy a strong current and even riffles as far down as Rte. 615 (providing, of course, that there is enough flow over the dam). Conversely, keep in mind that if you come here with both low flow and a low tide, you will be dragging through these riffles and lifting over a horrible web of tangled timber that sits in the stream bed below the dam.

The scenery along most of the tidal South River is drab. Perched on the shores are grimy commercial structures, noisy sand and gravel operations, big industry, bulkheading, etc. On the other hand, more positive types might derive some satisfaction from the patch of woods below Duhernal Lake, the feathery phragmites reeds that populate the spoil-pile banks, and finally, the more extensive wetlands that survive below the town of South River. And no doubt, as the years go by, the man-made landfill mountains, that rise on the left and across the Raritan, will soften in appearance as more variable vegetation covers them.

This river has two mouths. It used to loop inefficiently to its confluence with the Raritan. So long ago they dug out a shortcut, the Washington Canal. You can probably take either route at high tide (the author has only tried the canal); hence the two distances and times specified above. But the main tidal flow surges through the canal, so that, at low tide, much of the old channel is just glistening mud. Keep this in mind if you planned on finishing at the nice boat ramp at Varga Memorial Park in South River. You just cannot reach it at low tide. There is no access at either of the mouths of the South, but a half mile down the Raritan from the mouth of the canal is a good public boat ramp at the end of River Road in Sayreville.

HAZARDS: Duhernal Dam can be a hazard, though there is no excuse, other than in a fog or at night, for someone washing over the spillway.

WATER CONDITIONS: This being mostly tidal, water levels are not a problem. But at low tide on the section from Duhernal Lake to Rte. 615, the best odds for adequate water come between November and early May, within a week of hard rain.

GAUGE: Use the staff gauge on the Mundy Avenue bridge over Matchaponix Brook. Probably any level is sufficient to get down to Duhernal Lake. But to traverse the section from the dam to Rte. 615 at low tide, a level of at least 3.7 feet is advisable.

Rahway River

INTRODUCTION: The Rahway River demonstrates that a river and a city can coexist in harmony. Its name is a corruption of the Lenni Lenape phrase for "middle of the forest," which is still descriptive of much of this waterway's place in the universe. Enveloped by a string of roomy city parks and neighborhoods that regard the Rahway as an asset, this brook (for it is a "river" in title only) will give canoeists in Union County a reason to celebrate the next time that it rains.

Section 1. Springfield (N.J. Rte. 82) to Rahway (Grand Avenue)					
Gradient	Difficulty	Distance	Time	Scenery	Map
6	A to 1	12.2	5.5	Good	45

TRIP DESCRIPTION: The two tiny forks of this stream join together to form the Rahway above Morris Avenue (Rte. 82). Because there is no place to stop along Morris Avenue, you should turn onto Washington Avenue, where you will find parking and easy access. At this point, you are in a city park, and parks will follow most of the Rahway all the way to Grand Avenue. After the developed area at the start, the park becomes a woodland preserve that gives no hint to the paddler of the endless suburbs that surround it. Following an initial stint in an altered channel, the stream returns to its natural bed with high mud banks that occasionally anchor some nasty strainers. The gradient is slight, with few riffles but good current. Just above Kenilworth Boulevard, the Rahway flows through a concrete flood control dam. This dam functions on the principle that, at high water, the orifice in the structure cannot convey the entire flow of the river. So the water then backs up onto empty park land, thus preventing flooding downstream.

As the Rahway enters Cranford, the park shrinks to a narrow green strip, and on some stretches the banks are private property. This is a beautiful, old neighborhood of well-cared-for houses and yards. Where private property abuts the river, the residents maintain the riverfront as nicely as they do the street side of their houses. If you have seen many rivers, then you know that this is a rare practice. Paddle through here in May, and the whole place is a garden.

The creek now changes to an almost continuous chain of pools behind old milldams. The first is a sloping drop of three and a half feet (Cranes Mill) just above North Union Avenue. It has a powerful reversal, so carry on the left. Next comes a four-and-a-half-foot weir just above Lincoln Avenue. You will easily recognize this by beautiful, old Droeschers Mill on the left. Once a blanket mill, it dates back to 1740. A pleasant passage through more park resumes, but is interrupted by the crossing of the Garden State Parkway. Beneath its span lurks the next weir. This is a troublesome spot because of a walled channel that permits no riverside portage. So land on the right, carry up to Raritan Road, and follow it left across the Parkway. At the east end of the bridge, you can descend to the water. The next mile follows the noisy Parkway and broadens into another pool. This ends with another weir. Carry on the left. A woodsy stretch leads you into another wide pool. The responsible weir is just above Valley Road, and again you can carry on the left. You cruise quickly past Clark, on the right, and Springfield, on the left, and enter another big chunk of park land. When you spot a water treatment plant on the right bank, get out on the left and carry a three-foot weir. That should be the last of your portages. Now in the town of Rahway, the creek drops over a little gauging station weir and down a nice series of riffles until slowing in tidewater at Grand Avenue.

The remaining miles of the Rahway are mostly uninteresting. The setting is filled with industry, noise, busy roads, and more crowded towns. Little natural quality remains.

HAZARDS: Seven of the dams or weirs described above require carries. Some strainers may block the upper creek.

WATER CONDITIONS: It does not take much water to run this creek, but then again, this creek seldom carries much water. Catch within 24 hours of a hard rain to do the whole creek. If you just desire a short paddle around some of the weir pools, you can come any time other than when they are frozen.

GAUGE: There are USGS gauging stations by the downstream left end of the eastbound lane of U.S. Rte. 22 and just above St. George Avenue, on the left. Outside staffs should read 1.7 feet and 2.1 feet respectively when you float by them. Because the water level fluctuates so rapidly in this urban watershed, the pre-run gauge reading should be at least a few tenths higher.

Passaic River

INTRODUCTION: The Passaic has the distinction of being the longest river entirely within New Jersey. From its head spring near the village of Mendham to its meeting with the Hackensack, where they form Newark Bay, it flows over 81 miles via the most erratic route imaginable. What is really amazing is that for most of this distance, it passes through an unbroken blob of city and suburb, home to 2.5 million people. The name Passaic is Native American for "peaceful valley." While that may no longer be the best way to describe the Passaic Valley, you will be amazed to find that at least half of this waterway continues to provide a peaceful refuge from the bustling, crowded world that surrounds it. And as for the rest of the river, it will reinforce all of your negative stereotypes of New Jersey.

That so much of the natural Passaic is left, we can partly thank the last glacier, which retreated about 12,000 years ago. The glacier scooped out a basin, and when it melted, it left a huge lake dammed by the Watchung Mountains. The waters eventually found an outlet near what is now Paterson, mostly draining away, but leaving a classic mess in the form of clay bottom sediments in a flat valley. These relatively impervious sediments impeded complete drainage, resulting in the formation of extensive wetlands such as the 6,000-acre Great Swamp, and smaller parcels such as Great Piece Meadows, Troy Meadows, and Hatfield Swamp. For the most part, these soggy acres came to be the last pieces of real estate anyone cared to try to develop. This delay bought enough time for today's protective laws and attitudes on wetlands and floodplains to catch up and assure the survival of these areas. But there was a particularly close call back in the 1960's, when the Port Authority proposed building a jetport in Great Swamp. Public sympathy swung towards the frogs and ducks, however, and a new national wildlife refuge and a county park emerged instead.

Section 1. White Bridge to head of navigation

Gradient	Difficulty	Distance	Time	Scenery	Map
1	A	1.7	1.5	Good	46

TRIP DESCRIPTION: It is conceivable that you could start exploring the Passaic a few miles above White Bridge at Osborn Mill (Rte. 663), northeast of Basking Ridge. But the heavily posted put-in and miserably tree- and shrub-choked stream bed clearly make the suggested route more appealing.

White Bridge is Lord Stirling Road on the Somerset County side and White Bridge Road on the Morris County side. There is a fisherperson/boater access area on the west bank, part of Lord Stirling Park. The suggested trip takes you upstream on the Passaic for a mile, then up Great Brook to Pleasant Plains Road, and then back to the start, a round trip of almost three and a half miles. This is a beautiful trip that offers minimally disturbed vistas of perennial swamp, intermittent swamp, marsh, and one farm. The water is fairly clear and, below the confluence of the aptly named Black Brook, it is dark.

The stream is tiny and generally shallow, and its channel is even narrower. It is a crooked path and sometimes complicated by snags or even a deadfall. At moderate levels, the current is noticeable, but not too stiff to overcome. The water, of course, is smooth. If you try to ascend the Passaic above Great Brook, you will quickly develop an appreciation for the wisdom of your starting point.

Passaic River

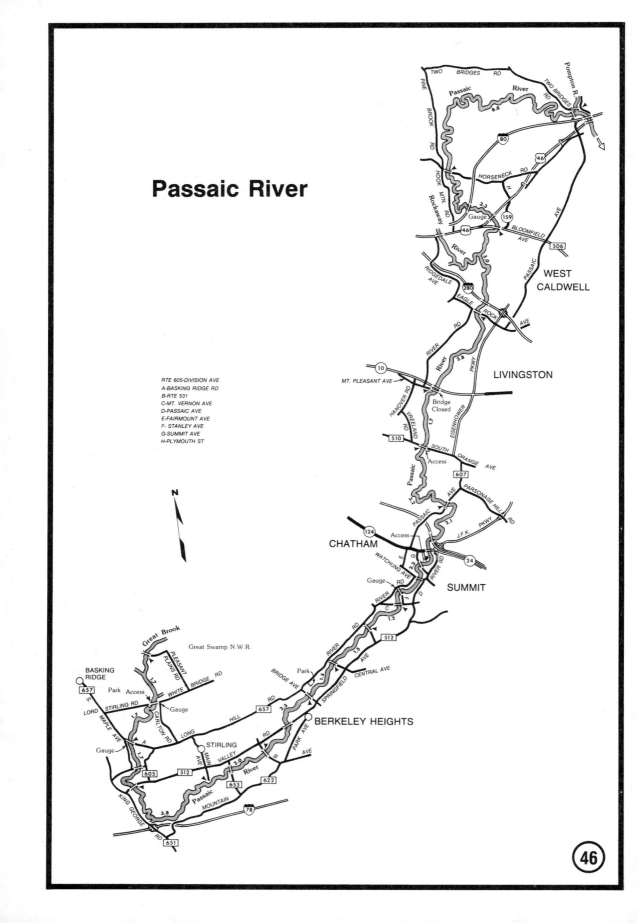

RTE 605-DIVISION AVE
A-BASKING RIDGE RD
B-RTE 531
C-MT. VERNON AVE
D-PASSAIC AVE
E-FAIRMOUNT AVE
F- STANLEY AVE
G-SUMMIT AVE
H-PLYMOUTH ST

Most of this run is through public lands. The west bank is Somerset County's Lord Stirling Park, most of which is set aside as an environmental education center. With an interpretive center, over eight miles of foot trails (including two miles of boardwalks), and two observation towers, the park offers you an unusual opportunity to thoroughly enjoy and understand the setting through which you are paddling. The other side of the creek is within the Great Swamp National Wildlife Refuge. The Refuge is more focused on its mission as a preserve than as a place for recreation. While boating on the Passaic and Great Brook is tolerated, access via the Refuge is not. That is why you can only start at White Bridge.

HAZARDS: None

WATER CONDITIONS: This uppermost section is runnable without dragging from late fall through, on the average, the end of May.

GAUGE: There is a USGS gauging station at Millington (right bank about 100 feet downstream of Rte. 657). You can call Philadelphia or inspect on site. If you visit the gauge, there is both a vertical and sloping staff. Use the vertical staff. At least 4.9 feet is desirable. There is also a staff gauge on the upstream side of the left abutment of White Bridge. A level of 223 units is delightful, zero is unknown.

Section 2. White Bridge to Two Bridges (Rte. 613)					
Gradient	Difficulty	Distance	Time	Scenery	Map
2	A to 1	42.7	17.0	Ugly to Good	46

TRIP DESCRIPTION: This is a long section that ends at the confluence with the Pompton River, north of Fairfield. Most of the Passaic's natural qualities will be found in these miles. You can actually feel that you have left the city here. In spite of numerous sewage treatment plants contributing to the flow, the water seems acceptably clean and is often clear. Access is plentiful, so you can tailor a trip to your energy.

Put in at the Lord Stirling Access Area. The course initially exposes you to more of the same natural beauty that exists upstream. But after a half mile, the suburbs crowd in. The water is initially quiet. Then at Rte. 657, the Passaic cuts a hemlock-shaded gap in Long Hill, called Millington Gorge. There are lots of simple riffles in this short ravine, but they become fewer below and disappear by the confluence with the Dead River. Below the Dead River, the Passaic commences its northward journey. The suburban scenery resumes below the gorge, but ends shortly below Rte. 512 as the Passaic burrows into its gloomy swamp. This swamp is only inundated at high water levels. Normally you will see a deep and damp forest, low mud banks, and even some mud flats. Often the swamp is broad enough that you can see little or none of the surrounding development, even when there is no foliage. After the trees green up, you feel even more remote. You are likely to start seeing the first of many deer. With hunting prohibited so close to residential areas, the deer are overabundant. As a result, you may see more game on the Passaic than you would paddling a comparable distance through Yellowstone National Park.

The most serious flaws to this stretch are the persistent presence of power lines and trash. You just cannot escape the old tires, plastic, etc. The water through here is sluggish at moderate levels and all flat, and fallen trees are seldom a problem.

Conditions change temporarily approaching Chatham and Summit. Hilly terrain closes in on the river, and below Mount Vernon Avenue, the waters begin a gentle descent through a series of rocky riffles. Scattered riffles persist as far as Passaic Avenue (Rte. 607). Most would wash out at higher levels. Other relatively lively spots are the 18-inch concrete weir at the gauging station below Stanley Avenue, Chatham (run center), some old ruins of a little weir about 300 yards

Passaic River

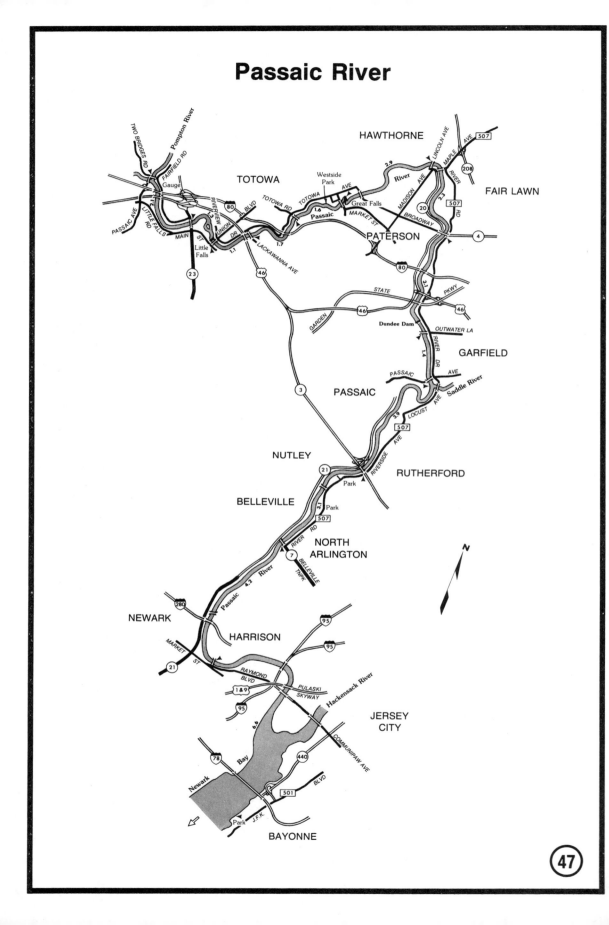

upstream of Main Street, Chatham (might develop a strong reversal at high water, so scout), and a hard-to-see, foot-high weir about a mile or so below Chatham at a pumping station (this could develop a strong reversal, so scout this, too).

Not only hills crowd the river around Chatham and Summit, but also unsightly commercial and industrial development and a lot of riverside junk. Contrasting with this blight is the beautiful, old, stone arch railroad bridge below Stanley Avenue.

From Passaic Avenue to just above Bloomfield Avenue (N.J. Rte. 159), the river again stays mostly secluded in a fairly mature forest. One might even get away with canoe camping in places. The big flaw remains that ubiquitous trash. Every strainer filters out a trash jam. The persistence of some level of distant road noise also lessens the illusion of wilderness.

Around Bloomfield Avenue and U.S. Rte. 46, there is some more ugly commercial activity perched on the banks and lots of road noise. These are busy highways. The river then eases into Great Piece Meadows. The name is no longer descriptive. Supposedly, this was once a vast meadow that was harvested for hay. But today it is mostly a swamp forest, though some portions of it are a mix of grass and trees. Initially, you can see houses off to the left, but in time this stretch really isolates itself. It is obvious that this is the biggest tract of undeveloped land along the Passaic below Great Swamp.

Unfortunately, the lower end of Great Piece was filled in years ago. The old, residential neighborhoods around Two Bridges sit on this "reclaimed" land, which rises only a few feet above the river. The occupants quickly became experienced at living with floods. Though it would probably be cheaper to buy the occupants out, there is currently a proposal in Congress to divert high flows from the Pompton River and upper Passaic River into 19.5 miles of tunnels that would run beneath suburban Jersey and dump the unwanted water into Newark Bay. We can cheerfully add the 1.2-billion-dollar cost of this porky project onto our modest federal budget deficit.

HAZARDS: The ruins of a weir above Main Street in Chatham and the intact weir below Chatham, at the Canoe Reservoir pumping station, could create dangerous rollers at high water. Treat with caution. There is a railroad trestle about two miles below N.J. Rte. 10 that is often totally jammed with logs and other debris. If there is no clear passage, you must face the miserable carry over the high railroad grade.

WATER CONDITIONS: This reach is generally up from late fall through mid-May. If you are not paddling through the rocky sections, the season may extend into mid-summer, unless it has been unusually dry.

GAUGE: There are USGS gauges below Rte. 657 at Millington, below Stanley Avenue at Chatham (staff is attached to downstream end of left pier of the bridge and is difficult to read), and at U.S. Rte. 46. at Pine Brook, near West Caldwell (west end of westbound span, downstream side). Note that the staff of the Pine Brook gauge is difficult to read from the shore angle. Stopping on the shoulder of Rte. 46 is extremely dangerous. But there is a narrow break in the guardrail through which you can back and park in safety. Call Philadelphia for each gauge or inspect on site. Respective minimums of 4.95 feet, 3.8 feet, and 13.1 feet are needed to avoid scraping in any of the riffles. For the flatwater stretches, minimum is unknown, but is probably around 4.7 feet, 3.5 feet, and 11.3 feet respectively. The gauge at Pine Brook is less reliable for the river above Rte. 46 because of the influence of flows from the Rockaway River.

Section 3. Two Bridges (Rte. 613) to N.J. Rte. 3					
Gradient	Difficulty	Distance	Time	Scenery	Map
3*	A to 1	21.4	11.0	Poor to Good	47
*above tidewater, not counting falls					

TRIP DESCRIPTION: The Passaic now clearly becomes an urban river. It will appeal to few, but two picturesque falls, some interesting architecture, and just a different perspective of the city may make it worthwhile.

With the contribution of the Pompton River's flow, the Passaic is much larger now. Its placid waters curve around the back of huge Willowbrook Mall, a quiet prelude to its sudden, violent plunge over Little Falls. The falls are beautiful, as are some of the old mills along the bank. You will appreciate little of this beauty though, if you are involuntarily plunging over the brink. So plan on pulling over well upstream. About three quarters of a mile past the Rte. 23 bridge, the river splits around an island. At the foot of the island, land on the left bank, find your way up side streets to River View Drive, follow River View across Union Boulevard and downhill past the huge water treatment plant to its lower end, and relaunch. You can shorten this slightly by taking out on the left a little downstream of the island, just above the water intake structure, and following a canal to Union Boulevard. The portage is a little over a half mile. Ugh. Be sure to paddle back upstream though, past the plant, for a spectacular view of the cataract.

A series of riffles below the falls helps you forget the pain of portaging. Relax for awhile. But in about three and a half miles, after passing between a pair of parks, you will be approaching Great Falls. This is a spectacular 70-foot plunge into a crack in the black rock where the river takes an unusual zigzag shift. At moderate levels, much of the stream flow bypasses the falls through a hydroelectric station. At such levels, it is reasonably safe to paddle almost to the Wayne Avenue bridge (and dam beneath it), take out by a fast food carry-out on the right, carry down McBride Avenue, cross the bridge, and then turn right onto the first street. Follow this a hundred yards, enter the city park, and follow a bicycle path downhill into the gorge. If water is high, the conservative approach would be to land farther upstream, on the left, at the end of the twin parks (Westside Park), and carry downstream. This adds two strenuous blocks to the portage, but lessens worry. Once again, after portaging, be sure to paddle upstream for a grand view.

Once again, a long stretch of riffles grace the river. But there is little else that graces the river. The neighborhood is in decay, as are some of the grand, old mills that once ran on the power from the falling water. It is difficult to appreciate the proud industrial past of this city — the home of the Colt revolver, the submarine, and cotton duck sails, and major producer of silk, locomotives, and airplane engines. Those factories that remain, including some huge operations like the Marcal Paper Company, and the grimy, old bridges are this section's most interesting features. Though the Passaic is not the sewer that it once was, water quality still becomes detectably worse than above.

The river now rounds its big bend and heads southward. About a half mile past the Garden State Parkway is your last obstacle. The river makes a 15-foot plunge over the stepped face of the Dundee Dam. A hydroelectric plant diverts most of the water around the right end of the dam at moderate levels, so that you can just carry down the face of the dam. If water is passing over the crest, a carry on the left is easy. Tidewater begins shortly below this point at high tide. But at low tide, you can enjoy about a mile and a half of exposed riffles, ending at the mouth of the Saddle River.

The remaining miles are through both industrial and residential neighborhoods. The banks are incredibly trashy. Access is minimal as many of the riverside parks are fenced off on their waterfront side. This being commercially navigable water, most of the bridges on this reach are drawbridges. The variability of their design and control house architecture is the most interesting feature of this section. While you can probably get out beneath Rte. 3, a much better place to exit — not to mention leave your car — is at Riverside County Park, on the left about 0.6 miles downstream. There is even a boat ramp there.

HAZARDS: Take care to avoid washing over Little Falls, Great Falls, and Dundee Dam. It is a good idea to visit at least the first two drops before your trip, so you will recognize their approach. During low flows and power generation, the latter two are more inconveniences than hazards.

WATER CONDITIONS: This section carries enough water to run anytime, if you do not mind dragging over some of the riffles. Good conditions, even in the riffles, occur from late fall through June.

GAUGE: There are USGS gauges about 400 feet down the left bank from the Pompton River at Two Bridges and at Little Falls. You can inspect Two Bridges on site and call Philadelphia for either. A low but adequate level to float the riffles would be 4.0 feet at Two Bridges and 2.1 feet at Little Falls. Zero is unknown.

Section 4. N.J. Rte. 3 to mouth					
Gradient	Difficulty	Distance	Time	Scenery	Map
0	A	10.5	4.0	Fair to ugly	47

TRIP DESCRIPTION: Even fewer people would find reason to paddle all of this section. This is entirely tidal. Initially there are some riverside parks to soften the scenery. The skyline of Newark and the vertical-lift drawbridges are interesting. Once past Newark though, the river enters a world of freeways, railroads, factories, and chemical plants. Approaching the mouth, the sickening smell of solvents permeates the air. A wide mud flat separates the mouth of the Passaic from the mouth of the Hackensack. The cranes of the Port of Newark lie ahead, like an Erector Set mirage. There is not a trout fisherman in sight.

Access to the mouth or anywhere nearby is nonexistent. Best ideas are to double back to where you started, cross Newark Bay to the county park in Bayonne, or ascend the Hackensack, where you can get to a road beneath the west end of the Belleville Turnpike bridge.

HAZARDS: Motorboat traffic and fumes from chemical plants

WATER CONDITIONS: This is tidal and commercially navigable, so it is more than deep enough.

GAUGE: None

Rockaway River

INTRODUCTION: The name Rockaway is common in these parts. But it has nothing to do with rocks. In fact, its rough translation from Native American is "sandy place." It really takes more than just two words, however, to describe this variable waterway.

The Rockaway follows a whiplash path across the heart of Morris County, coming to rest in the Passaic just west of West Caldwell. Overall, this is a poor canoe stream. Roads, industry, the crush of suburban development, and wear and tear from 200 years of civilization have taken their toll on the aesthetics of the surroundings. If you are content with short excursions, however, you can find some silver linings in the gloom, not the least of which includes some of the most challenging whitewater in Jersey.

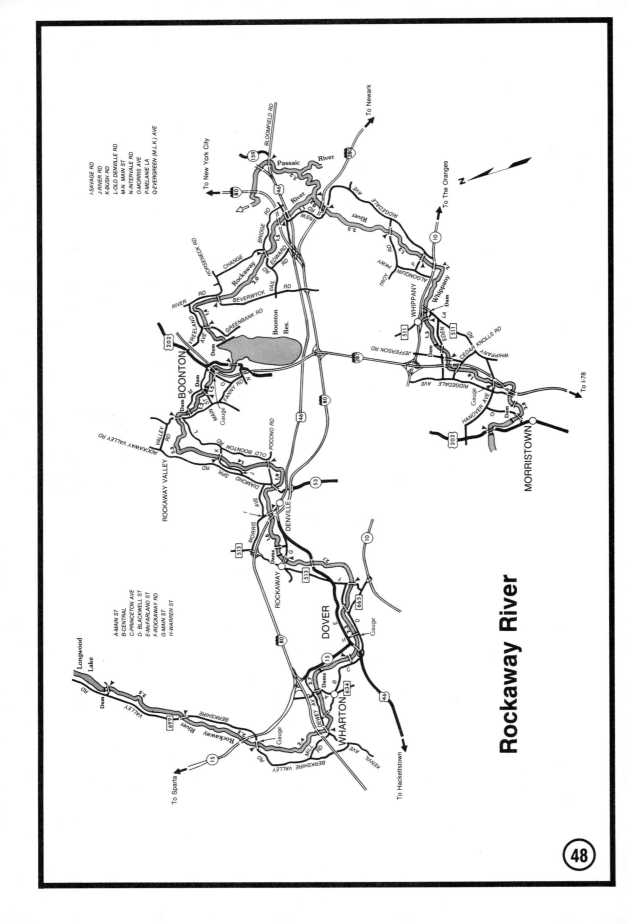

Rockaway River

I-SAVAGE RD
J-RIVER RD
K-BUSH RD
L-OLD DENVILLE RD
M-N. MAIN ST
N-INTERVALE RD
O-MORRIS AVE
P-MELANIE LA
Q-EVERGREEN (M.L.K.) AVE

A-MAIN ST
B-CENTRAL
C-PRINCETON AVE
D-BLACKWELL ST
E-McFARLAND ST
F-ROCKAWAY RD
G-MAIN ST
H-WARREN ST

Section 1. Longwood Lake to Wharton (West Dewey Avenue)					
Gradient	Difficulty	Distance	Time	Scenery	Map
8	A to 1	7.4	3.0	Good	48

TRIP DESCRIPTION: The upper Rockaway offers ministream canoeing in a mostly natural setting. The put-in is about 200 yards below the dam that forms Longwood Lake. A dirt road leading to the development on the lake's east side gets you to a bridge over the stream. Be sure to ask permission before parking here.

Initially the Rockaway occupies a narrow, wooded valley between two relatively high ridges. The winding channel allows one good views of their attractive, pine-dappled slopes. This is some of the better mountain scenery that you will find in New Jersey.

Approaching N.J. Rte. 15, the slopes diverge, and the surroundings become swampy. Houses occupy the nearby high ground and interrupt the natural setting just above and below this highway. But after passing Berkshire Valley Road, the Rockaway wanders into the many protected acres of a state fish and wildlife management area. In here you will find an undisturbed tract of extensive swamp and marsh, fringed by wooded hills.

Though mostly a gentle stream at moderate levels, the upper Rockaway is variable and sometimes challenging. The clear waters initially speed over riffles, but much of the path is smooth, especially in the swampy stretches. The channel on the reach between Longwood Lake and Rte. 15 is small enough to be periodically obstructed by deadfalls, some in fast water. The path through the swamps is surprisingly unobstructed, even by alder sieves. Finally, just above I-80, the stream hits a bouldery deposit that causes the channel to disperse amongst both rocks and live trees. There are lots of choices here of where to go, all of them bad, except at very high water. So those desiring to do just some swamp exploring in the fish and wildlife area might be best off to launch at Berkshire Valley Road, paddle down, and then paddle back.

HAZARDS: Be ready for some strainers, particularly above Rte. 15.

WATER CONDITIONS: The upper Rockaway is most often up between November and early May. To start at Longwood Lake, catch within three days of hard rain. To do just the wetlands between Berkshire Valley Road and I-80, floatable water usually remains for 10 to 12 days after a hard rain. Water enough for those final, shallow riffles, however, only persists for three days after hard rain.

GAUGE: There is a USGS gauging station at Berkshire Valley Road with an outside staff. A level of about 5.0 feet is adequate for starting at Longwood Lake, 4.5 feet is minimum for negotiating the rock gardens at I-80, and 4.0 feet is enough for the section in the fish and wildlife area. For long distance checking, use the USGS gauging station just above Boonton Reservoir at Boonton (call Philadelphia). Roughly, 2.7 feet corresponds to 4.0 feet at Berkshire Valley Road and 3.4 feet corresponds to 5.0 feet.

Section 2. Wharton (West Dewey Avenue) to Boonton (West Main Street)					
Gradient	Difficulty	Distance	Time	Scenery	Map
13	A to 2	15.5	7.0	Fair to Poor	48
2 mi. @ 38					

TRIP DESCRIPTION: The Rockaway now settles into its long, hard journey through civilization. The assault is relentless and has been long-standing. Industry's impact goes back to the early 19th century when iron mining and manufacturing dominated the upper valley. In fact, Dover was supposedly called the "Pittsburgh of New Jersey." Other industry, boom, bust, and, ultimately, the tide of suburbia have followed. So the paddler views a landscape often framed by crumbling retaining walls, trash, auto graveyards, factories, roads, railroads, and the backside of drab commercial structures. In all fairness, there are also strips of bottomland woods, little parks, golf courses, and even attractive residential areas. But there is never enough of the good stuff to make a lasting impression.

Some streams make up for a dearth of good scenery by offering entertaining whitewater. The Rockaway provides inadequate compensation. As far as Denville, there are plenty of easy rapids and riffles, mostly concentrated in the first few miles. A twisting chute through the remains of an old dam, just below the start, is particularly fun. These first miles, however, also contain more of those spread-out, rock-garden rapids like the one found near the end of Section 1. Without lots of water, these segments can be hikes. Below Denville, flatwater dominates the way. You must also deal with five weirs on this 15-mile section and that means probably five portages.

HAZARDS: There are five weirs. The first, a six-footer, is about 100 yards below Main Street in Wharton and easily carried on the right. The second is a sloping, diagonal three-footer located about a half mile below Main Street. Carry this. The third is a seven-footer about 100 yards above Main Street in Rockaway. Carry on the left. The fourth is a sloping three-footer about a quarter mile downstream of Main Street. This may be runnable, but the carry on the left is easy. The fifth is a sloping eight-footer just above North Main Street in Powerville. Carry on the left. Strainers are also a possibility, particularly above Dover.

WATER CONDITIONS: This section most often comes up between November and early May. The reach above Dover (a major tributary boosts flow just above Dover) seldom stays high enough for more than three days after a hard rain. The rest of the section should last as long as 12 days after hard rain.

GAUGE: The USGS gauge at Berkshire Valley Road should read at least 4.5 feet to start at West Dewey Avenue, and 3.9 feet is getting down near minimum for paddling below Wharton. There is a staff gauge in Dover attached to the river left retaining wall about 100 feet above North Warren Street (above fire hall, behind convenience store). You probably need about 3.0 feet to start at West Dewey, but 2.5 feet is fine for below Wharton. The USGS gauge above Boonton Reservoir, in Boonton (call Philadelphia or visit), should probably read over 3.0 feet to start at West Dewey and 2.7 feet for below Wharton.

Section 3. Boonton (West Main Street) to Boonton (U.S. Rte. 202)					
Gradient	Difficulty	Distance	Time	Scenery	Map
126	3 to 4 +	1.5	1.0	Good to Poor	48

TRIP DESCRIPTION: The Rockaway now plunges through the rugged Boonton Gorge. This has been traditionally considered the premier whitewater run in New Jersey, and it is not for everybody. Actually, in the eyes of the authorities, it is not for anybody. For the take-out is on Jerseys City's water supply reservoir, and its managers have zero tolerance for floating trespassers. The put-in is at a town park that is posted with signs demanding a use permit for nonresidents. So bring your passport, for if you paddle Boonton Gorge, you will have left the United States of America, "Land of the Free."

The put-in is not really at West Main Street. You first want to portage down the nice foot trail on the right at least a hundred yards to bypass an eight-foot dam followed by a beautiful but lethal waterfalls. You will probably also want to carry the drop below the falls and another drop beneath the arch bridge. If so, end your carry on river left just below that bridge.

What follows is an almost continuous series of rapids formed by boulders and jagged bedrock. The rock is black and sinister-looking. The surrounding gorge is initially attractive, though the demanding whitewater gives you little opportunity to appreciate that. The creek plunges over a sharp gauging station weir at Morris Avenue, passes under I-287, and then heads south, parallel to the freeway. Here starts a particularly long and powerful rapid, a grand finale. This slows in the backwater of the reservoir, leaving you with a third of a mile paddle to Rte. 202, a steep climb, and probable meeting with the security guard.

HAZARDS: The whole run demands respect. Scout the weir at the gauging station before attempting, as it has a powerful reversal.

WATER CONDITIONS: Most often up between November and early May within 10 days of hard rain.

GAUGE: Use the USGS gauge in Boonton (visit or call Philadelphia). To reach the gauge, turn off of Main Street at the east end of downtown Boonton onto the southbound ramp to I-287. In a few yards, a one-way street (which leads to Morris Avenue) branches off to the right and under the railroad. The gauge is on your right, beneath the bridge. A level of 2.6 feet is about bare minimum.

Section 4. Greenbank Road to mouth					
Gradient	Difficulty	Distance	Time	Scenery	Map
7	A to 1—	7.2	2.0	Fair to Good	48

TRIP DESCRIPTION: The Rockaway has now completed its plunge into the Passaic Valley. There are only a few riffles left. Then the path is smooth. The surrounding land flattens, and much of it near the river was probably once swamp and meadows. Residential and light industrial development has claimed many of these acres, degrading much of your view. Only the final two miles give a taste of what this place was like when it was wild. There is no access to the mouth, so continue a mile down the Passaic to N.J. Rte. 506.

HAZARDS: None

WATER CONDITIONS: Flow depends on how full the reservoir is. Barring a drought, there is usually adequate water anytime from December through May.

GAUGE: There is a USGS gauge below the reservoir (no access, so call Philadelphia). Minimum is unknown, but at least 2.1 feet should be enough.

Whippany River

INTRODUCTION: The Whippany River is a tiny tributary to the Rockaway River, starting in the hills just above historic Morristown. The name is Native American, meaning either "tooth place" or "arrow stream," the latter translation given because this was supposedly the source of wood for their arrows. But little remains of the primitive valley those native craftsmen once roamed. The stream now flows past decaying neighborhoods, shiny new office parks, crumbling factories, and a remaining patch of wild, open space. If you are looking for arrow wood, you might as well try the shopping mall up Rte. 10. So the Whippany is not the sort of stream for which one drives long distances, but it can be a rewarding, after-a-hard-rain special for local paddlers.

Section 1. Morristown (U.S. Rte. 202) to Melanie Lane					
Gradient	Difficulty	Distance	Time	Scenery	Map
15	A to 2	8.3	3.0	Poor	48

TRIP DESCRIPTION: How many houses, crossroads, or small towns reach for just a little place in the sun merely because George Washington once spent a night there? The answer is plenty. So just think how envious they must be of Morristown, New Jersey, where Mr. Washington spent not just one evening, but two long, cold winters. Remember this, and may the knowledge that you are paddling through such historic, hallowed ground (and water) be just compensation for bumping down this dismal ditch.

The runs starts out nicely enough, in a park at the foot of Speedwell Lake. It is just a brook here, but after a few bends the water spreads out into Lake Pocahontas. Pocahontas is fairly attractive for an urban lake, with the town perched upon the hill to your right. The carry around the dam (left) is easy. Your journey resumes on a tiny, dirty, trashy creek. The creek winds through the dirty and decaying poor side of town, past retaining walls and forlorn buildings. Rusting shopping carts, tattered plastic film, and a sea of styrofoam decorate your path. While Morristown may have only 17,000 inhabitants, it seems like a city from the water.

Leaving town, the Whippany hugs noisy, smelly I-287, while also bumping against industrial parks, a sewage treatment plant, and a shopping mall. Luckily, a good gradient provides strong current and lots of riffles to at least make the paddling fun. Finally shaking free of the interstate highway, the creek then slows in another pond, a relatively attractive reach surrounded by a park. The dam at the end has a short but steep portage on the left. Just below this is a treat. There is an exhilarating stretch of easy whitewater where a big, crumbling factory has narrowed the rocky stream bed to form a fast, powerful, and tortuous series of rapids (still only Class 2). The rapids extend to the town of Whippany. Riffles follow, and then comes a five-foot weir located about a hundred feet above Whippany Road. Carry this. Now the water becomes entirely smooth as it winds about remnant bottomland woods and sprouting office complexes.

HAZARDS: Two dams and a weir are all unrunnable. Strainers are also possible.

WATER CONDITIONS: The best chance for favorable conditions occur from November through early May. Catch within three days of hard rain.

GAUGE: There is a USGS gauging station on the left bank behind the lower end of the sewage treatment plant below Hanover Avenue. Call Philadelphia or visit. If you choose the latter, you will find access a challenge. Most likely you will have to struggle down the left bank through a thorny, brushy jungle. However, if you can walk through the treatment plant to its downstream corner, the approach is easy. A level of 2.3 feet is minimal but adequate for the shallowest spots.

| *Section 2. Melanie Lane to mouth* | | | | | |
Gradient	Difficulty	Distance	Time	Scenery	Map
5	A	4.0	1.5	Good	48

TRIP DESCRIPTION: The remainder of the Whippany flows through Troy Meadows. Though infringed upon by industry and housing, the landscape that you behold is mostly natural. An unusual facet of Troy Meadows is that, unlike the "meadows" on the Passaic, it actually includes open, grassy meadows. The path through here is crooked and the water smooth, with only a possible deadfall to complicate things. There is no access at the mouth. So continue down the Rockaway and then the Passaic to N.J. Rte. 506, an additional 2.2 miles of woodsy paddling.

HAZARDS: Normally there are none.

WATER CONDITIONS: The best season is from November through May. Catch within a week of hard rain.

GAUGE: The USGS gauge at Hanover Avenue (call Philadelphia or visit) should read at least 2.1 feet.

Pompton River

INTRODUCTION: The Pompton is the Passaic's largest tributary, collecting the drainage from over 350 square miles of North Jersey and southwest New York. It is formed by the confluence of the Pequannock and Ramapo rivers near Pompton Plains. This river has a short life, ending only six and a half miles later in the brooding waters of the Passaic at Two Bridges. The Pompton is only a mediocre canoe route at best, and it will thus probably appeal only to those who live nearby. But since this is such a densely populated, congested patch of suburbia, there just may well be more than a few takers. Whatever the aesthetics, it is a relatively safe destination for beginners.

| *Section 1. Pompton Plains Cross Road to mouth* | | | | | |
Gradient	Difficulty	Distance	Time	Scenery	Map
4	A to 1−	6.4	2.0	Fair	49

TRIP DESCRIPTION: The trip starts at Pompton Plains Cross Road (also called Jackson Avenue) because there is no access at the confluence of the Pequannock and Ramapo. But you do not miss much, the confluence being only a few hundred yards above the bridge. By putting in on the downstream right end of the bridge, you avoid the nasty little weir at the pumping station.

The following miles are easy. The water is mostly smooth, with only a straightforward riffle or two per mile. Except for near the end, where there are a few islands, the channel is wide and free of any obstructions.

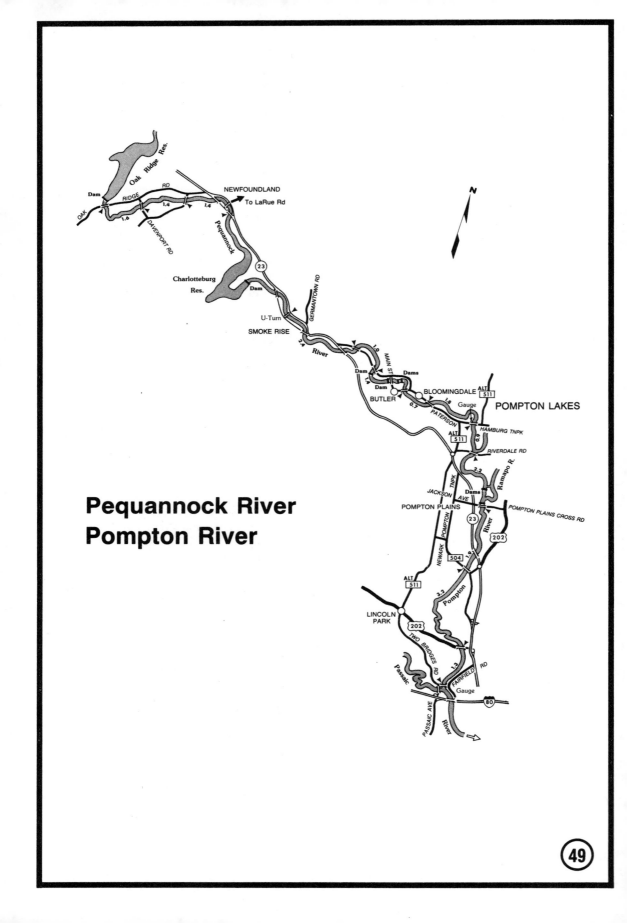

Pequannock River
Pompton River

49

The scenery is a softened version of the sprawl that lies beyond. The often murky waters flow past high, wooded mud banks. The banks are generally built upon, and you are usually paddling past someone's backyard. If you come here after May, at least the full foliage helps dilute the effect. You can end the trip right at the mouth, where a sometimes slippery scramble up the steep right bank at the bridge (Two Bridges Road) delivers you to a roomy parking lot.

HAZARDS: Beware of the weir at the put-in bridge. The churning hole in its center chute is dangerous. At moderately high water, the right edge of the weir can be safely run.

WATER CONDITIONS: Best levels usually persist from November through mid-June. If you do not mind a little scraping, it is often passable into August.

GAUGE: There is a USGS gauge at the pumping station at the put-in, but you must call Philadelphia to get a reading. Zero canoeing level is unknown, but it is probably around 7.6 feet. There is a staff gauge on the upstream left abutment of Two Bridges Road. Zero is unknown, but 159.0 feet is an acceptable level. Keep in mind that this reading can be influenced by water backing up from the Passaic when the Passaic is high but the Pompton is not.

Pequannock River

INTRODUCTION: The Pequannock is a Passaic County stream, gathering its waters along the western boundary and feeding them to the Pompton River at Pompton Plains. It cuts across the geologic grain of a mountainous swath, and in doing so, is blessed with some inherently good whitewater and good scenery. The city of Newark, unfortunately, has usurped much of the upper watershed (not to mention the water) to quench its thirst. Highways and towns have taken their toll on the beauty of the rest of the river. But there are still enough scraps remaining to please the adventuresome paddler.

Section 1. Oak Ridge Road to Newfoundland					
Gradient	Difficulty	Distance	Time	Scenery	Map
9	A to 1	4.4	1.5	Good	49

TRIP DESCRIPTION: This is the section of free-flowing river that survives between Oak Ridge and Charlotteburg reservoirs, part of the water supply for Newark. The watershed people also own the land along this reach and prohibit boating on these waters. People who have snuck through anyway have found it a delight.

The put-in is just below the tailrace of Oak Ridge Dam. Moving downstream, about the first three miles of this passage is swift but smooth. The water is usually a clear brown and follows a twisting channel bordered by thick stands of willow, alder, and other shrubbery. The channel width fluctuates, ranging from wide pools to brook-like narrows. Wooded hillsides, generally covered with pine, rise steeply just behind the swampy floodplain. You see no houses until Davenport Road. Then the surroundings become increasingly developed. Approaching Rte. 23, the water dashes through a bouncy chute, and soon the bed tilts to form an almost continuous series of riffles. Before long, you realize that you are now paddling down the roomy, wooded median strip of this divided highway. Finish your run where the river cuts back underneath the eastbound lane in Newfoundland.

It would certainly be nice if the water supply people would abandon their medieval attitudes towards canoeing and kayaking. In addition to controlling this lovely stream, Newark has five beautiful, mountain-rimmed reservoirs in the watershed of the upper Pequannock. The Newark Watershed Conservation & Development Corp., the authority that administers the system, permits rowboats on some of these, but no paddle craft. This is stupid. Write them (P.O. Box 319, Newfoundland, NJ 07435) and your elected state and local officials and urge them to change this policy. This is a great recreational resource — the kind of thing that more enlightened watershed agencies in other parts of the country see fit to make available to us. The general public derives no benefit when Newark ties up these waters.

HAZARDS: You might meet some blood-thirsty reservoir guards.

WATER CONDITIONS: This is seldom up. The best odds for water are March, April, and early May of a winter or spring that was wet enough to fill the reservoirs to overflowing.

GAUGE: None. The widest and shallowest riffles are at the bridge to Larue Road in Newfoundland. So scout the stream at that spot.

Section 2. U-turn near Smoke Rise to mouth					
Gradient	Difficulty	Distance	Time	Scenery	Map
40*	1 to 3	10.2	4.0	Good to Poor	49
*but exceeds 70 at times					

TRIP DESCRIPTION: This can be a delightful whitewater run, though some nasty portages and poor aesthetics would probably limit its appeal. The run starts at the U-turn in N.J. Rte. 23, six tenths of a mile west of Germantown Road. This is on the edge of (actually just inside) Newark Watershed property. Note that there is an additional mile and a half of mostly free-flowing river from Charlotteburg Reservoir down to here, much of it good whitewater, that you cannot legally run. A walk through the woods gets you to a small, steep, boulder-clogged brook of clear water. The flow is initially spread thinly through the rocks and live trees. So at high levels, this is a dangerous place with potential for pinning. The channel soon narrows though, and the water begins to dash down, at an erratic gradient, what is basically the median of Rte. 23. This is not as bad as it seems, however, as the road is relatively high above the water, and there is a good screen of rocks and vegetation. It is actually attractive through here. Sometimes there are pools, and sometimes the rapids just go on and on.

Entering Butler (and leaving Rte. 23), the creek drops down a particularly memorable rapid where the water filters through a maze of big boulders. Not far below, it drops over a five-foot weir. Carry this on the left, through the woods (at very high water there might be a sneak chute on the left). A little over a quarter mile farther is a railroad bridge and, on the right, a factory. Get out here, carry down the railroad to Main Street, follow Main back to the river, and put in below its bridge. This is a long, miserable carry (over 500 yards), but you do this because just below the railroad bridge the creek files between vertical retaining walls that allow no portage around a lethal five-foot weir just above Main Street bridge. Avoid this trap. A series of three weirs soon follow. The first two are only about three feet high and certainly runnable at moderate levels. But the last forms a vertical, seven-foot plunge into a churning reversal. Carry this on the right. After that drop, you can relax on an easy, delightful flush down more rock-studded, continuous whitewater that will distract you from the dismal scenery.

The gradient gradually subsides, and by the time the stream turns south, just past Bloomingdale, the way is mostly on flatwater. The scenery becomes suburban, but below the confluence with the Wanaque River, the river banks once again assume a fairly wild appearance as the Pequannock courses through jungle-like, wooded bottomlands. You will be surprised to find a final weir down there — a six-footer. You can carry this immediately, or paddle through a connecting channel to the Ramapo and carry a comparable weir on that stream. Take out on the Pompton River a few hundred yards below the mouth at Pompton Plains Cross Road.

HAZARDS: Watch out for those trees that grow in the stream bed at the start and, for strainers throughout the run. Three of the five weirs in Butler are definitely dangerous. So is the last one near the mouth. Carry all of them. Be alert for the little weir at the end, if you paddle to Pompton Plains Cross Road.

WATER CONDITIONS: This is seldom runnable because much of the watershed's runoff is intercepted and bottled up by those five water supply reservoirs. The best bet for finding water is after a wet winter or spring that fills these reservoirs. At such time, most likely during March, April, or May, catch within three days of hard rain.

GAUGE: There is a staff gauge on the upstream right abutment of Paterson Hamburg Turnpike. A level of 3.9 feet is about minimum level.

Wanaque River

INTRODUCTION: The Wanaque River (Native American for "place of the sassafras") is a tiny tributary to the Pequannock River. It gathers its waters from up near the New York-New Jersey line in northern Passaic County. Most of its length has been converted to a chain of reservoirs to slake the thirst of suburban Jersey. Thus we can now only enjoy a short stretch of beginner-level canoeing in its last few miles.

Section 1. Rte. 511 to mouth					
Gradient	Difficulty	Distance	Time	Scenery	Map
5	A to 1+	4.9	2.0	Good to Poor	50

TRIP DESCRIPTION: Right now, much of this run provides a pleasant escape to the outdoors. Confined between two mountain ridges, the path takes you through a woodsy setting with little development. The lower end of Ramapo Mountain first looms ahead, and then on your left, displaying some pretty cliffs. The current is fair, and there are scattered riffles. Just above Wanaque Avenue, you can bounce down a nice chute through the remains of an old dam that once converted much of this reach into Lake Inez. Because the proposed alignment of I-287 is due to slash through the middle of all this, the quality of this section may diminish.

Below Wanaque Avenue, residential development crowds the banks. It is similar to what you see along the Pompton or lower Ramapo. Riverdale Road crosses the water right at the mouth, but it is a poor take-out. So you might consider continuing down the Pequannock and Pompton for another two miles to Pompton Plains Cross Road. Enveloped by a mostly wild floodplain, this addition makes a pleasant end for the trip.

HAZARDS: There are none on the Wanaque. But if you continue down to the Pompton Plains take-out, watch out for a sharp weir near the mouth of the Pequannock and a weir with a deceptively dangerous hole at the take-out bridge.

Ramapo River
Wanaque River

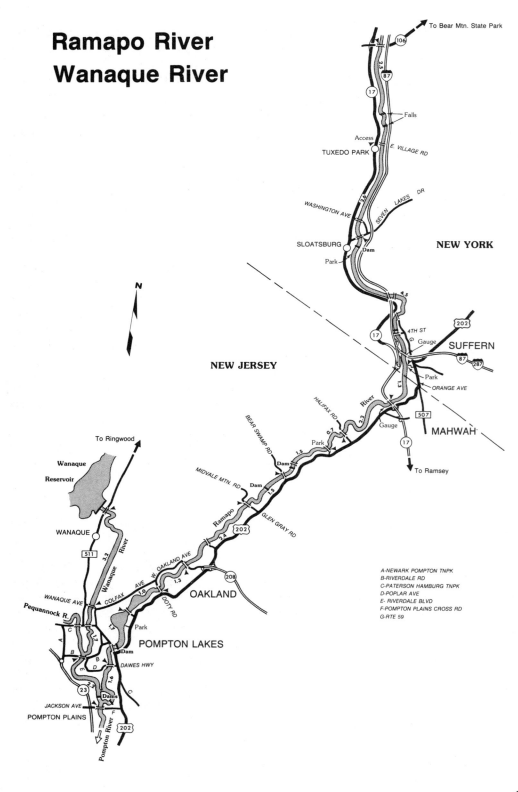

To Bear Mtn. State Park

106

2.5

87

17

Falls

Access

E. VILLAGE RD

TUXEDO PARK

WASHINGTON AVE

2.8

SEVEN LAKES DR

SLOATSBURG

Dam

NEW YORK

Park

4.5

4TH ST

202

17

Gauge

SUFFERN

87

287

NEW JERSEY

River

1.3

Park

ORANGE AVE

HALIFAX RD

2.2

507

0.7

Gauge

MAHWAH

Bear Swamp Rd

Park

To Ramsey

1.5

17

Dam

MIDVALE MTN. RD

Dam

1.5

To Ringwood

Wanaque
Reservoir

Ramapo

202

2.4

GLEN GRAY RD

WANAQUE

511

3.2

Wanaque River

W. OAKLAND AVE

COLFAX AVE

1.3

208

1.0

OAKLAND

WANAQUE AVE

DOTY RD

Pequannock R.

1.7

Park

C

POMPTON LAKES

A
B
m
D

1.7

Dam

B

DAWES HWY

23

2.2

1.6

C

Dams

JACKSON AVE

F

POMPTON PLAINS

202

Pompton River

A-NEWARK POMPTON TNPK
B-RIVERDALE RD
C-PATERSON HAMBURG TNPK
D-POPLAR AVE
E- RIVERDALE BLVD
F-POMPTON PLAINS CROSS RD
G-RTE 59

50

WATER CONDITIONS: This is seldom up. Nature has to fill those big upstream reservoirs before there is water for you. So wait for a wet winter or spring. If the reservoirs are then full, a hard rain may sustain canoeable flows for a week.

GAUGE: There are none. Judge at Rte. 511.

Ramapo River

INTRODUCTION: The Ramapo (Native American for "round pond") has been a favorite novice canoe destination for generations of North Jersey paddlers. Once a country cruise, its environs have since been overtaken by the advance of suburbia. Still, part of the creek remains a de facto refuge — a good springtime run that is convenient to many.

This is an interstate stream of varying character. The river's source is a smattering of ponds set in the mountainous, eastern edge of Orange County, New York, about 10 miles north of the New Jersey line. Often a close companion of the New York Thruway, its upper reaches see relatively few paddlers. Next the stream clips a corner of Rockland County and then enters Bergen County to show its best face. Here it has always been a popular place to cruise. As it reaches Oakland and heads into Passaic County, it is smothered by suburbia. It is a place to paddle, but by no means an escape from crowds and civilization. In contrast, the Ramapo enjoys a quiet, lonely finish in a patch of woods near Pompton Plains. Might any of this appeal to you?

Section 1. Co. Rte. 106 to N.J. Rte. 17					
Gradient	Difficulty	Distance	Time	Scenery	Map
18	A to 2—	10.9	4.0	Good to Poor	50

TRIP DESCRIPTION: Rte. 106 is not the absolute head of navigation, but it is the first good access point. The bridge crosses high above the river. So to reach the water, follow the ramp off Rte. 17 at Rte. 106 (sign says "Bear Mountain Park"), cross over Rte. 17, and immediately turn left (beneath the power lines) onto a steep dirt road. This bears to the right, ending at a trashy but easy put-in spot.

They say nature abhors a vacuum. But that is nothing compared to the aversion held by highway builders for empty spaces. So it is no wonder that, long ago, transportation engineers wired the New York Thruway, Rte. 17, and a railroad through the convenient portal followed by the Ramapo through the 12-mile-wide swath of mountains and plateau that spans southeast New York. You would think, therefore, that the upper reaches of the Ramapo would be ruined. There is certainly no denying that the highways make it noisier here than on some Adirondack lake. But otherwise, thanks to either distance, high banks, or riverside vegetation, the roads' visual presence is hardly overpowering.

You do not have to paddle far to appreciate the finest quality of the upper river — its good views of the surrounding mountains. They are particularly striking where they display their black rock outcrops and cliffs. Sometimes though, you see little of this because the stream files down a trough of high banks. Within a half mile of the start, the Ramapo begins to pass through a series of pond-like pools separated by ledgy rock masses. In these spots, the stream tumbles over delightful rapids and riffles. Delightful, that is, until about a mile and a half below Rte. 106. When the creek bends left and then slides beneath a railroad bridge, get out immediately. Just around the bend to the right is a rugged waterfall — a beautiful sight if you ignore the power line above and the graffiti on the rocks. The best portage is on the right. At the end of the attractive pool below, get out again on the right to portage a dam that caps another beautiful falls. This was originally the site of an 18th-century iron furnace (Augusta Furnace), but only some industrial ruins of a more recent era remain along your portage path and downstream. A rocky rapid and exciting, sloping ledge wait for you at the end of the portage. The stream continues at a fast pace, with many riffles, but no real rapids. The pleasure of the ride may partially compensate for the checkered aesthetics. For when the Ramapo passes behind towns, the banks are often trashy, and nearby buildings are unsightly.

In Sloatsburg, about 200 yards below Seven Lakes Drive, there is a four-foot weir to carry. About a mile farther, as you approach the first Thruway bridge, watch out for a row of timber pilings — a potential pinning hazard. Only 50 yards farther, at what seems to be a more significant danger, an apparent dead end against the concrete mass of an old dam turns out to have an easy bypass through a breach on the left. A mile farther, an intact, five-foot weir, with a steep, trashy rubble rapid at its base, invites another carry (right).

You then get to enjoy more good current and riffles as you float past the ugly backside of Suffern. Now the Ramapo breaks out of its narrow, mountain-rimmed valley and enters New Jersey. Greeting the paddler is the dazzling sight of a towering Sheraton Hotel, scenery the rest of the world expects one to see upon paddling into New Jersey. But things improve vastly on Section 2, so do not give up on this river.

There is no ideal take-out for this section. Probably the most popular spot is at a small parking lot on U.S. Rte. 202 just upstream of Rte. 17. Another option is the ball field in Suffern. To find it, turn west off Orange Avenue onto Chestnut Street, dip beneath the railroad tracks, and bear right. Walk around the left edge of the ball field and, assuming the gate in the fence is unlocked, walk through and put in beneath the old railroad bridge.

HAZARDS: The first falls, about a mile and a half below the start, can really surprise you. The next falls and the two weirs described above are more easily recognized. Carry all four. Beware of those pilings in the channel above the first Thruway bridge.

WATER CONDITIONS: Best levels mostly occur from November through early May. In that period, catch within four to seven days of hard rain.

GAUGE: Your first choice should be a USGS gauging station at Mahwah, along Rte. 202 about a hundred yards downstream of Rte. 17 (call Philadelphia or visit site). It has an outside staff that may be difficult to read at high levels. A level of 3.8 feet is about zero. Your second choice should be the USGS gauging station at Suffern, located beneath the Thruway's bridge. To reach it, park at the commuter railway station, cross the tracks, follow a fishermen's path downhill, and then follow a dirt road to the right for about a hundred yards. The staff is in the fast-moving water, and its reading fluctuates because of pillowing water. Roughly, 2.7 feet is minimal. There is also another staff gauge beneath the Thruway bridge above Suffern. But visiting it involves trespassing.

Section 2. N.J. Rte. 17 to Oakland (Doty Road)					
Gradient	Difficulty	Distance	Time	Scenery	Map
6	A to 1	9.6	4.0	Good to Poor	50

TRIP DESCRIPTION: This is the most pleasant part of the Ramapo. The flavor is relaxed. The busy highways are finally gone. The country is more open now with chunks of land preserved in a park, college campus, and various estates. To the right, the wooded wall of Ramapo Mountain is your constant companion. If you are an admirer of durable works of engineering, you will appreciate the spindly iron form of Cleveland Bridge (Bear Swamp Road), in service since 1888.

As you pull into Oakland, the population density rises and, by the last mile, suburban clutter robs the view of any redeeming scenic value. So if you can get permission to take out at West Oakland Avenue, which is about a mile upstream of Doty Road, you will not have missed much.

You get to enjoy this reach at a mild pace. The water is primarily smooth, but still expect some riffles. You will need to carry two weirs. First comes a four-footer about four miles into the trip. The owner of the private bridge just upstream has been kind enough to hang up a warning sign. A carry on the left is short and easy. Then about three quarters of a mile farther, there is a three-footer. Carry this on the right. Barring any newly fallen trees, you should find no more obstructions.

HAZARDS: There are two weirs to carry.

WATER CONDITIONS: Most probable season is November through mid-May. During that period, if weather has been wetter than average, the creek will almost always have enough water for canoeing. In dry periods, it should remain up for a week after a hard rain.

GAUGE: Use the USGS gauging station at Mahwah, along Rte. 202 about a hundred yards downstream of Rte. 17 (call Philadelphia or visit). A level of 3.3 feet is about as low as most would tolerate. Note that, because the staff is bent, the staff gauge reads 0.05 feet higher than the true level, which Philadelphia reports.

Section 3. Oakland (Doty Road) to mouth					
Gradient	Difficulty	Distance	Time	Scenery	Map
7	A to 1—	4.1	2.5	Fair to Poor	50

TRIP DESCRIPTION: This is a forgettable stretch. The creek immediately spreads out as a lake. Except for a few tiny parks, the lake shore is entirely built up. While it is a nice enough neighborhood, this means that there are few places where you can land without being in someone's backyard. At the end of the lake, a dam forces you into a short, steep carry on the left. There is a nice rapid at its foot, then mostly flatwater for the rest of the way. In fact, much of this reach is the backwater of a seven-foot weir located just above the confluence with the Pequannock. The carry on the right is easy. Washing over its brink might shorten your life.

These final, mellow miles lead you mostly through more suburbs. But there is a relatively isolated, woodsy flourish near the mouth. There is no access to this point, so continue down the Pompton River for a few hundred yards to Pompton Plains Cross Road.

HAZARDS: Stay away from the big dam at the end of Pompton Lake, and watch out for fast traffic when you portage it. The seven-foot weir near the mouth is particularly dangerous because of its strong reversal. Please carry. Take out above the three-foot weir at Pompton Plains Cross Road, or run it only along the right end.

WATER CONDITIONS: Pompton Lake is always paddleable. The river below the dam is passable usually from November through May.

GAUGE: None. The shallowest spot is in the rapid below Pompton Lake Dam, so judge conditions there.

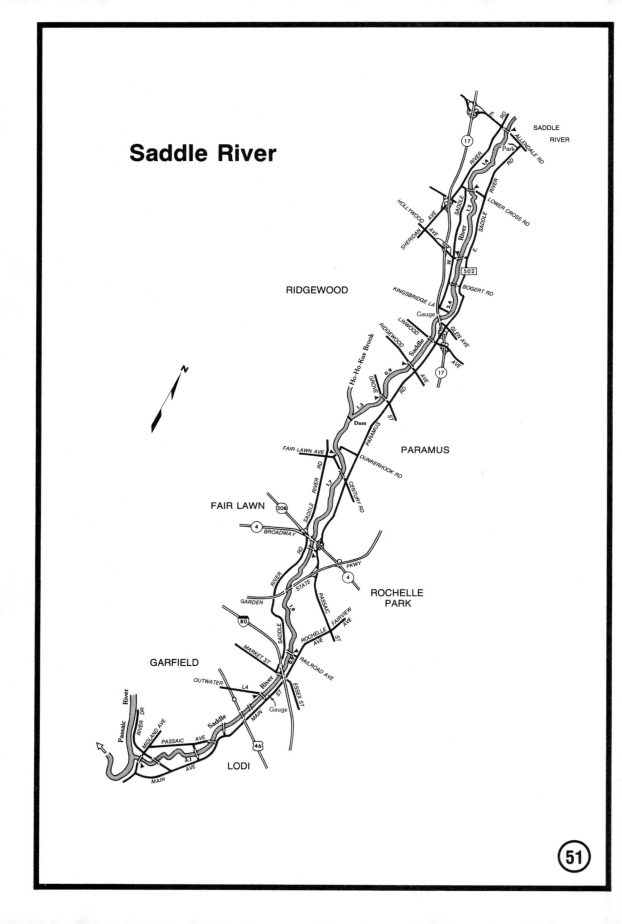

Saddle River

SADDLE RIVER

ALLENDALE RD
17
RIVER 1.4
Park
SADDLE
E. RD
SADDLE RIVER
LOWER CROSS RD
HOLLYWOOD AVE
SADDLE 1.3
SHERIDAN AVE
River E. SADDLE RIVER
W.
502
BOGERT RD

RIDGEWOOD

KINGSBRIDGE LA
2.4
Gauge
LINWOOD
GLEN AVE
Saddle
RIDGEWOOD
0.9
Ho-Ho-Kus Brook
GROVE
AVE
17
ST
1.3
RD
Dam
PARAMUS
FAIR LAWN AVE
DUNKERHOOK RD
SADDLE
RIVER
1.7
CENTURY RD
RD
PARAMUS

FAIR LAWN
208
4
BROADWAY
RIVER
PKWY
4
RD
STATE
ROCHELLE
PARK
GARDEN
1.9
PASSAIC
FAIRVIEW
AVE
80
SADDLE
ROCHELLE
AVE
ST
MARKET ST
RAILROAD AVE

GARFIELD
OUTWATER
LA
River
ESSEX ST
Passaic River
ST
RIVER DR
Saddle
MAIN
Gauge
MIDLAND AVE
PASSAIC
AVE
46
3.1
AVE
LODI
MAIN

51

Saddle River

INTRODUCTION: The Saddle River rises just over the New York line in Rockland County, and then flows southward through Bergen County to join the Passaic River at Garfield. Its watershed is completely urbanized and suburbanized, and one might expect to write this creek off as another ravaged victim of civilization. But the Saddle is different. It has weathered its trauma well. Coursing through fine neighborhoods and a string of parks, it makes a satisfying — albeit ephemeral — destination for, at least, Bergen County boaters.

Section 1. *East Allendale Road to mouth*					
Gradient	Difficulty	Distance	Time	Scenery	Map
12	A to 1	14.9	5.0	Fair to Good	51

TRIP DESCRIPTION: This is just a tiny brook at East Allendale Road. The recommended put-in is just downstream of this bridge, approached from Rindlaub Park. The park is located behind the borough hall off East Saddle River Road. The first few miles twist past the backyards of the rich and famous. The opportunity to study the architecture and landscaping are the best attractions of this stretch, though this may just serve to remind you that you really should be home cutting the grass or planting tulips, not flushing down a storm drain in a canoe. Fortunately, most paddlers quickly develop immunity to such guilty feelings and should enjoy the setting.

From N.J. Rte. 17 to Railroad Avenue in Rochelle Park, a chain of public parks grace the banks. A nice feature of these parks is a bicycle trail that follows most of this reach. The trail allows you to enjoy the Saddle even when it is too low to float upon. These parks are popular, so on a nice day, expect plenty of company up on the banks.

The remainder of the Saddle finally looks like an urban creek. Industrial plants, apartments, and commercial buildings crowd its banks, and more trash appears. There is no bicycle trail down here. Yet, even on this reach, there are some leafy interludes, and the general level of abuse is less than on most built-up streams. There is no access at the mouth, so take out just upstream at Midland Avenue.

At moderate levels, the Saddle is suitable for novice boaters, even beginners for much of the way. There are lots of riffles, especially at the start. But much of the path is smooth and sometimes channelized, with a shallow, sandy or gravelly bottom. The path is often free of strainers, and there are only two weirs. The most serious of these, just below the confluence with Ho-Ho-Kus Brook, is a recommended carry.

HAZARDS: Strainers are uncommon here, but they are always a potential problem on so small a stream. There is a four-foot weir just below Ho-Ho-Kus Brook, easily carried on the right. The gauging station above Outwater Lane has an 18-inch weir, but this should cause no difficulty at moderate levels.

WATER CONDITIONS: This being an urbanized watershed, runoff is usually quick and intense. Even under these conditions, winter and spring sustain the longest high flows. To start at Allendale Road, catch within a day of hard rain. To float below Ho-Ho-Kus Brook, catch within four to six days of hard rain.

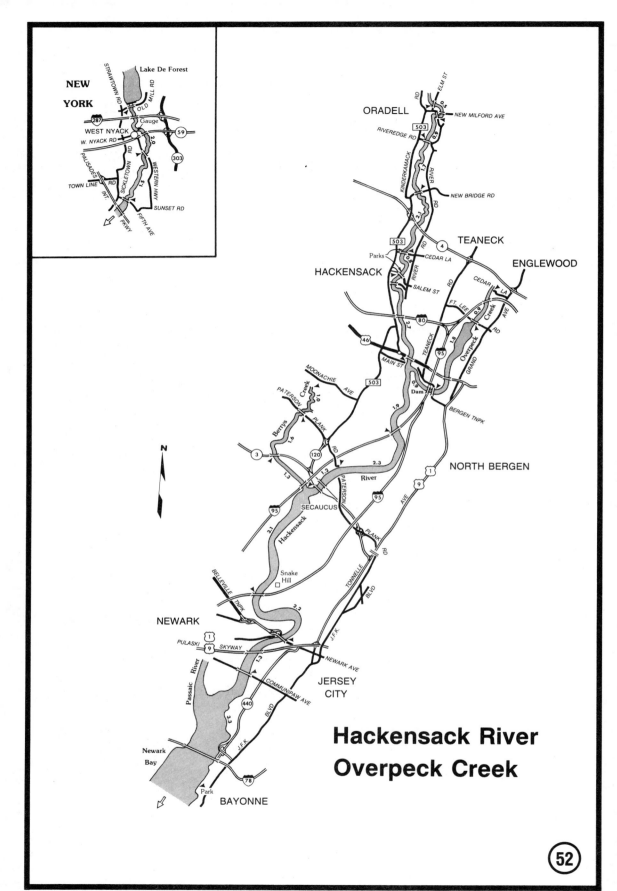

Hackensack River
Overpeck Creek

NEW YORK

Lake De Forest

WEST NYACK
Gauge

Lake De Forest
STRAWTOWN RD
OLD MILL RD
W. NYACK RD
SICKLETOWN RD
WESTERN HWY
SUNSET RD
TOWN LINE RD
PALISADES INT. PKWY
FIFTH AVE
287
59
303
2.0
1.2

ORADELL
ELM ST
RD
0.5
New Milford Ave
503
0.5
RIVEREDGE RD
KINDERKAMACK
RIVER RD
NEW BRIDGE RD
2.1
503
RD
4
TEANECK
Parks
CEDAR LA
RIVER RD
0.6
SALEM ST
HACKENSACK
ENGLEWOOD
CEDAR LA
FT. LEE RD
80
TEANECK
2.7
95
Creek
RD
1.8
Overpeck
GRAND AVE
46
MAIN ST
503
0.5
Dam
1.9
MOONACHIE AVE
Creek
1.0
PATERSON
PLANK RD
BERGEN TNPK
Berry's
1.6
120
2.3
NORTH BERGEN
3
1.3
1.2
PATERSON
River
95
1
9
SECAUCUS
PLANK RD
95
2.1
Hackensack
TONNELLE BLVD
Snake Hill
BELLEVILLE TNPK
2.2
NEWARK
1
PULASKI SKYWAY
9
1.3
J.F.K.
Newark Ave
JERSEY CITY
COMMUNIPAW AVE
Passaic River
440
BLVD
3.3
J.F.K.
Newark Bay
78
Park
BAYONNE

52

GAUGE: There are USGS gauging stations just above Rte. 17 in Ridgewood, on the left bank, and about a hundred yards above Outwater Lane in Lodi, on the left. You can call Philadelphia for both or inspect on site. Neither gauge has easy access. For the first, there is no stopping at the Rte. 17 bridge. So park a quarter mile upstream at the end of Kingsbridge Lane, cross the footbridge, and walk down Saddle River Road to the Rte. 17 bridge. For the Lodi gauge, pull off Outwater Lane, and park at the fence gate near the northeast end of the bridge. Walk around the fence at the bridge, and then follow the grassy right-of-way to the gauging station. A level of 2.0 feet at Ridgewood is zero for starting at Allendale Road. A level of 2.6 feet at Lodi is zero for starting at Allendale Road, but 2.3 feet is zero for the creek below Ho-Ho-Kus confluence.

Hackensack River

INTRODUCTION: The Hackensack is probably the least likely river in New Jersey to garner one's attention. But, like rivers everywhere, it is filled with water, or at least some liquid substance. And being within a few miles of millions of people, some of whom paddle, it may just come in handy as at least a place to exercise.

The Hackensack rises only a mile from the Hudson River near Haverstraw, New York. It follows a winding course, but overall runs parallel to the Hudson to join the Passaic at the head of Newark Bay. Roughly half of this river is nontidal. But that is of no benefit for you the paddler, because most of that half is a chain of municipal water supply reservoirs. About all that the authorities allow you to do with these lakes is look at them, and even that is from behind high chain-link fences. So that leaves the paddler with one short stretch through West Nyack, New York, and those miles of tidewater through The Meadowlands that most of us know best as scenery from the Turnpike.

Section 1. Old Mill Road to 5th Avenue (Rockland County, New York)					
Gradient	Difficulty	Distance	Time	Scenery	Map
2	A	3.5	1.5	Fair to Good	52

TRIP DESCRIPTION: This section is entirely inside New York and is detached from the other river segments described below. The run starts just below the fenced and guarded grounds of Lake DeForest, the first of three taboo water supply reservoirs. The left downstream end of the bridge is your easiest access to the sluggish stream. There is a brief wooded section followed by an unscenic view of the backside of West Nyack, with lots of road noise from the New York Thruway.

In compensation, below Western Highway, the creek slips into a beautiful marsh, the head of Lake Tappan. Fortunately, the next fenced no-mans-land does not start until the downstream side of 5th Avenue. Many might choose to just start at 5th Avenue and paddle upstream and back.

HAZARDS: None

WATER CONDITIONS: This route is always deep enough below Western Highway and most of the time OK above there.

GAUGE: There is a USGS gauge on the right bank a few feet downstream of the railroad bridge
in West Nyack, about 200 yards west of the N.Y. Rte. 59 bridge. Zero is unknown, but is probably around 2.7 feet for the shallowest spots.

Section 2. Oradell (Elm Street) to Hackensack (Salem Street)					
Gradient	Difficulty	Distance	Time	Scenery	Map
0	A	6.0	2.5	Fair to Good	52

TRIP DESCRIPTION: This is the head of tidewater and, for the most part, is upstream of
the ugliness. You cannot put in at Elm Street, as it is water company property (Oradell Reservoir
is just upstream). But, if the tide is in, it is easy to enter from the side of New Milford Avenue
just a few feet east of where the road crosses the commuter railroad line. The three-quarters-of-a-
mile paddle upstream to Elm Street is pleasant, tree-shaded, and legal.

The trip downstream is a pleasant surprise, as a wooded buffer generally separates the river
from the tidy surrounding neighborhoods. There are occasional patches of marsh. The river remains
narrow. After about two miles you start seeing more houses, some shiny office buildings, a college
campus, and even a shopping mall. But it remains a pleasant setting. The finish is at either Foschini
Park, west bank, or either of two small parks at the east end of Salem Street bridge.

HAZARDS: None

WATER CONDITIONS: This is all tidal, so it is always deep enough. But high tide at the
upper end greatly eases your ability to launch or land.

GAUGE: None

Section 3. Hackensack (Salem Street) to mouth					
Gradient	Difficulty	Distance	Time	Scenery	Map
0	A	16.5	6.0	Poor	52

TRIP DESCRIPTION: The remainder of the Hackensack will appeal to few, though it can
function nicely as some badly needed open space in this crowded area. But do not expect much
of aesthetic value.

The first stretch, from Salem Street to Little Ferry, has heavily developed banks. Bulk oil termi-
nals, commercial buildings, apartments, and junk replace trees and marshes. About the only really
interesting spot is the USS Ling (in Hackensack) — a rusting, old submarine with tours and an
accompanying museum. At Little Ferry, Overpeck Creek joins, and the river widens. Overpeck
Creek also offers some paddling and is described below as Section 4.

Below Little Ferry, the Hackensack enters the Meadowlands. This was probably once a vast
expanse of beautiful marsh meadows. But today, that which has not been dredged or built upon,
has most likely been used as a giant depository for the area's trash. Thus, much of the "meadows"
is now just raised acres of buried refuse. On the bright side, great stands of phragmites occupy
the fringes of the landfills and those wetlands that remain, softening the area's appearance. Probably the most interesting sight on this reach is Snake Hill. This big chunk of black volcanic rock,
at least what is left of it, rises improbably out of otherwise soggy surroundings a few miles below
the Sports Complex. Official access to The Meadowlands area is poor, though local fishers and
crabbers seem to find numerous back roads to the banks.

On the right, just below the busy spans of N.J. Rte. 3, is Berrys Creek Canal. The Canal is a straight, mile-long man-made channel that is now the outlet for Berrys Creek. You can ascend the Canal and Berrys Creek for almost four miles, not quite making it up to Moonachie Avenue. This phragmites-lined passage offers views of the Sports Complex, the Manhattan skyline, a hotel, and industrial parks. Near its headwaters, the narrow, reed-lined channels finally take on a natural appearance. You actually feel a bit hidden from the world at this point.

Below Snake Hill, the Hackensack rounds a bend and enters an area of heavy industry that lasts until the mouth. There are ocean-going ships, power plants, tank farms, and big factories. Bridges down here are interesting, especially the Pulaski Skyway. The last place to take out is beneath the right end of the Belleville Turnpike bridge. Below the mouth, the Hudson County Park in Bayonne might also suffice.

HAZARDS: Watch out for motorboats and commercial shipping.

WATER CONDITIONS: Always canoeable

GAUGE: None

Section 4. Overpeck Creek. Cedar Lane to Bergen Turnpike					
Gradient	Difficulty	Distance	Time	Scenery	Map
0	A	3.3	1.5	Fair	52

TRIP DESCRIPTION: Overpeck Creek provides a nice place to get some exercise paddling on flat water, if you live in that neighborhood. The described section is really a lake formed by a wooden dam that hides beneath I-95. The suggested put-in is from a cul-de-sac at the end of Cedar Lane in Englewood. The creek here is only a few feet wide. It quickly broadens to about a hundred yards, shaping up as an attractive lake bordered first by a golf course, then by a park. At Fort Lee Road the waters really balloon out. Though the surroundings are still mostly park, the phragmites-fringed shores and high ground reveal that these are all reclaimed trash dumps on what was no doubt once wetlands. Though it is an acceptably pleasant setting from the middle, close inspection of the eroded banks exposes the paper, plastic, and steel stuffing that underlies it all. Approaching and below U.S. Rte. 46, the surroundings assume a commercial and industrial appearance similar to the Hackensack. The take-out at Bergen Turnpike is easy.

Do not bother to do the last mile of this creek. To get around the dam, you must follow Bergen Turnpike over I-95. There is, unfortunately, no good way to reach the water for at least a few more blocks. There is a bad way though, through a hole in the fence along the west side of I-95, over another fence, and down a steep embankment to the river. All this work would be to see a 100% ugly riverscape. Save yourself the pain, and let not the author's suffering be in vain.

HAZARDS: Dam beneath I-95

WATER CONDITIONS: Always canoeable

GAUGE: None

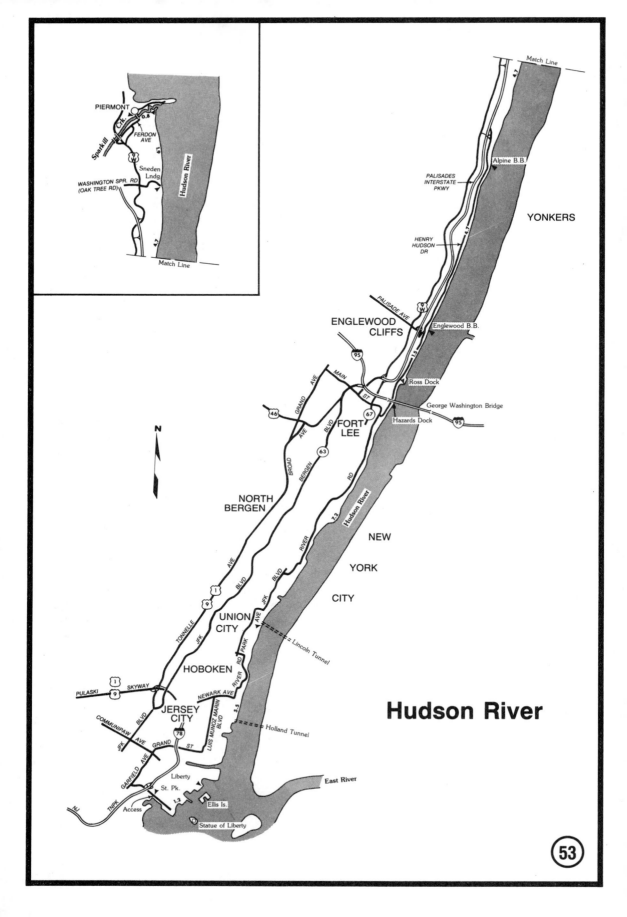

Hudson River

Match Line

YONKERS

PALISADES INTERSTATE PKWY

Alpine B.B.

HENRY HUDSON DR

4.7

PALISADE AVE

ENGLEWOOD CLIFFS

Englewood B.B.

95

MAIN ST

GRAND AVE

67

Ross Dock

George Washington Bridge

46

BERGEN AVE

BROAD AVE

FORT LEE

63

Hazards Dock

95

RD

7.2

Hudson River

NORTH BERGEN

NEW YORK CITY

1

9

RIVER BLVD

JFK BLVD

AVE

UNION CITY

JFK AVE

Lincoln Tunnel

TONNELLE AVE

JFK BLVD

HOBOKEN

PARK RD

RIVER RD

PULASKI SKYWAY

1

9

NEWARK AVE

3.5

Holland Tunnel

COMMUNIPAW AVE

JFK BLVD

JERSEY CITY

78

GRAND ST

LUIS MUNOZ MARIN BLVD

East River

GARFIELD AVE

NJ TNPK

Liberty St. Pk.

Access

1.2

Ellis Is.

Statue of Liberty

Inset (upper left)

PIERMONT

0.8

Sparkill Ck.

FERDON AVE

9W

19

Sneden Lndg.

WASHINGTON SPR. RD (OAK TREE RD)

Hudson River

4.7

Match Line

N

53

Hudson River

INTRODUCTION: Just about anybody in the country has heard of the Hudson River. It is in New York. Right? Yes, so interwoven is the Hudson's identity with that of the Big Apple that it is easy to forget that the last 20 miles of this majestic waterway form New Jersey's border. Even fewer people would ever guess that this might also be a good place to go paddling. But it is.

Let us first do a background check on the Hudson. It starts nearly 300 miles above New York Bay in the Adirondack wilderness near Mount Marcy, New York's highest point. Its passage through the Adirondacks is one of great beauty, and the whitewater of its gorge is famous among boaters of the Northeast. The river leaves the plateau in great steps that long ago were harnessed to power mills and generate electricity. The resulting industries in towns like Glens Falls and Fort Edward prospered, but fouled the river mightily. Even after much cleanup, aftereffects still linger.

The Hudson reaches sea level near Troy. In a way, its estuary is a river in retirement. For at one time, the Hudson was the country's premier transportation corridor. In series with the Erie Canal, it was the gateway to the American frontier. It is not nearly so vital now, though some barges still ply its waters and busy railroad lines follow its banks.

For many miles the Hudson estuary cuts through a raised landscape to form a scenic, gorge-like passage that is so grand that it is nicknamed "the American Rhine." In fact, one of the Hudson's most unusual characteristics is that, unlike most rivers, the closer it gets to the sea, the more impressive the scenery gets, even where part of that scenery is man-made. And part of this section is what is described below.

Section 1. Piermont, New York, to George Washington Bridge (Ross Dock)					
Gradient	Difficulty	Distance	Time	Scenery	Map
0	A	13.6	4.0	Good to Very Good	53

TRIP DESCRIPTION: This trip can start on tiny Sparkill Creek, where Ferdon Avenue crosses it in Piermont, New York. The creek twists through town, past docks and lawns, and then through a phragmites marsh for three quarters of a mile before spitting you out into the broad Hudson. The Hudson here is huge, widening to two and a half miles just upstream. In fact, it is so huge that it once fooled Henry Hudson into thinking that this might just be the fabled Northwest Passage. The marshes cling to the west shore for about the next two miles, with Tallman Mountain rising behind them. The far side also rises well above the river, but more gently, with a chain of towns clinging to the hillsides. Looking back to the western shore, after passing some houses around Sneden Landing, you enter the Palisades.

The Palisades are just grand. Rising 500 feet almost straight up from the riverside, they at least take the form of wooded bluffs. But for much of this stretch, they do better than that, presenting a fearsome exposure of black, jagged basaltic cliffs, often with barren talus slopes at their base. Most people have to travel to Wyoming's Devil's Tower or Oregon's Columbia Plateau to see such rock. You have it here, right in your own backyard. If you ignore the east shore and just focus on this wonderful view, it is easy to pretend that you are Henry Hudson and the time right now is the 17th century. There are at least two wet-weather waterfalls dashing down the escarpment. Particularly pretty is the northernmost cascade, just a mile or two south of Sneden Landing. Some crumbling white columns mark the spot — a memento of a time when this was a wealthy family's private retreat. Now it belongs to you and me, as Tallman Mountain, and all of the New Jersey portion of this reach, are part of Palisades Interstate Park.

We are fortunate that the Palisades are protected. At one time, they were looked upon as an exploitable resource, and used they were. People quarried the hard rock of the cliffs. The Englewood Boat Basin was once the busy terminus of the Dyckman Street Ferry, before the George Washington Bridge was built. And up near the state line is High Gutter Point, where logs were hurled down a chute to the riverside to provide fuel for steamboats.

In the park, you can find launching ramps at Alpine Boat Basin, Englewood Boat Basin, Ross Dock, and Hazards Dock. In season, all of these ramps have user fees. But the park has no problems with or fees for paddlers launching at other convenient locations. For that reason, the recreation area next to Ross Dock is chosen as the finish for this section.

HAZARDS: Stay relatively close to shore to avoid commercial shipping. Even there, watch out for careless recreational motorboaters.

WATER CONDITIONS: The Hudson is tidal and deep, so it is always runnable. Keep in mind that the Hudson tide can be fierce, so be sure that you are running with it.

GAUGE: None

Section 2. George Washington Bridge (Ross Dock) to Liberty State Park					
Gradient	Difficulty	Distance	Time	Scenery	Map
0	A	13.9	4.0	Unique	53

TRIP DESCRIPTION: Welcome to the big city. The park ends just below the bridge, but the Palisades do not, continuing south and slowly shrinking. But there is flat land now at their base, mostly heavily built upon, and high above, high-rise apartments perch just beyond the rim of the cliffs. Just south of the Lincoln Tunnel, the bluffs finally turn away from the river.

Much of the immediate Jersey shore is a mess. Miles of this side have ceased to function as a port. Piers and warehouses are either crumbling or have been leveled. Some new development is going on, and it seems as if gentrification will ultimately fill the void. In spite of much vacant land, you will find few spots where you are free to land.

The real glory of this section is the view from the Jersey side of the New York side. If you are unaccustomed to this town, the sight of block after block, mile after mile of continuous, multistory development is mind boggling. This seems all the more impressive because much of the city is perched upon already high ground. That Manhattan has two downtown, high-rise office districts, each one bigger than almost any other city's, is even more amazing. Particularly stunning is the financial district, at the tip of the island, rising like a steel and glass mirage above the water.

Passing the tip of Manhattan, it is time to turn your attention back to the Jersey side. Immediately ahead is the fortress-like Ellis Island, perhaps a stepping-stone in your ancestry. And just a little farther ahead is the Statue of Liberty, the ultimate and most beautiful of rock ornaments. At this point, it is time to turn due west, towards the picnic area of Liberty State Park. You can get out of the water easily here, at the old pier sites by the parking area. Or you can go all the way to the formal boat ramp, but you may face a user fee for the luxury.

Just because the lower Hudson is "flat water," that does not necessarily mean that it is smooth. The tidal currents here are so fast that they actually throw up boils and whirlpools along the eddy lines. A little wind can stir up some nasty chop, not to mention blow you around. Boat wakes can also be sizable. And once you reach the mouth, big, rolling swells can rock you even on a calm day. Be on the lookout for wild motorboat jockeys, and be sure to give a wide berth to the fast-moving ferry that operates between Port Imperial and 38th Street.

One should note that there is one pronounced drawback to such urban paddling — extremely poor access. It is difficult to find convenient or friendly places to put in between George Washington and Liberty. Even landing for lunch is difficult, as some of the landowners, particularly absentee ones with security guards, are totally selfish. Other stretches are inaccessible unless you can scale the high bulkheads. As for finding a private spot at which to relieve yourself, forget it. So plan accordingly.

Finally, you have some hard shuttle choices to decide upon. The most direct route traverses the most congested territory in the state. If you plan to paddle this entire section, a slightly better route is just to follow the west side of town via U.S. Rte. 1/9 and connecting streets. The best route, though there was inadequate room to show this on the shuttle map, is to take I-95, the N.J. Turnpike (also I-95), and the I-78 extension of the Turnpike. This route is roughly 23 miles each way verses 16 miles via Rte. 1/9. But the tolls and few extra miles are well worth missing 10 million traffic lights, double-parked cars, unpredictable pedestrians, and creeping traffic.

HAZARDS: Be prepared for variable weather, particularly wind. Boat wakes can be troublesome. Steer clear of boats and ships.

WATER CONDITIONS: Always up. Once again, remember that the tide really rips through this relatively narrow channel. So read the tables so that you can travel every inch with the tide.

GAUGE: None. A tide table and a clock are your gauge.

Wallkill River

INTRODUCTION: Do not fall for that myth about rivers not flowing north. Plenty of them do — big ones, too. What about the Nile, the Ob, or the Rhine? And more importantly, what about the Wallkill? This noble stream starts near Sparta, in Sussex County, gathering its first waters in a narrow basin between Sparta Mountain and the Pimple Hills (probably the only realistically named uplands in the state). It flows north into New York to join Rondout Creek and ultimately feeds the Hudson River near Kingston. Flowing about 90 miles total, the Wallkill is the third longest river in this book, though most of it is in New York. The New Jersey portion and its tributaries drain the entire eastern half of Sussex County. It is a stream of many moods, with its best one (in Jersey) being mellow. Many will find that the Wallkill offers the finest flatwater paddling this side of the Pine Barrens.

Section 1. Ogdensburg (Brooks Flat Road) to Sussex (Rte. 565)					
Gradient	Difficulty	Distance	Time	Scenery	Map
18	A to 2	12.0	6.0	Good to Poor	54
1 mi. @ 47					

TRIP DESCRIPTION: The defining characteristic of this first section is that it seldom stays the same for very long. So only a paddler of diverse tastes and skills is likely to be happy here for more than two miles at a time.

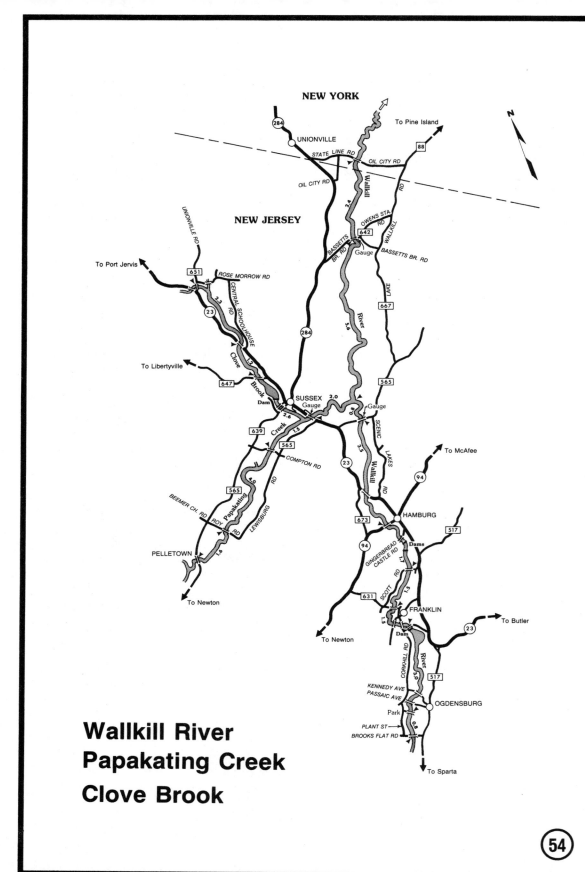

NEW YORK

284 UNIONVILLE

To Pine Island

88

STATE LINE RD

OIL CITY RD

Wallkill

OIL CITY RD

2.4

OWENS STA. RD

642

WALLKILL RD

BASSETTS BR. RD

Gauge

BASSETTS BR. RD

NEW JERSEY

UNIONVILLE RD

To Port Jervis

651

ROSE MORROW RD

CENTRAL SCHOOLHOUSE

LAKE

667

2.3

23

RD

River

284

5.6

565

To Libertyville

Clove

1.2

647

Brook

SUSSEX

Gauge

2.0

Gauge

Dam

2.6

0.8

565

Creek

1.5

SCENIC

639

565

COMPTON RD

3.5

LAKES

Wallkill

RD

565

4.0

Papakating

23

BEEMER CH. RD

ROY.

RD

LEWISBURG RD

To McAfee

94

PELLETOWN

1.4

673

HAMBURG

517

94

Dams

GINGERBREAD CASTLE RD

1.7

631

SCOTT RD

1.5

To Newton

To Newton

1.5

FRANKLIN

23

To Butler

Dam

CORKHILL RD

River

3.0

517

KENNEDY AVE

PASSAIC AVE

Park

OGDENSBURG

PLANT ST

0.8

BROOKS FLAT RD

To Sparta

N

Wallkill River
Papakating Creek
Clove Brook

54

The Wallkill "River" that you find at Brooks Flat Road looks like a refugee from South Jersey — an eight-foot-wide dribble disappearing into a swamp. Surprisingly, the twisting passage through that beautiful swamp, while tortuous, is practically unobstructed. Though this is a hardwood forest swamp, the channel is lined mostly by alder, willow, and other shrubs. The water is clear, smooth, and swift.

After about a mile, the channel breaks out of the jungle, allowing you to behold the ugly side of Ogdensburg, to the right, and a big scab of mine devastation on the hillside, to the left. The mine is inactive. Formerly owned by New Jersey Zinc, this was once one of the biggest zinc mines in the country. But the mine lives again, now for the amusement of tourists, operating as Stirling Hill Mine. You can tour the underground mine and view equipment and exotic minerals at the museum.

If you continue down the river, you will eat wood. For although the stream now assumes some gradient and easy rapids, the path is plagued by too many strainers. There follows temporary relief in a pleasant and unobstructed passage through a well-kept horse farm, and then it is in and out of more little swamps. A short, slow paddle across a pond at Franklin (the pond, by the way, is posted "For Residents Only") brings you to a dam. Carry on the right. More ugly views of towns and pretty interludes in woods follow. The water intermittently flows placidly or tumbles down sets of easy rapids (Class 1 +). Strainers continue to be a repeated annoyance.

Approaching Scott Road, the gradient steepens. A long rapid dances past Scott Road, but dies in a pool. If industrial history interests you, watch for a path on the right bank shortly below the head of this pool. It leads up to a splendid battery of old lime kilns (or you can reach this by auto via Limekiln Road at the south end of Hamburg). The pool is formed by a 20-foot dam beside a crumbling, old factory. Carry the dam on the left, where a tangled landing is followed by an easy path. There is a delightful Class 2 stretch just below, but watch out for a dangerous iron spike in the middle of the channel beneath the factory's concrete bridge. Then comes another short pool, this one backed up behind a 15-foot dam beside an active factory. After a tight carry on the right, you can relax on about a mile of easy rapids. Much of this lively reach is along the backside of Hamburg. Dominated by industrial and commercial structures and lots of trash, it is a good place to be distracted by rapids. Between N.J. Rte. 94 and N.J. Rte. 23, the Wallkill escapes back into the woods, and the rapids yield to fast but quiet water.

Below Rte. 23, the Wallkill blossoms. The widening valley is carpeted by a marshy meadow. Wooded hillsides dappled with cedar form the backdrop. It is a lovely and peaceful setting. If you like this, you will love Section 2.

HAZARDS: Three small dams require carries. There are lots of strainers, often in fast water. Watch out for a metal spike in the rapid at the foot of the 20-foot dam below Scott Road.

WATER CONDITIONS: You can usually catch this stream only up between November and early May, within three days of hard rain.

GAUGE: There is a staff gauge on the downstream side of the right abutment of Rte. 565. Consider about 3.3 feet to be your minimum level for clearing the shallowest rapids.

Section 2. Sussex (Rte. 565) to Unionville, N.Y. (Oil City Road)					
Gradient	Difficulty	Distance	Time	Scenery	Map
1	A to 1—	8.8	3.0	Very Good	54

TRIP DESCRIPTION: This stretch of the Wallkill offers what is a rare commodity in New Jersey — open space and an uncluttered view. The river now meanders down a wide, flat valley (probably the bed of an old lake) whose mushy bottom is either marsh meadow or swamp forest.

At one point (just below Bassetts Bridge Road), the river bumps up against pretty cliffs. Generally though, banks are low or nonexistent, allowing expansive views of the countryside. The gentle hills to the west are a patchwork of pasture and woods. Pochuck Mountain, to the east, presents a bold, wooded face. There are few structures on the valley floor. You have so much space down here that even background road noise is negligible. With so much wetland, your chances of seeing waterfowl are good. But there are fewer acres of wetlands here than there once were, as towards the end of this segment, the valley turns agricultural. Though a wooded buffer screens it from you, the land beyond is now drained and dedicated largely to growing onions, celery, and other crops best suited to loose soils.

HAZARDS: None

WATER CONDITIONS: You will most often find the lower Wallkill up from November through the end of May, within 10 days of hard rain. If you are lucky enough to have some wet weather in October, this would be a great fall colors trip.

GAUGE: There are staff gauges on the downstream side of the right abutments of both Rte. 565 and Bassetts Bridge Road. Zero is unknown, but respective levels of 3.0 feet and 5.0 feet are just fine.

Papakating Creek and Clove Brook

INTRODUCTION: Papakating Creek and Clove Brook gather most of their water off the east slope of Kittatinny Mountain. Clove Brook is a tributary of Papakating, the latter joining the Wallkill below Sussex. Though so close, they possess distinct personalities. Papakating is a mellow stream that runs with the geologic grain of the land, while Clove is a lively passage that cuts across the grain. Both are only ephemeral targets and, thus, only for the dedicated or nearby paddler.

Section 1. Papakating Creek. Pellettown (Rte. 565) to mouth					
Gradient	Difficulty	Distance	Time	Scenery	Map
3	A to 1	9.1	5.0	Good	54

TRIP DESCRIPTION: The run begins just below the confluence of two equal-size forks of the creek. Do not even think about starting any farther upstream, or the strainer-strewn flume will teach you what a lump of cotton feels like after it has passed through the gin. Papakating is as tiny as you could ever want at Rte. 565, where it dashes over a riffle and around the bend into the unknown. The creek takes you on a twisting path through bottomland woods, swamps, and meadows. The wooded reaches can be particularly pleasant, being graced with some fine specimens of beech. Occasionally the path approaches a farm, but generally the surroundings are undeveloped. Depending on water level, most banks are medium or low, allowing ample views of the valley and distant mountains. In its final reach, Papakating meanders through the marshy meadows of the Wallkill.

Papakating's murky waters are gentle enough, with only an occasional riffle, the best being at the put-in. But persistent complications by strainers will make this more of a challenge than most beginners or unathletic paddlers would care to face. Addition of water from the West Branch and Clove Brook reduces the number of obstacles in the last three miles.

There is no access to the mouth. The most expedient option is to paddle almost a mile up the Wallkill to Rte. 565. A more pleasant approach would be to allow time for a leisurely five-and-a-half-mile float down the Wallkill to Bassetts Bridge Road.

HAZARDS: There are many strainers and one low private bridge. There is also the possibility of a fence.

WATER CONDITIONS: This is most often up between November and early May, within three days of hard rain.

GAUGE: There is a staff gauge beneath N.J. Rte. 23 bridge, left bank (approach from side road on north side of highway), attached to the concrete head wall of a sewer pipe outlet. Zero is unknown, but a level of 2.7 feet is adequate. Also, you can count grooves in the concrete of the left abutment of the Rte. 565 bridge, southeast of Sussex. Zero is unknown, but a level at the third groove down from the top is adequate.

Section 2. Clove Brook. Unionville Road to mouth					
Gradient	Difficulty	Distance	Time	Scenery	Map
25	A to 1 +	5.3	2.0	Fair to Good	54

TRIP DESCRIPTION: If your pleasure is riding the tiny creeks, then you well know the skepticism nonboaters hold for the targets of your delight. "Ain't that too small to float" is the common refrain, usually because most of those doubters have only observed these streams in fair weather when they are but a dribble. You, of course, know better. But even you, Mr. or Ms. Experienced, may have your doubts when standing at the Unionville Road put-in for Clove Brook.

There is not much creek at Unionville Road, even after a big rain. But it is big enough for a canoe. The dash down its rocky bed can be a delight, though some ill-placed strainers may diminish the pleasure. After a few hundred yards, an unnamed side stream pumps in some valuable flow. The creek then turns southeast, remains tiny, but becomes flat. It initially bursts through some more wood and briers but then settles into peaceful meanders through a rolling, pastoral setting. The channel is so narrow that you can almost touch both banks at once. Turns are sharp and tight. With fast current, simple gravel riffles, and maybe even some fences, the stretch can be stimulating. Then the gradient begins to increase. The stream provides a continual assortment of rapids formed by cobble bars, rock gardens, and even some little ledges. All the while, you speed past roads and more houses. As Clove Brook slides into Sussex, it pauses in a short pool formed by a 20-foot dam. There is a steep carry on the left. Riffles then begin to decrease, and in the final half mile, flat water and high, vegetated mud banks make this look much like the swamp creek that it soon will join.

The last exit on Clove Brook is at the ball field at the south corner of Sussex. If you paddle to the mouth, continue down Papakating Creek two thirds of a mile to N.J. Rte. 23. There is an easy, though probably slippery and muddy, take-out on the left beneath the bridge. You can drive to this spot by a side road off the north side of the highway.

HAZARDS: Gird for a repeated assault of deadfalls, overhanging vegetation, and fences. There is a 20-foot dam in Sussex.

WATER CONDITIONS: This is usually just a late fall or springtime run. Catch within two days of a hard rain.

Pochuck Creek
Wawayanda Creek

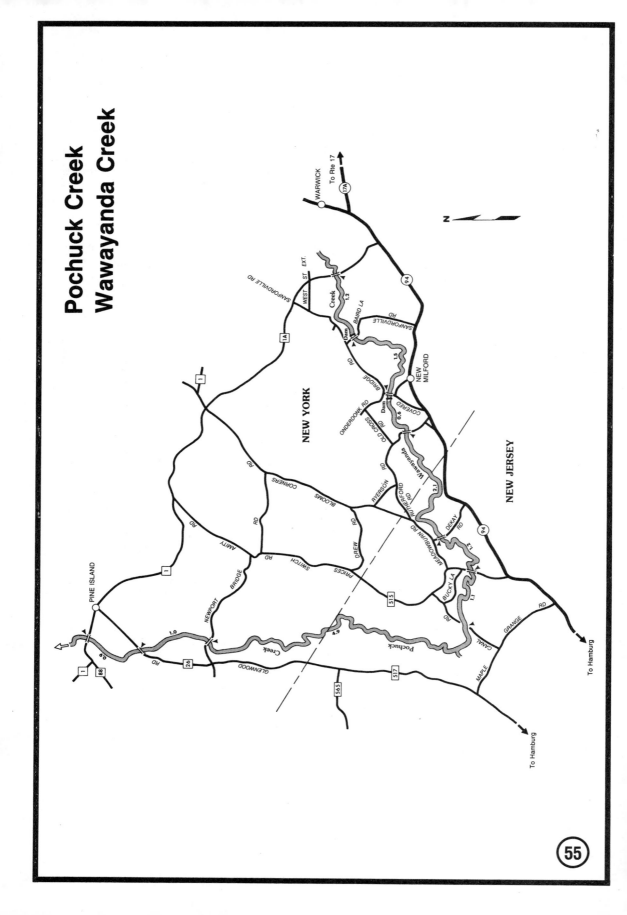

55

GAUGE: None. Judge riffles at the put-in. Enough water here is enough water everywhere.

Wawayanda Creek and Pochuck Creek

INTRODUCTION: Pochuck Creek is a tributary to the Wallkill. It starts northeast of Warwick, New York, but above its confluence with the tributary Black Creek, it is called Wawayanda Creek (pronounced "way way yonda"). Most of this little stream is within Orange County, New York. But its path dips into New Jersey for several miles, just north of Highland Lakes. It offers a delightful run with beauty and temperament comparable to the Wallkill.

Section 1. *Warwick, New York (Rte. 1-A) to Pine Island, New York (Rte. 1)*					
Gradient	Difficulty	Distance	Time	Scenery	Map
7*	A to 1+	14.5	5.0	Good to	55
*3 mi. @ 25				Very Good	

TRIP DESCRIPTION: Warwick is a classic, beautiful upstate New York town filled with big frame houses and possessing a grand, old railroad station. You can start in or above this town, but alas, all you see from the water is an ugly, trashy panorama. If you put in at Rte. 1-A, you bypass all of this, though the sluggish creek still shows little promise of being a winner. So it is quite a pleasant surprise when its waters burst through the remains of an old dam and dash down an easy, twisting rapid. Better yet, rapids and riffles caused by cobbles and little ledges fill the next three miles. Shortly into this stretch, you are confronted by a five-foot dam at Baird Lane. This is an unrunnable drop, creating an awkward situation, as the surrounding land is heavily posted by a rod and gun club. Below that dam, the creek winds through a beautiful patch of open, rolling countryside and then enters New Milford.

In its heyday, New Milford was a busy, little industrial center with several water-powered mills. There is little hint of that today. You might find New Milford forgettable if it were not for a four-foot weir just below Covered Bridge Road. Though probably runnable, most will choose to carry this on the left. And when you do, you will find a unique portage through a yard full of strange metal sculptures — an outdoor art gallery. You have just wandered into "Pacem In Terris." The creation of artist Frederick Franck, this display and restored old inn and mill are set aside as a nondenominational spiritual sanctuary. You are free to trespass and inspect. Just step lightly. There is so much some of the landowners upstream could learn from this man.

After passing Ryerson Road, the creek loses its steam, and in the spirit of "Pacem In Terris," it becomes a docile ribbon meandering through the most beautiful of valleys. To the south, there are good views of Pochuck Mountain, whose imposing profile makes it one of the few mountains in Jersey that looks like a mountain. The creek rolls by some pretty farms and just a few houses. It then enters a big, flat valley, just like the Wallkill does. The surroundings are mostly wet meadows and swamps. But the flatness is repeatedly broken by rocky, cedar-covered hillocks that rise like islands out of a green, grassy sea. A dash through a bouncy chute at Newport Bridge Road interrupts the quiet water momentarily. Then the scenery changes again, because drainage projects have changed this part of the valley into prime crop land. You can finish the trip at either Rte. 26 or Rte. 1, near the village of Pine Island.

HAZARDS: Watch for the two dams at and above New Milford. Also, Wawayanda has many strainers.

WATER CONDITIONS: Most often up between November and mid-May. Catch the upper section within three days of a hard rain. The flat lower reaches stay navigable for a week or more after a hard rain.

GAUGE: None. Very roughly, you want over 3.3 feet on the staff gauge at Rte. 565 on the Wallkill to do Wawayanda Creek and over 3.0 feet to do Pochuck Creek.

It Ain't Easy Writing A Guidebook or
Some of My Beast Memories of Paddling

I often eat animal crackers for my river lunch. It is so appropriate and symbolic. Animals are a memorable part of the river experience. They stimulate every sense. Routinely, we see herons, ducks, deer, and muskrats. We hear the splash of fish, the whir of cicadas, and moo of cows. We smell skunks. We feel the bite of the mosquito. And when we overlook that critical rock in that tough rapid, we learn the taste of eating crow.

Whether wild or domestic, animals of the riverside are always interesting. But they are not just scenery. You will inevitably interact with them, as I have. And they will leave their impact.

One possible impact that animals may have on you is that they might actually help mold your personality. For example, if you have ever paddled streams through cow pastures, as I have often done, you will discover that cows are quite curious. Once they spot you, they inevitably stare. In a herd of 50 cows, I guarantee that you will have 50 sets of eyeballs glued to your every motion. Thanks to several experiences like this, I never again suffered stage fright or shyness. Even more extreme, whole herds sometimes follow you down a river. On fast creeks, I have started thundering stampedes of curious cows running to pace me downstream. After these experiences, I began to believe that I had exceptional leadership qualities. So as you can see, animals can boost your self-confidence, and they are also cheaper than visiting a therapist.

Animals can endanger your life. Now I have no hair-raising tales of marauding grizzlies, venomous serpents, and charging pachyderms. For these, you will have to buy a tabloid from the check-out line at your supermarket. But I can tell you about real-life adventures, like you may find in New Jersey. For example, once I rounded a bend on a country brook and found a giant sow standing in the only passage through a shallow riffle. Bigger than Rhode Island, this blue-ribbon porker spanned the entire channel and clearly had absolutely no intention of moving. I mean, she was so stubbornly territorial that I am positive that she was responsible for posting the 200 no trespassing signs that I had seen along the last mile. And when she turned her massive head and glared at me, I know she was thinking about paddler chops for supper that night. No canoeing textbook ever prepared me for strainers like this. Only her keen desire to go round up her scattering piglets prompted her to eventually yield the right-of-way. After that brush with annihilation, I didn't eat bacon for a year.

Animals can sometimes be just plain aggravating, such as in my brush with dogs on a small creek in Delaware many years ago. I was exploring this creek alone. And to do so, the first item of business was to set up the shuttle. This meant dropping off the boat at the start, driving to the finish, and then hitchhiking back. Before taking to the road, I always try to leave my boat in a safe place, ideally at some stranger's house. At the put-in for this run, I was fortunate to find a beautiful old home perfectly situated on a nearby hillside. So on this cold winter morning, I knocked on this unfamiliar door, and as I waited for a response, I noticed a big, furry canine sniffing (but not gnawing) at my leg. A pretty young woman answered the bell, and I politely requested permission to park my boat and gear in her yard while I was away on my shuttle. That was OK with her, but she warned me that I had better keep my gear out of reach of the dog as it liked to chew on things. That remark served to explain why the packed earth of the backyard was strewn with such curiosities as dolls without heads and limbs, sticks without bark, tennis balls without fuzz, and a toy truck without tires. So I carefully stashed my gear far back inside my canoe*, sneered at the dog, and hurried off.

The shuttle went incredibly well, and I was back at the house in about 45 minutes. To my relief, I found my boat intact, free of tooth marks, not even scratched, and my equipment was fine, too. But to my puzzlement, the grab loops were missing. I looked at the dog, and Ole Blue gave me this big, wide-eyed, innocent look and burped. Another minute of searching uncovered bits and pieces of grab-loop rope strewn about the yard. I just shook my head in disgust, muttered a few obscenities at the mutt, and carried down to the river.

As I was stepping into my boat, I sensed evil in the air. Glancing over my shoulder, I noticed Rover charging down the hill towards me. Now it just might have wanted to say goodbye. Or it might have just wanted to be petted. But remembering those grisly dolls without heads and sensing a hungry hostility in its gait, I quickly shoved off. Much to my surprise, Lassie leaped into the water in hot pursuit. And even more to my surprise, that beast could swim like a fish. And by only 200 feet downstream, Bowser had almost closed the gap. With only a few inches to go, I saw it make a final lunge forward, shark-like mouth agape, ready to clamp onto my stern. BUT, with the grab loops gone, there was nothing for it to bite (grab) on to. Yes, Spot was a victim of its own foul play. Finally hitting a deep pool, I accelerated and left the frustrated pooch wallowing in the foam.

I thought I had had it with "man's best friend." But about four miles downstream, I encountered this beautiful, husky-type dog running along the bank and wagging its tail. It stole my heart, so I decided to go over and pet it. The delighted dog quickly scrambled down the steep mud bank and, after a few scratches behind the ear, turned around and, to my surprise, hopped aboard the stern deck of my boat. It just stood there, licking my ears and sending doggy vibes to me indicating that it would like to be ferried across the stream to another dog that was waiting longingly on that bank. It is a awesome responsibility being the potential catalyst in a canine Romeo and Juliet affair. But this being a frosty day, I just really didn't feel up to performing such a delicate whitewater maneuver with a giant critter making me top-heavy. So I just sat there and presented compelling, rational arguments to the dog as to why it should get off my boat. The dog was unmoved, and didn't. A battle of wills ensued, which I eventually won. The lonesome dog finally jumped overboard, almost taking me in also, and swam the icy torrent. I spoke to no more dogs that day, and no more dogs spoke to me.

So as you can see, paddling in Jersey can offer you every bit as much excitement as an African Safari. And if you still are not convinced, just remember that somewhere out in those Jersey backwoods, eager to meet you, is some horrible creature called the New Jersey Devil. Yes indeed, animals can make your canoe trips more interesting.

---

*I usually paddle a decked whitewater canoe called a C-1. To the uninitiated, it looks like a kayak, but I kneel in it.

Index

(+ denotes stream with Class 3 whitewater or greater)
(* denotes stream with exceptional scenery)

Pequannock River, + 187
Pequest River, 37
Pochuck Creek,* 209
Pohatcong Creek, 40
Pompton River, 185
Raccoon Creek, 67
Rahway River, 171
Ramapo River, 191
Rancocas Creek, 57
Raritan River, 143
Ridgeway Branch, 128
Rockaway Creek, + 156
Rockaway River, + 179
Saddle River, 195
Salem River, 70
Sandy Hook, 140
Scotland Run, 89
South Branch Metedeconk River, 131
South Branch Rancocas Creek, 64
South Branch Raritan River, + 145
South River (Great Egg trib.),* 108
South River (Raritan trib.), 167
Southwest Branch Rancocas Creek, 66
Still Run,* 89
Stony Brook, 161
Stow Creek, 76
Swimming River, 142
Toms River,* 127
Tuckahoe River, 109
Union Branch, 128
Wading River,* 117
Wallkill River,* 203
Wanaque River, 189
Wawayanda Creek, 209
West Branch Wading River,* 117
West Creek, 93
Westecunk Creek,* 122
Whippany River, 184
Wickecheoke Creek,* + 50